SEXUAL BOUNDARY
VIOLATIONS

SEXUAL BOUNDARY VIOLATIONS

Therapeutic, Supervisory, and Academic Contexts

ANDREA CELENZA

JASON ARONSON
Lanham • Boulder • New York • Toronto • Plymouth, UK

Published in the United States of America
by Jason Aronson
An imprint of Rowman & Littlefield Publishers, Inc.

A wholly owned subsidiary of
The Rowman & Littlefield Publishing Group, Inc.
4501 Forbes Boulevard, Suite 200, Lanham, Maryland 20706
www.rowmanlittlefield.com

Estover Road
Plymouth PL6 7PY
United Kingdom

British Library Cataloguing in Publication Information Available

Library of Congress Cataloging-in-Publication Data

The hardback edition of this book was previously cataloged by the Library of
Congress as follows:

Celenza, Andrea, 1954–
    Sexual boundary violations : therapeutic, supervisory, and academic contexts /
Andrea Celenza.
        p. cm.
    Includes bibliographical references and index.
    1. Psychotherapists—Sexual behavior. 2. Psychotherapy patients—Sexual
behavior. 3. Psychotherapists and patients. 4. Psychotherapists—Professional ethics.
I. Title.

    RC480.8.C4 2007
    616.89'14—dc22   2007001450

ISBN: 978-0-7657-0471-9 (cloth : alk. paper)
ISBN: 978-0-7657-0853-3 (pbk. : alk. paper)

Printed in the United States of America

♾ The paper used in this publication meets the minimum requirements of American
National Standard for Information Sciences—Permanence of Paper for Printed
Library Materials, ANSI/NISO Z39.48-1992.

For my husband, Bruce, who makes all my dreams come true.

CONTENTS

ACKNOWLEDGMENTS

This book is, in great measure, a compilation of my personal experience and reflections with many therapist-transgressors and clergy-transgressors to whom I owe a debt of gratitude. I worked with them during a most trying time in their lives. As this book amply demonstrates, most were highly self-critical and remorseful. They also had been badly stereotyped. I will always be indebted to them for opening up to me and allowing me to get inside their hearts and minds so that we, together, could come to some understanding of how their treatments had gone so awry.

In similar measure, this book compiles my personal experience with enormously courageous victim-survivors of therapist and clergy sexual abuse. They too had been stereotyped and degraded, by their trusted therapist or pastor as well as others who were skeptical of them or too defensive to be compassionate. Though there is still a long way to go, the profession has progressed tremendously in the last fifteen years due to these victims' ability to transcend their shame and step forward, bringing this complicated and harmful problem to light. I admire them greatly and thank them for trusting me to help them.

I am deeply grateful to my good friend, Mark Hilsenroth, who worked closely with me on two empirical projects and cowrote the two appendices in this book. He has been a tremendous source of encouragement, urging me to submit my ideas to the empirical test, and devoting his time and energy on these projects. Not only has it been immensely satisfying to bring these projects to fruition, but it has been great fun as well.

A huge and heartfelt appreciation goes to Gary Schoener for his generosity, careful critique, and for writing the foreword to this book. Gary was open to my efforts in this area from the very start, when studying and writing about transgressors was barely tolerated. His encouragement was and continues to be pivotal in cementing my commitment to this work. I am also profoundly grateful to Glen Gabbard for his crucial support and invaluable collaboration over the years. It is truly a pleasure to share this interest with such a generous and terrific colleague, especially when the subject matter is so divisive.

I am also greatly indebted to many more colleagues and friends who share my desire to make the problem of sexual boundary violations a less perplexing, more deeply understood, and consequently, perhaps preventable problem. Many of these colleagues offered essential feedback at various stages of my writing and I remain grateful for their involvement, either directly in this book or at various stages of my professional career and in my life. I am especially grateful to Mary Gail Frawley O'Dea, Tom Gutheil, Linda Jorgenson, Karen Schwartz, Ginny Theo-Steelman, and Jan Wohlberg.

I would also like to thank the countless Episcopal bishops, rabbis, and other clergy who are committed to taking a compassionate approach to their congregants, ministers, pastors, and rabbis in need. It is not easy to extend a hand to both the victim and the transgressor, resisting the pressures of polarization and oversimplification. In particular, I thank Attny. Paul Cooney, the Rt. Rev. Wendell Gibbs, the Rt. Rev. Ronald H. Haines, the Rt. Rev. Mark S. Sisk, Rev. Anne F. C. Richards, the Rt. Rev. Catherine S. Roskam, Rev. David Ryder, and the Rt. Rev. Stewart Wood.

Another source of valuable feedback and stimulating discussion came from my COPE Study Group on Boundaries, with whom I have been meeting for over ten years, including Dean Brockman, Kathy Brunkow, Glen Gabbard, Axel Hoffer, Larry Inderbitzen, Peg Keenan, Howard Levine, Malkah Notman, Morrie Peltz, Rhonda Shaw, Brenda Solomon, Sarah Tucker, Judy Yanof, and Alan Zeints. I have felt a continuing source of support and camaraderie through many thoughtful discussions with this group.

Many colleagues and friends offered enormously valuable insights and support throughout the writing of this book. They took time out of their busy lives to read drafts of chapters and gave me very helpful suggestions from their thoughtful reading. Most have been terrific colleagues and friends throughout my professional career and I am forever grateful to have them in my life. I am particularly grateful to Salman Akhtar, Lew Aron, Dan Brown, Murray Cohen, Steven Cooper, Jennifer Ellwood, Ellen Golding, Andy Harlem, Axel Hoffer, Randy Paulsen, Alan Pollock, and Jim Walton.

I will always be grateful to Jay Aronson who supported me from the start. His warmth, encouragement, and belief in my writing gave me the energy to make this project a reality. My editors, Art Pomponio, Mary Catherine La Mar, and Kat Macdonald have helped to make writing this book a surprising pleasure. They have the ability to offer suggestions without making the task too onerous and at the same time convey an abiding respect for my authorship.

I am also deeply touched by the continual encouragement and support I have received from my father who always believed I would write this book. I look forward to hours of discussion and debate with him about it. From my mother, I feel pride and respect for both my professional achievements and for my mothering. How she did it with four kids is a continual mystery to all of us! It is through both my parents that I have learned to have the courage of my convictions and to write about controversial subjects.

I could never have written this book without the love, unfailing support, patience and involvement of my husband, Bruce. He is my most attentive editor and constructive support and critic. I am infinitely indebted to him and our two sons, Derek and Ethan. Their ability to tolerate the hours of my preoccupation with this work has allowed this book to become a reality and I am boundlessly grateful to all of them for their patience and love.

I am grateful to the periodicals cited below for their permission to republish these articles with revisions: Sexual boundary violations: How do they happen? *Directions in Psychiatry*, 25:141–49, 2005; The misuse of countertransference love in sexual intimacies between therapists and patients. *Psychoanalytic Psychology*, 8:501–9, 1991; Precursors to therapist sexual misconduct: Preliminary findings. *Psychoanalytic Psychology*, 15: 378–95, 1998; Sexual boundary violations in the office: When is a couch just a couch? *Psychoanalytic Dialogues*, 16:113–28, 2006; Sexual boundary violations in the clergy: The search for the father. *Studies in Gender & Sexuality*, 5:213–32, 2004; Love and hate in the countertransference: Supervisory concerns. *Psychotherapy: Theory, Research & Practice*, 32:301–7, 1995; Analytic love and power: Responsible responsivity, *Psychoanalytic Inquiry*, in press; Personality characteristics of mental health professionals who have engaged in sexualized dual relationships: A Rorschach investigation. *Bulletin of Menninger Clinic*, 61:1–20, 1997.

FOREWORD

This book focuses on *sexual* boundary violations, but does so in the context of an examination of boundary issues which are far broader than those connected with sexual desires. Boundaries are key to defining relationships between nations and between people. In professional relationships they help ensure that professional work is maximally effective. In situations where there is a power differential—doctor-patient, employer-employee, supervisor-student—they help protect the integrity of the relationship. Professional boundaries are central to the core definition of a profession.

The first of the helping professions to define its role was medicine. Socrates (*The Republic, book 1, section 342*) quoted Plato (427–347 BC):

> Is it not also true that no physician, insofar as he is a physician,
> considers or enjoins
> What is for the physician's interest, but that all seek the
> good of their patients?

It was more than twenty-three centuries ago that a document entitled *The Oath* became part of the *Corpus Hippocratum,* a body of medical writings in the ancient Library of Alexandria in Egypt. Later called *The Oath of Hippocrates* (although he did not write it), this oath brought sexual boundary violations into focus with the oft-quoted words:

> Whatever houses I may visit, I will come for the benefit of the sick, remaining
> Free of all intentional injustice, of all mischief and in particular of sexual
> Relations with both female and male persons, be they free or slaves.
>
> (Reiser, Dyck, & Curran, 1977)

References to sexual contact with patients are recorded at various times during the centuries that followed. In 1784 the French king, Louis XVI, concerned about a new medical technique, *mesmerism* or *animal magnetism,* developed by Frederick Anton Mesmer, commissioned a group of prominent scientists and doctors to examine the possibility that unethical French physicians might use this technique to sexually exploit female patients. The *Commission of Inquiry,* chaired by Benjamin Franklin, concluded that such a risk existed (Franklin, et. al., 1965; Laurence & Perry, 1988).

Similar concerns appeared throughout the Middle Ages concerning sexual misconduct by clergy, including both cases involving debauchery and also those involving sexual abuse of children. America's first "psychological novel," Nathaniel Hawthorne's *The Scarlet Letter,* which was published in 1850, dealt with a case of sexual misconduct by a clergyman and chronicled its destructive impact on both the clergyman and the victim (Hawthorne, 1991). In 1974 renowned clergyman Henry Ward Beecher was the subject of public attention concerning his alleged sexual exploitation of Elizabeth Tilton, a parishioner whom he was counseling. The battle in the press pitted Beecher's sister, Harriet Beecher Stowe (author of *Uncle Tom's Cabin*), a leading New England Feminist, against Victoria Woodhull, a feminist publisher (Gabriel, 1998; Waller, 1982).

The early psychoanalytic movement in Europe, Canada, and the United States brought with it cases of sexual involvement between therapist and patient as well as recognition of both the role of erotic transference and countertransference. Many of these examples of sexual boundary crossings have become far better known in more recent times due to the publication of books such as Carotenuto's *A Secret Symmetry: Spielrein between Freud and Jung* published in Italy in 1982 and in English translation in 1984. Indeed, analyst Carl Jung's romantic relationship with his patient, Sabina Spielrein, was to lead to interesting correspondence with Sigmund Freud. Jonathan Kerr's (1993) extraordinary examination of this relationship, *A Most Dangerous Method,* provided further analysis, masterfully putting it into historical and cultural context.

Popular literature also dealt with this topic. F. Scott Fitzgerald's *Tender Is the Night* (1933) described protagonist Dr. Diver, a psychiatrist, as having lost control in his struggle with sexual feelings for a patient. In 1912 Corra Harris's book *A Circuit Rider's Wife* discussed the problem of clergy-parishioner sexual contact, largely framing it as a case of needy women parishioners seducing naive pastors. This book was serialized in the *Saturday Evening Post* and although it may seem dated was reprinted in the 1980s. According to Corra Harris:

> When we hear of a minister who has disgraced himself with some female member of his flock, my sympathies are all with the preacher. I know exactly what has happened. Some sad-faced lady who has been "awakened" from a silent, cold, backslidden state by his sermons goes to see

him in his church study. . . . This lady is perfectly innocent in that she
has not considered her moral responsibility to the preacher she is about
to victimize. She is very modest, really and truly modest. He is a little on
his guard until he discovers this. . . . That is the way it happens nine times
out of ten, a good man damned and lost by some frail angel of the church.
(Harris, 1988, pp. 81–83)

None of this public discussion seems to have led to much review of these
matters within the various professions. But change was due to come, as I will
attempt to examine by reviewing the history of our attempts to deal with the
issues surrounding sexual boundary violations. Throughout all those centuries and up through much of the last century the focus was on the male professional as either a victim of manipulation, or on mutual responsibility for what
had happened. The remedy, to the degree that one was deemed necessary at
all, was adherence to codes of ethics.

This was all to change in the latter part of the twentieth century. I will
examine the various decades from the 1960s through the present to attempt to
propose a historical framework.

The 1960s are the decade of the initial framing of the discussion of professional sexual boundary violations. The human sexuality movement and the
evolving feminist movements provided a base for further examination of these
issues in the 1960s, with a debate over McCartney's (1966) article on "Overt
Transference" in which he described sexual contact with his patients. Renowned sex researchers Masters and Johnson also charged that many patients
who had come to them for help with sexual performance problems had alleged
sexual misconduct by a prior treating professional (Masters & Johnson, 1970,
1975; Schoener, et al., 1989, p. 15).

In the early 1970s the publication of Phyllis Chesler's (1972) *Women and Madness* and Dr. Martin Shepard's (1971) *The Love Treatment* brought the topic of therapists' sexual misconduct into a much broader light. This same time period brought
a highly publicized lawsuit in New York City, *Roy v. Hartogs*, which received
considerable attention and was eventually chronicled in a book (Freeman & Roy,
1976) and made into a movie, *Betrayal,* which is still available on videotape.

Starting in 1973, studies and articles began to appear in the American
psychiatric and psychological literature detailing the incidence and prevalence
of sexual contact between professionals and their patients. These tended to be
of two types. First, self-report studies wherein a group of professionals was
asked questions about their sexual contact with patients. Secondly, studies
(typically Ph.D. dissertations) which involved in-depth interviews with clients
who had sex with former psychotherapists.

Our own Walk-In Counseling Center in Minneapolis began support groups for women who had been sexually victimized by therapists, counselors, and clergy in 1976. Groups ran regularly for nineteen years lead by Ellen Luepker, ACSW, in Minneapolis (Schoener, et al., 1989).

By the early 1980s lawsuits alleging sexual misconduct by a professional had become more common and were garnering publicity. The American Psychological Association's Insurance Trust estimated that about 18 percent of all malpractice cases and about 50 percent of the total costs of defense and pay-out were due to "sex cases." Even in the earliest cases the violations of boundaries other than just sexual contact had been an issue. In fact, far earlier, in the landmark decision in the *Zipkin vs. Freeman* in 1968, the court found that Dr. Freeman, the psychiatrist, had mishandled the transference phenomenon, and concluded:

> the damage would have been done to Mrs. Zipkin even if the trips outside the state were carefully chaperoned, the swimming done with suits on, and if there had been ballroom dancing instead of sexual relations.

Concerns about clergy began to explode by the mid-1980s achieving high visibility with the case of Fr. Gilbert Gauthe in Lafayette, Louisiana, which was publicized around the country (Berry, 1992) and led to a report to the Roman Catholic Bishops about the sexual abuse of children (Berry, 1992). During the same period many cases emerged involving sexual exploitation of adults by clergy from a wide range of faith groups (Fortune, 1989; Bisbing, Jorgenson & Sutherland, 1995). The 1980s were marked by many efforts to develop therapies to help victims of sexual exploitation by professionals and this work came in the context of a general interest in the treatment of victims of sexual abuse.

The issue of understanding and treating the offending professional emerged in the 1980s but was given far less attention than was the treatment of victims. Furthermore, starting with Wisconsin's criminalization of therapist-client sex in 1984, a succession of states began to look at how they go beyond codes of ethics as a mechanism of control. Minnesota, in 1985, made sexual contact with a psychotherapy client a felony. This trend continued into the 1990s and several state legislatures appointed commissions to study the problem and how the state might try to respond to it. Best-known was Minnesota's in 1985–1988, which led to a major text, *It's Never O.K.* (Sanderson, 1989).

Interdisciplinary committees were established which often had victims or consumer advocates as members. States like Massachusetts, California, New York, and Maryland developed legislative task forces. A few consumer advocacy groups emerged in the 1980s and functioned for a few years. Television "talk shows" and magazines and newspapers reported on cases and gave the problem more public visibility.

By the early 1990s the issue of sex between physicians and patients became a major issue in the Province of Ontario in Canada and eventually swept through Canada. Unlike the earlier work, this was focused on sexual misconduct by physicians. Soon other health professions followed suit, and in the early 1990s two major studies were done in Canada which for the first time surveyed the public. The provinces varied dramatically as to their response, with Ontario on one end creating mandatory reporting of offenses and much stiffer penalties.

Starting in the mid-1980s, the professions refocused on ethics codes as solutions. New standards were defined, ethics codes modified, and a great many articles and books appeared on this topic. A primary area of change was as regards post-termination relationships/sexual involvement and romantic involvement with former patients. Furthermore, the issue as defined was *sexual exploitation by professionals*. Common themes were warnings to clients and trying to teach them how to choose a therapist and what were early warning signs that one might be seeing in an offender.

Major international conferences were held in Minneapolis, Minnesota (1986 and 1992), Toronto, Canada (1994), and Boston (1998). Two Australia-New Zealand conferences were held in 1996 and 1998. Local and regional workshops on this topic were held in various places, including Norway, England, Ireland, and Denmark. In September 2000 AGAVA held the First Swiss Congress on *Exploitation of Professional Relationship*. Another such conference was held the following year.

During this same period of time attention began to shift toward understanding how it was that clergy, psychotherapists, and others in helping roles ended up having sexual contact with their patients. This involved a concern about *early warning signs* that patients, or other professionals might take seriously, but also an interest in understanding how such relationships evolved. While some professionals were sociopathic and simply seeking to exploit the vulnerability of those in their charge, it was clear that others who appeared to be ethical professionals could fall into such relationships. It also became clear that this was simply not just an issue of compulsive sex offenses since some only had a single instance.

As clinical experience and research weighed in, the concept of *the slippery slope* emerged in the writings of psychiatrists such as Robert Simon, M.D. But it was not until a decade ago that much was understood about the slippery slope (Simon, 1991). Research and clinical writings began to examine a variety of issues related to the boundaries between professionals and their patients, clients, or parishioners. Instead of examining just *sexual* contact, all physical contact came under scrutiny. Should a psychiatrist hug a patient? Should a pastor hug a parishioner? Does age matter? What about gender? This expanded to examinations of giving and receiving gifts, personal self-disclosure by the professional, social contacts outside the office, and many other issues.

Clinical experience echoed the fact that patients, clients, and parishioners could be harmed by boundary violations of this sort even if sexual contact did not occur. The development of a close, personal, but nontherapeutic relationship could undermine the helping process or cause harm in and of itself, even without sexual contact. Furthermore, regulatory bodies such as licensure boards were receiving complaints of boundary violations other than sexual ones.

It wasn't until 1994 when psychiatrist Richard Epstein published his book *Keeping Boundaries: Maintaining Safety and Integrity in the Psychotherapeutic Process* that there was a major text relative to this issue. In 1995 Psychiatrists Glen Gabbard and Eva Lester's book *Boundaries and Boundary Violations in Psychoanalysis* was published. Other books followed. Some were specific to issues such as the use of touch in psychotherapy, but they all dealt with various boundaries.

During the same period writings began to appear relative to the assessment and treatment of professionals who had sex with their patients, or clergy who had sexual contact with parishioners. These too evolved into methods of assessment and treatment of professionals who violated boundaries of all types—not just sexual ones. Dr. Celenza was one of a relatively small group of professionals who became active in examining and researching these issues. This was not a popular area of work and it was not uncommon for those of us who did presentations on the topic of assessment and rehabilitation of offenders to find ourselves talking to a very small group.

Throughout this period there were some who objected to rehabilitation, focusing on the need to properly punish offenders or simply run them out of the field. Others like myself and Dr. Celenza argued that this was overly simplistic. For example, Gabbard wrote:

> Any attempt to understand the phenomenon of sexual misconduct requires a detailed examination of the characteristics of therapists who have become involved in sexual transgressions. A fair-minded and scientific assessment of these therapists has been hindered in recent years by the increasing politicization of the problem of sexual misconduct. In some segments of the mental health professions there is an insistence on a "politically correct" view of the phenomenon that ascribes all sexual misconduct to evil and thoroughly corrupt male therapists. . . . This perspective may have particular appeal to other practitioners of psychotherapy, who

can reassure themselves that those colleagues who transgress sexual boundaries have characteristics that set them apart from all other therapists. The problem can thus be solved by eliminating these "bad apples" from the various professions.

This politically correct model depends on the projective disavowal of the universal vulnerability to sexual transgressions that is inherent in anyone who practices in the mental health professions. The most sensible approach is to assume that we are all at risk for boundary violations under certain circumstances. . . . All systematic studies of psychotherapists who have been involved in sexual boundary violations indicate that sexual misconduct occurs among a diverse group of clinicians who become involved with patients for a variety of reasons. Any attempt to lump all the transgressing therapists into one politically correct category is reductionistic and misguided. (Gabbard 1994, pp. 438–39)

While behaviorists and those who have traditionally treated sex offenders have adapted some of their tools and methods to the professional who has offended, the reality is that only a subset of professionals who offend are compulsive offenders. Taking a behavioral approach can be very effective with some types of offenders, but it does not come close to addressing the broader range of problems which have emerged as significant in assessments done by people like our group, Dr. Glen Gabbard, and Dr. Celenza.

As the end of the twentieth century approached Americans and Canadians were experimenting with *boundaries training*. This ranged from finding ways to better train professionals so as to prevent them from engaging in boundary violations once they were practicing, to ways of providing remedial training or treatment to those who had violated boundaries. This was not aimed at sociopathic offenders or repeat offenders, but rather professionals who were not basically predatory but who had the potential to fail to maintain boundaries.

While certainly debates rage on about appropriate penalties, the wording of licensure laws and codes of conduct, administrative safeguards, and the like, the major issue on the horizon today is what this book is all about. Health care and psychotherapy professions, pastoral counseling, and clergy are all seeking answers as to how sexual misconduct occurs from the perspective of problems in the offending professional. This is designed to give guidance as to how to structure rehabilitation and how to decide who can safely return to practice. It is also designed to provide instruction for those who train those in the helping professions, and those who supervise them.

In this book Dr. Celenza takes us further along on that journey. She effectively pulls together what has been learned to date, including her own contributions, and presents us with insights and observations, as well as direction for the future. The decade we are in is a decade which will be focused on more clearly understanding how and why sexual misconduct and related boundary violations occur in counseling, psychotherapy, health care, and pastoral work. This is essential if we are to make further progress at finding solutions. The current text takes us additional steps along that pathway.

—Gary R. Schoener, M.Eq.
licensed psychologist and executive director,
Walk-In Counseling Center,
Minneapolis, Minnesota

REFERENCES

Berry, Jason. (1992). *Lead Us Not Into Temptation: Catholic Priests and the Sexual Abuse of Children.* New York: Doubleday.

Bisbing, Steve; Jorgenson, Linda; & Sutherland, Pamela. (1996). *Sexual Abuse by Professionals: A Legal Guide.* Charlottesville, VA: Michie Company.

Braceland, F. (1969). Historical perspectives of the ethical practice of psychiatry. *American Journal of Psychiatry*, 126, pp. 230–237.

Carotenuto, Aldo. (1984). *A Secret Symmetry: Sabina Spielrein between Jung and Freud.* New York: Pantheon Books.

Chesler, Phyllis. (1972). *Women and Madness.* New York: Avon Books.

Donn, Linda. (1990). *Freud and Jung: Years of Friendship, Years of Loss.* New York: Collier Books.

Epstein, R. (1994). *Keeping Boundaries: Maintaining Safety and Integrity in the Psychotherapeutic Process.* Washington, DC: American Psychiatric Press.

Fitzgerald, F. Scott. (1933). *Tender Is the Night.* New York: Charles Scribner's.

Fortune, Marie. (1989). *Is Nothing Sacred?* New York: Harper and Row.

Franklin, B.; deBory, G., Lavoisier, A.L., Bailly, J.S., Majault, S. D'Arcet, J., Guillotin, J. & LeRoy, J.B. (1965). Secret report on mesmerism or animal magnetism. In R.E. Shor and M.T. Orne (Eds.) *The Nature of Hypnosis: Selected Basic Readings.* New York: Holt, Rinehart & Winston. (Original work published in 1784.)

Freeman, L. & Roy, J. (1976). *Betrayal.* New York: Stein & Day.

Gabbard, G. (1994). Sexual misconduct. In J. Oldham & M. Riba (Eds.) *Review of Psychiatry, Vol. 13*, pp. 433–456, Washington, DC: American Psychiatric Press.

Gabbard, G. & Lester, Eva. (1995). *Boundaries and Boundary Violations in Psychoanalysis.* Washington, DC: American Psychiatric Press.

Gabriel, Mary. (1998). *Notorious Victoria: The Life of Victoria Woodhull, Uncensored.* Chapel Hill, NC: Algonquin Books of Chapel Hill.

Harris, Corra. (1988). *The Circuit Rider's Wife.* Wilmore, KY: Bristol Books. (Originally published as *A Circuit Rider's Wife* in 1910.)

Hawthorne, Nathaniel. (1991). *The Scarlet Letter*. Philadelphia, PA: Courage Books. (Originally published in 1850 by Ticknor, Reed, and Fields.)

Jones, Ernest. (1953). *The Life and Work of Sigmund Freud, Vol. 1*. New York: Basic Books.

Kerr, Jonathon. (1993). *A Most Dangerous Method*. New York: Alfred A. Knopf.

Laurence, J.R. & Perry, C. (1988). *Hypnosis, Will & Memory: A Psycholegal History*. New York: Guilford Press.

Lloyd, G.E.R. (Ed.). (1983). *Hippocratic Writings*. London: Penguin Classics.

Masters, William & Johnson, Virginia. (1970). *Human Sexual Inadequacy*. Boston, MA: Little, Brown & Co.

Masters, William & Johnson, Virginia. (1975). Principles of the new sex therapy. Paper delivered at the annual meeting of the American Psychiatric Association, Anaheim, California.

McCartney, J.L. (1966). Overt transference. *Journal of Sex Research*, 2, pp. 227–237.

McGuire, William. (Ed.). (1988). *The Freud/Jung Letters: The Correspondence between Sigmund Freud and C. G. Jung*. Cambridge, MA: Harvard University Press.

Reiser, S.J.; Dyck, A.J.; & Curran, W.J. (1977). *Ethics in Medicine—Historical Perspectives and Contemporary Concerns*. Cambridge, MA: MIT Press.

Rutter, Peter. (1989). *Sex in the Forbidden Zone: When Therapists, Doctors, Clergy, Teachers and Other Men in Power Betray Women's Trust*. Los Angeles, CA: Jeremy P. Tarcher.

Sanderson, Barbara (Ed.). (1989). *It's Never O.K.: A Handbook for Professionals on Sexual Exploitation by Counselors and Therapists*. St. Paul, MN: Minnesota Dept. of Corrections

Schoener, Gary; Milgrom, Jeanette; Gonsiorek, John; Luepker, Ellen; & Conroe, Ray. (1989). *Psychotherapists' Sexual Involvement with Clients: Intervention and Prevention*. Minneapolis, MN: Walk-In Counseling Center.

Shepard, Martin. (1971). *The Love Treatment: Sexual Intimacy between Patients and Psychotherapist*. New York: Peter H. Wyden.

Simon, Robert. (1991). Psychological injury caused by boundary violation precursors to therapist-patient sex. *Psychiatric Annals*, 21, pp. 614–619.

Sipe, A.W. Richard. (1990). *A Secret World: Sexuality and the Search for Celibacy*. New York: Brunner/Mazel.

Sipe, A.W. Richard. (1995). *Sex, Priests and Power: Anatomy of a Crisis*. New York: Brunner/Mazel.

Turnbull, Agnes. (1948). *The Bishop's Mantle*. New York: Macmillan Co.

Waller, Altina. (1982). *Reverend Beecher and Mrs. Tilton*. Boston: University of Massachusetts Press.

Weber, M. (Jan. 1972). Should you sleep with your therapist? The raging controversy in American psychiatry. *Vogue*, pp. 78–79.

INTRODUCTION

The problem of sexual boundary violations has a long history but only a short time in which it has been studied. There are many taboos preventing the discussion of it, not the least of which is the incest analogy. When a colleague transgresses, he or she brings shame upon the profession much like an incestuous father brings shame upon the family. Hence, the secret is kept even when many are aware of its existence. There can be a simultaneous "knowing and not-knowing" characteristic of trauma in general, aptly described as the unthought known (Bollas, 1987; Stern, 1997). Differing levels of awareness divide individual psyches, and the splits can be sustained by a group-level (tacit) pressure not to tell, which adds to the perverse nature of the act. A profession whose basic tenet revolves around the importance of awareness blinds itself to harm in the very context that is designed for healing.

One of the aims of this book is to dispel several myths that make the awareness and discussion of the problem all the more difficult. For one, the problem of sexual boundary transgressions is more frequent than we would like to believe. Another is that there are many types of transgressors and, most importantly, the most prevalent type is one with whom we can all identify. The circumstances are also quite familiar. This is the instance of a narcissistically needy male or female mental health practitioner who is at a highly stressful time in his or her life. The practitioner may be a therapist, psychoanalyst, teacher, or member of the clergy. The inability or unwillingness to accept the now well-documented fact that we are all vulnerable to this type of transgression can stimulate a reactive anger (for all involved, including transgressor, victim, spouse, colleague, and friend), which blocks the capacity to come to terms with this vexing problem.

There are other complications associated with the unwillingness or inability to accept our universal fallibility to this type of sexual boundary transgression. There is often a highly punitive response by members of the mental health profession to the transgressor, especially when he or she masochistically welcomes such an overly wrought reaction. There is also an unconscionable and inexplicable rage against the victim who may have had the courage to bring the problem to light—a "kill the messenger" kind of response. On top of this, there is a way in which we all back ourselves into an impossible corner by insisting that "this could never happen to me." Such a sweeping prediction of future mental health and stable life circumstance is a tempting but omnipotent wish.

Another myth that must be dispelled is the notion that all victims of sexual boundary transgressions are borderline women. This notion is the result of at least two factors. One is the deplorable tendency to blame the victim and/or to perceive women as dangerous seductresses—an all too common way of devaluing women and maintaining the status quo (especially along gender and power stereotypes). The other is an overgeneralization from the fact that some victims do fall within this spectrum. Overall, however, the victims of sexual boundary transgressions span the full range of diagnostic categories and the majority are highly appealing women who tend toward meeting others' needs at the expense of their own.

Experience has shown that the victims of sexual boundary transgressions are often empathically gifted. This is a tragic scenario because these victims trusted and were betrayed in a most egregious manner. Often the transgressors have told them they were special and that it was "true love," and the revelation of other victims (sometimes simultaneously exploited) is shocking. Understandably, it is very difficult for some of these victims to ever seek help in a therapeutic setting again. Another unfortunate but inescapable observation is that many of these victims have been exploited by psychopathic predators. They often react with an understandable rage for transgressors of this sort. These predators show no remorse and are clearly exploitative by premeditation and design. It is hard for anyone who has been victimized by such a character to believe that all practitioners do not have such nefarious motives or to accept that this type of transgressor is not the most prevalent.

Most of the discussions in this book revolve around a different and more prevalent type of sexual boundary transgression. These discussions are an attempt to make explicable the case of the remorseful and rehabilitatable practitioner whose transgression is part of a subjectively experienced love affair. Since loving is the essence of any therapeutic effort, we must acknowledge the ways in which loving can go astray. This is equally true for both the transgressor and the victim. Just as the potential to transgress is a universal fallibility, we are all also vulnerable to *being exploited* when we open ourselves to love. Since mental health treatment of all kinds requires a deep emotional involvement, we are all potential victims to the extent that we, as clients or patients, can open ourselves to the process. In this way, there is a potential transgressor and a potential victim in us all.

This book aims to address all of the misconceptions noted above as well as the largely unhelpful responses that typically ensue. It is hoped that greater awareness and understanding of the problem of sexual boundary transgressions will aid prevention and resolution for mental health practitioners and consumers alike. It is not a sufficient preventative measure to say to oneself, "This could never happen to me." Nor is it helpful to create or sustain an overly punitive legal and professional atmosphere with the misguided notion that some form of extreme punishment will serve as a deterrent. The great majority of transgressors are well aware of the unethical nature of their behavior and its untoward consequences. Many express the despairing notion (in retrospect) that they had nowhere to turn. For many, this was in fact true.

The final aim of this book is to outline the various attitudinal and structural factors that are necessary to establish a safe and healthy atmosphere for both practitioners and consumers of mental health services. A professional atmosphere that facilitates openness, honesty, and support for all involved will make it safer for victims to come forward and receive recompense as well as for transgressors to seek and receive the help they need. In this effort, it is wise to keep in mind Sullivan's basic tenet: We are all much more human than otherwise (1953).

The essential nutrients through which mental health services thrive are all fortified with love. As people allow themselves greater access to deep-seated desires, this love becomes infused with all kinds of passionate longings and intensely felt pressures. It should not be surprising that sometimes a couple will lose their bearings. It should not be surprising that sometimes, especially for some practitioners under unusual stress, the capacity to maintain the treatment frame will be compromised. Like a perfect storm, the only response is to rescue both members and provide help in the specific ways that are needed.

One of the more unfortunate misconceptions about sexual boundary violations is that by the time a treatment has gone awry—the point at which a sexual boundary transgression feels inevitable but has not yet occurred—it is too late for help and the transgressor is unlikely to *want* to stop. Clearly, this is true in some cases. However, it is also common enough for both the client/patient and the potential transgressor to want help but have nowhere to turn. Consultations often fail to address the underlying issues (especially for the transgressor), and since the likely outcome of a more formal complaint is nothing short of professional ruin, the problem becomes stalemated. With the appropriate structures and attitudes in place, however, it is possible for both the client/patient and the potential transgressor to be helped in the specific ways that each needs. At present there is not enough belief in this possibility, including the hope or expectation that the situation will be compassionately and forthrightly understood.

A nonpunitive atmosphere that reflects the true nature of sexual boundary transgressions must be present for anyone to make use of help. It is not enough for consultants to be available; they must exist in a context that is conducive to coming forward. Unfortunately, the attitudes and structures that make up such a context are lacking in most professional networks. This book aims to address those factors that must be put in place so that receptivity toward rehabilitation, support, guidance, and consultation are all present and are avenues more likely to be used.

It is also true that some transgressors are in no way amenable to the potentially helpful influence of support, consultation, or any kind of guidance. It must be acknowledged that there are psychopathic predators who contaminate any profession and who should be expelled from any service-providing occupation. It is my strong conviction, however, that at least in the mental health professions, this type of transgressor is less common today than in decades past. It is likely that this is a salutary effect of the courageous actions of the many victims who have risked their reputation and mental stability in order to bring this problem to light. The "powers that be" always resist loss of face and status; the efforts of countless victims deserve nothing but respect for their willingness to come forward. This book is an effort to make the mental health profession a context in which future victims do not have to take such personal risk when shining the spotlight on a problem that sorely needs to be addressed.

Part I

NATURE AND SCOPE OF THE PROBLEM

1

HOW DO THEY HAPPEN?

It has long been my impression that a major reason for therapists' becoming actually sexually involved with patients is that the therapist's own therapeutic striving, desublimated to the level on which it was at work early in his childhood, has impelled him into this form of involvement with the patient. He has succumbed to the illusion that a magically curative copulation will resolve the patient's illness which tenaciously has resisted all the more sophisticated psychotherapeutic techniques learned in his adult-life training and practice.

—H. F. Searles (1979, p. 431)

It has been said that all therapy revolves around one basic question, "Why can't we be lovers?" Posed as a hypothetical, a "what if" kind of mental exercise, this sometimes burning question prompts the most useful exploration of the patient's deeply cherished wishes, longings, fantasies, and sexual desire. What happens when this question does not remain at a hypothetical level? Is it then answered once and for all? Is there a therapeutic aspect to actualizing such deeply held longings? Why are there such strong prohibitions against sexual contact between therapist and patient? Why do sexual boundary violations occur—at a relatively high prevalence rate, it might be added—despite the strong prohibitions against them?

Mental health practitioners consider sexual boundary violations to be the most egregious kind of ethical violation. Despite this, the problem has a long history and it has only been addressed in the past 15 to 20 years. Many of Freud's inner circle became involved with one or more patients—Carl Jung with Sabina Spielrein, Sandor Ferenczi with Gizella and Elma Palos (mother *and* daughter, both of whom were patients), and Ernest Jones with Loë Kann, who eventually became his common-law wife. At one time or another, Freud became involved in each of these relationships, ostensibly to help disentangle the various boundary violations; however, he added several of his own in the mix (see Gabbard and Lester, 1995a, and Kerr, 1993, for historical reviews within psychoanalysis; Strean, 1993, for an historical review in mental health professions in general).

Today, therapists who have crossed boundaries in this way are usually expelled from their professional organizations, lose their licensure, and typically lose the majority of their colleagues and friends along the way. Nor do marriages usually survive this cataclysmic event. Because the consequences are so grave, the question is often posed, Why aren't therapists deterred by the threats of losing their livelihood, career, and social network? What is it that causes a therapist to violate boundaries in this most extreme way?

Taking into account the long history of boundary violations as well as the recognition of the intensely personal involvement that psychoanalysis and psychotherapy entail, perhaps we should also ask why therapists *don't* violate boundaries more often. This question is the other side of this most troubling problem that will be addressed from a variety of vantage points throughout this book.

The answer to all of the questions posed above rests on an understanding of how power issues and loving feelings intersect in therapeutic, supervisory, and academic settings. Among all mental health and academic professionals, sexual boundary violations are recognized as unethical due to the power imbalance inherent in the structure of the relationship. This imbalance derives from many sources, but revolves primarily around the *unequal distribution of attention* paid to the client, patient, or student as compared to the therapist, analyst, teacher, or clergy-person.[1] The way in which the therapist acquires more and more knowledge of the patient articulates and elaborates the power imbalance even further over time. This power is constituted by knowledge— in particular, the therapist's knowledge of the patient's inner life, his or her hopes, fears, shames, and longings.

Further, the patient comes to therapy seeking help, guidance, support, and self-knowledge, usually in a *state of emotional disequilibrium*, distress, or need. This is another dimension of the power imbalance between them since the therapist, vis-à-vis the patient at least, is not similarly disequilibrated. The therapist is experienced as having what the patient wants, realistically or not, and is thus imbued with fantasies of healing, repairing, correcting, bestowing what is needed, and other wish-driven expectations and hopes.

For these reasons and others that will unfold over time, the patient and therapist are not on an equal footing from the start. This is defining of the therapeutic context and the therapist's role. It is undeniable and irreducible. It is also desirable since the context of healing requires such an imbalanced focus.

There is yet another imbalance that intensifies over time and is derived from the fact that the therapy process encourages *unresolved transference-based relationships*. That is to say, the patient will, whether the therapy addresses it specifically or not, begin to experience the therapist as an important and conflictual figure from the past. Usually, this takes the form of an intense yet unresolved mode of relating derived from early childhood, most often with a parent. This is another aspect of the inherent disempowerment of the patient structured into the therapeutic setting and is a major focus of treatment in psychodynamic and psychoanalytic therapies. However, it is important to note that transference-based relationships will develop in any therapeutic context, whether the therapy is designed to make use of it or not.

It is through the structure of the therapeutic setting and the imbalance inherent in this structure that the patient is rendered particularly vulnerable to exploitation, especially of a sexual nature. Because of the design of the context, this structure renders the patient's consent moot, even if the patient desires erotic contact with the therapist. Indeed, it is fair to say that the patient is *very likely* to desire erotic contact with the therapist since sexualization and erotic longing naturally occur when transference-based relationships of many types are stimulated. It is the therapist's responsibility, therefore, to maintain the clarity of roles in the face of these inherent and developing pressures.

Given these structural and emotional imbalances, it is understandable that there is widespread concern about the problem of therapist-patient sexual boundary violations in the mental health profession. This chapter provides mental health practitioners with an overview of the problem of sexual boundary violations, reviews the characteristics of vulnerable therapists, and describes the most common scenario within which sexual boundary violations occurs. It is hoped that such a review will provide mental health practitioners with a useful guideline in maintaining boundaries as well as to alert vulnerable therapists to seek help and support at times of risk.

DEFINITION

Sexual boundary violations are defined as any kind of physical contact occurring in the context of a therapeutic relationship for the purpose of erotic pleasure. It should be noted that there is touching that can, though rarely, occur in the context of therapy that would not be included in this definition, such as the occasional handshake or even a hug (for example, at termination), when the intent, at least on the therapist's part, is not erotic. Already, however, it is possible to see a difficulty in the attempt to distinguish one person's intent from another's conscious or unconscious hope or reaction. Many affectionate gestures made by therapists are misconstrued, either at the time they occur or at some later point. This is why any kind of physical touch in the therapeutic setting is generally discouraged.

PREVALENCE

Prevalence studies consistently reveal an unacceptably high incidence rate (7–12%) of erotic contact between therapists and patients among mental health practitioners in the United States (Kardener, Fuller, & Mensch, 1973; Perry, 1976; Gechtman & Bouhoutsos, 1985; Pope, Keith-Spiegel, & Tabachnick, 1986; Pope, Tabachnick, & Keith-Spiegel, 1987; Holroyd & Brodsky, 1977; Pope, Levenson, & Schover, 1979; Gartrell, Herman, Olarte, Feldstein, & Localio, 1986; Akamatsu, 1988; Borys & Pope, 1989; Lamb & Catanzaro, 1998; Jackson & Nuttall, 2001). All of these studies are comprised of anonymous, self-report questionnaires and most are derived from a national pool of various disciplines, including psychiatrists, psychologists, social workers, and/or clergy. Since these studies rely on the willingness of therapists to report on their own behavior, it is likely that the results underrepresent the true prevalence rate. Studies of British psychologists' self-reported prevalence reveal data similar to the studies in the United States (Garrett & Davis, 1998).

Despite this high prevalence and widespread concern among therapists, patients, and the public at large, the problem of sexual boundary violations is not well understood. Several misconceptions hinder therapists' abilities to recognize and address risk factors and vulnerabilities that otherwise might facilitate prevention. Studies generally show remarkable consistency in age, gender, and practice characteristics: the typical transgressor is a middle-aged male therapist in solo private practice who engages in a sexual dual relationship with one female patient (Borys & Pope, 1989; Bouhoutsos, Holroyd, Lerman, Forer, & Greenberg, 1983; Butler & Zelen, 1977; Epstein, Simon, & Kay, 1992; Jackson & Nuttall, 2001; Lamb & Catanzaro, 1998; Lamb et al., 1994; Pope, Levenson, & Schover, 1979; Pope, 1990, 1993; Somer & Saadon, 1999). Some studies have suggested that as therapists age and gain more experience, ethical judgment falls below previously held standards (Borys & Pope, 1989; Epstein et al., 1992; Lamb et al., 1994; Rodolfa et al., 1994; Stake & Oliver, 1991). These and other risk factors have been identified (Schoener, Milgrom, Gonsiorek, Luepker, & Conroe, 1989; Gabbard, 1994a; Celenza, 1998) and are presented below.

In malpractice prevention and risk management consultation, boundary issues account for a considerable portion of legal and ethical complaints

(Gutheil & Gabbard, 1993) and the problem of sexual boundary violations between therapists and patients is a large proportion of these cases (Garrett, 2002). In all prevalence studies, male practitioners account for over 80% of the incidences. Interestingly, female practitioners account for a relatively low percentage of the prevalence yet engage in sexual boundary violations mostly with female patients (Kardener, Fuller, & Mensh, 1973; Holroyd & Brodsky, 1977; Pope et al., 1979; Gartrell et al., 1986; Borys & Pope, 1989; Schoener et al., 1989). Therefore, most victim/patients of sexual boundary violations are female, whether the therapist is male or female, and the patient population most likely to be harmed by sexual boundary violations is female. Schoener et al. (1989) reported 80% of their victim/patients were women who had been sexually abused by a male therapist, and more than 10% of their victim/patients were women abused by a female therapist. In general, the prevalence studies report approximately 4% of female therapists admit to having sexually exploited their patients/clients.

As mentioned, the prevalence studies consistently show an overrepresentation of male therapists in those who report having engaged in sexual boundary violations. In general, studies report 7–9% of male therapists engaged in sexual boundary violations, while female therapists account for only 2–3% of the incidence rate (Holroyd & Brodsky, 1977; Pope et al., 1979; Gartrell et al., 1986; Borys & Pope, 1989; Schoener et al., 1989; Parsons & Wincze, 1995; Jackson & Nuttall, 2001). Interestingly, some preliminary data suggest that the female therapists who engage in sexual boundary violations with female patients are not necessarily self-identified as homosexual prior to their involvement with their patient. Benowitz (1995) studied 15 female therapist–female patient pairs and found 20% self-identified as heterosexual, 20% as bisexual, and 40% as clearly lesbian. Benowitz suggests that some female therapists use the relationship with the patient to explore their own sexuality. (Though the prevalence rates are relatively low in this gender pairing, more research is clearly needed in this subset. One study [Albrecht, 2003] attributes the lack of research on this particular homosexual pairing to cultural factors involving the idealization of motherhood and Freud's legacy in viewing women as sexually passive.)

The least frequent pairings are male-male and female therapist-male patient. Gonsiorek (1989) found conflicts and insecurities revolving around sexual orientation in his study of male transgressors. One especially influential risk factor occurs when the therapist is in the throes of his or her own "coming out" process.

Although psychiatrists are three times as likely to be sued for sexual misconduct (Perr, 1975), epidemiological studies suggest no difference of prevalence rate among the disciplines. Psychiatrists and psychologists have equivalent prevalence rates, with a lower incidence among psychodynamic therapists and therapists who provide long-term intensive psychotherapy (Borys & Pope, 1989; Baer & Murdock, 1995; Pope, Tabachnick, & Keith-Spiegel, 1987). It is speculated that this derives from greater awareness of the importance of clear, nonexploitative, and therapeutically oriented roles, boundaries, and responsibilities, such as maintaining the frame, the holding environment, and appreciation for transference. These studies imply that the more loosely bounded maintenance of the therapeutic frame in humanistic and cognitive-behavioral approaches may predispose clinicians to boundary crossings, such as excessive self-disclosure and nonerotic touch (e.g., hugs, pats on the back).

One study reflected a divergent finding where psychodynamic clinicians were overrepresented in a group of nonsexual boundary violators (Ehlert, 2002). Interestingly, in Ehlert's study, the most frequently endorsed theoretical orientation in the group of sexual boundary violators was "eclectic," perhaps an easy catch-all category for those who conduct treatment in idiosyncratic or omnipotent ways.

Gechtman (1989) found a significantly lower rate of sexual boundary violations among social workers, the reasons for which are unclear. In a study of physician sexual misconduct, Dehlendorf and Wolfe (1998) found that psychiatrists, obstetricians and gynecologists, and family and general practitioners were overrepresented in the groups disciplined by medical boards.

Sexual boundary violations are also a special problem among clergy (Celenza, 2004; Lothstein, 2004; Richards, 2004, see chapter 7). Blackmon (1984) surveyed clergy in four denominations—Presbyterian, United Methodist, Episcopalian, and Assembly of God—and found 39% acknowledged sexual contact with a congregant and 12.7% reported sexual intercourse with a congregant. These figures are far higher than self-report data in other mental health professions (see Schoener, 2005, for a historical review of clergy sexual abuse of women), representing another area for future research. It should be noted that many of the training issues related to conventional practices in humanistic and behavioral approaches (such as hugging, dining, home visits, and so forth) also apply to pastoral care.

COMMON CHARACTERISTICS

Though sexual boundary violations have been a major focus of study in the past couple of decades (Schoener et al., 1989; Celenza, 1998; Gabbard & Lester, 1995a; Gonsiorek, 1995; Rutter, 1989; Strean, 1993; Bloom, Nadelson, &

Notman, 1999), several misconceptions about the nature of the problem continue to be held among therapists and patients alike. Some of these misconceptions are a consequence of the differential attention paid by the media to notorious, egregious cases that have attracted statewide and sometimes national attention. These usually involve a therapist who is psychopathic and who has sexually exploited multiple patients over many years. It is now well known, however, that this is neither the only nor most prevalent type of sexual boundary violation.[2]

Previous clinical observations have culminated in a range of profiles and diagnostic categories of the transgressing therapist. Six diagnostic categories were delineated by Schoener and Gonsiorek (1989), including: (1) uninformed/naive, (2) healthy or mildly neurotic, (3) severely neurotic and/or socially isolated, (4) impulsive character disorders, (5) sociopathic or narcissistic character disorders, and (6) psychotic or borderline personalities. A seventh category, bipolar disorders, was added in 1994 (Schoener, personal communication). Gabbard (1994a) proposed four underlying psychological profiles as an alternative classification scheme. These underlying characteristics include: (1) psychotic disorders, (2) predatory psychopathy and paraphilias, (3) lovesickness, and (4) masochistic surrender. The last two categories, lovesickness and masochistic surrender, can be conceived as occupying two ends along the same continuum (Celenza & Gabbard, 2003).

On a more descriptive level, Pope and Bouhoutsos (1986) have delineated ten common scenarios that characterize the mode of relating of the transgression: Role Trading, Sex Therapy, As If . . . , Svengali, Drugs, Rape, True Love, It Just Got Out of Hand, Time Out, and Hold Me. Groth and Birnbaum (1979) categorized the modes of relating into three major types: Power and Control, Anger, and Sadism. Knowledge of offender strategies is sometimes specifically tied to intervention programs (Tschan, 2005). Irons and Schneider (1994) found 54% of their sample of transgressors had a psychosocial disorder with addictive features while 31% were chemically dependent.

Little is known about the psychology of the psychopathic predator because these transgressors typically refuse to be evaluated, persistently lie about the misconduct (even when multiple complaints are filed), and, if they lose their license to practice, still display no motivation to rehabilitate themselves. One such case involved over 20 complaints from former patients; the therapist continued to deny the abuse over several years as the many complainants came forward. So-called multiple offenders tend to show no remorse or guilt and usually blame the patient for the seduction and transgression.

The dynamics of these psychopathically organized transgressors usually revolve around sadism and a need for power or control (Smith, 1984; Pope &

Bouhoutsos, 1986; Celenza, 2006c). On superficial observation, this type of transgressor is often described as charismatic, difficult (perhaps intimidating), and highly regarded, at least by some (see, for example, Sandler's [2004] depiction of Masud Khan). It is a sad fact that no profession has been wholly successful in weeding out these types of characters; indeed, it is a characteristic of the psychopathic personality to charm and mimic the behavior of a competent professional with great interpersonal skill (see Smith, 1984, for a description of several therapist/predators). After one or more complaints are filed and the practitioner loses his license, the psychopathic predator usually continues to practice as a psychotherapist, as this vocation does not require a license in most states.

It has been well documented that the one-time offender (usually narcissistically needy, lovesick, or from the masochistic-surrender category) is the most prevalent type of sexual boundary transgressor (Schoener et al., 1989; Gabbard & Lester, 1995a; Celenza & Gabbard, 2003). In contrast to the psychopathic predator, much has become known about these types of characters because they seek help, display genuine remorse, and can be effectively rehabilitated (Celenza & Gabbard, 2003). Indeed, it can be argued that these characters are more like you and me than is generally accepted or than is comfortable to acknowledge.

There are typical features and a common scenario associated with this most prevalent type of sexual misconduct (Celenza & Gabbard, 2003; Plakun, 1999). The scenario most often involves a heterosexual male therapist who becomes sexually involved with only one of his patients.[3] The therapist is usually midcareer, isolated in his practice, and is treating a difficult patient in a highly stressful time in his life. The relationship is usually intense, may last for several years, and the couple may feel that they have found "true love," at least initially. Sometimes the therapy relationship is terminated while the sexual relationship continues. If the relationship is brought to an end by the therapist, this is the time when an ethical complaint is most likely to be filed by the patient.

There are several common therapist characteristics that have been identified related to the therapist's personality, life circumstance, past history, and the transference/countertransference dynamics of this particular therapist-patient pair (Celenza, 1998; Twemlow & Gabbard, 1989; Gonsiorek & Schoener, 1987). My organization of these is presented below (see table 1.1) and further elaborated in chapter 3. While certain precursors may be long-standing, most researchers have found these therapists capable of conducting competent and ethical treatment for most of their professional career (Gabbard & Lester, 1995a). For this type of transgressor, the greatest risk involves a particular transference/countertransference (mis)fit at a highly stressful time of their lives. These precursors are presented not as a way to differentiate ourselves from transgressors but

Table 1.1.   Precursors of Therapist/Patient Sexual Misconduct

Clinical Findings
- Long-standing narcissistic vulnerability
- Grandiose (covert) rescue fantasies
- Intolerance of negative transference
- Childhood history of emotional deprivation and sexualized overstimulation
- Family history of covert and sanctioned boundary transgressions
- Unresolved anger toward authority figures
- Restricted awareness of fantasy (especially hostile/aggressive)
- Transformation of countertransference hate to countertransference "love"

$n > 100$ (therapists, analysts, and pastoral counselors) cases of therapist sexual misconduct in the context of evaluation, therapy, supervision, or consultation.

to recognize the potential transgressor in all of us. Though there is a ubiquitous temptation to apply an "us/them" type of disclaiming to these characteristics and warning signs, I have found that it is the therapist who insists he or she is not at risk who is most vulnerable.

It is important to state at the outset that for this type of transgressor, there is also a typical profile for the victim/patient in this context. This is not to blame the patient in any way. It is always the therapist's responsibility to maintain the frame of the treatment and to monitor and manage the boundaries of the relationship. Indeed, it is the patient's need to present the full intensity of her desires and affects in their full range; this is what she comes to treatment for and what she needs to explore and examine. However, it has been exceedingly difficult to take an investigative approach to this problem in a way that encompasses the transference/countertransference dynamics without appearing to either blame or denigrate the patient/victim (see, for example, Gutheil & Gabbard, 1992). This chapter and others that focus on this type of transgressor should not be understood as placing any responsibility or blame on the victim/patient.

PRECURSORS CONTEXTUALIZED
IN THE THERAPY RELATIONSHIP

The structure of the therapy situation is a template that replicates several of the familial dynamics outlined above. The therapeutic context is essentially a depriving situation for the therapist in that it is asymmetric. The patient is the recipient of the attention paid and it is her needs that are the focus of treatment. In contrast, it is the therapist's responsibility to put his needs aside for most of the hours in his day.

At the same time, the therapy situation may be overstimulating to the therapist in that the content of many therapy hours can involve intensely sexualized material. Thus, the therapy situation itself replicates the early childhood experience of these therapists in that it is simultaneously depriving and sexually overstimulating. It is also a context where it is overtly forbidden for the therapist to gain gratification of his wishes, paralleling the prohibitive atmosphere in these therapists' childhood experience (see chapter 3 for an elaboration of these dynamics).

The critical moments in a psychodynamic therapy that hold the greatest potential for change revolve around phases of the therapy where the patient is expressing dissatisfaction with and criticism of the therapy and/or the therapist himself. These are usually intense moments or phases and with certain patients, this part of the treatment may escalate into a crisis and/or include threats of suicide (Wheelis, Michels, Celenza, & Gabbard, 2003), self-mutilation, or blackmail. These and other kinds of implicit and explicit threats can render the therapist (subjectively) helpless and desperate (Gabbard, 1994a; Celenza, 1998; Gutheil & Gabbard, 1992, 1993). Because of the therapist's narcissistic fragility, he may be moved to transform the nature of the therapeutic process at this phase. Rather than tolerate and continue to explore the patient's dissatisfactions, the therapist becomes increasingly anxious and desperate, relying on sexualization to transform the way in which the patient is responding to him (see, for example, Eyman & Gabbard, 1991; Celenza & Gabbard, 2003; Gabbard, 2003). He may enact a masochistic scenario, linked to childhood wishes of self-sacrifice and "going out in a blaze of glory" by acting on incestuous wishes and courting punishment for the forbidden act of pleasure (Gabbard & Lester, 1995a).

Thus, the seduction occurs when the therapist believes that the therapy is at an impasse. In this way, the process shifts from one of enormous frustration and challenge to one of seduction and sexual gratification.

COMMON MISCONCEPTIONS

It is very important for therapists to be aware of the warning signs and particular vulnerabilities associated with the problem of sexual boundary violations. The misconceptions that surround this problem prevent therapists from adequately addressing these vulnerabilities before it is too late. Consultation, supervision, and regular discussion in peer study groups and the like are often absent as potential sources of support in cases of sexual boundary transgressions. The punitive atmosphere within the profession, including licensing boards, ethics committees, and overseeing professional agencies, also engenders a prohibition against reaching out for support and guidance, creating an additional barrier to therapists seeking help when they need it.

On a more psychological level, there is a tendency for most therapists to disown the problem, supported by the belief that therapists who engage in sexual boundary violations are psychopathic or grandiose, that is, fundamentally different from oneself (Celenza & Gabbard, 2003). This allows therapists to deny their own vulnerability to this problem. Through the use of a variety of defenses such as splitting, disavowal, and projection, many therapists attempt to console themselves that sexual boundary violations could never happen to them because they are educated, ethical, and well intended.

It is dangerous to hold the belief that one is immune to this type of boundary transgression because those who continue to deny their own vulnerability will more likely ignore warning signs and be less likely to seek help and support. It is also more likely that aspects of self-care will be underappreciated, since most therapists who have become sexually involved with a patient do so at a stressful time in their lives. Knowing the ethical code surrounding the maintenance of appropriate boundaries is not a safeguard against boundary violations since the great majority of transgressors did so knowing full well that they were violating the ethical code of their profession.

The absence of sexual attraction toward a particular patient also does not safeguard against sexual exploitation. This is another common misunderstanding of the problem itself and a way in which sexual boundary violations are commonly portrayed in film. In real life, sexual boundary violations are not about a physically appealing patient or a romantic/sexual spark between two people. When the transgressor is a psychopathic predator, he may select particularly attractive and appealing patients among his entourage. However, in the most prevalent kind of sexual boundary violation, the seduction is most often the result of a defensive reaction to a difficult patient at a stressful time in the therapist's life. It is most common to hear the transgressor say (in retrospect), "I never thought I'd be sexual with any patient and certainly not with this one."

SUMMARY

Loving feelings are inevitably stirred up in therapeutic contexts. Because of the defining structure of the therapeutic setting, however, and its inherent power imbalance, erotic contact is exploitative of the patient's vulnerability, even when sexual contact is consciously desired by the patient. It remains the therapist's responsibility to maintain the clarity of roles in all types of therapy.

Sexual boundary violations continue to be a misunderstood and under-treated problem within the helping professions. Eight risk factors are presented to enhance practitioners' knowledge of the problem. These risk factors include: long-standing narcissistic vulnerability, grandiose (covert) rescue fantasies, intolerance of negative transference, childhood history of emotional deprivation and sexualization, family history of covert and sanctioned boundary transgressions, unresolved anger toward authority figures, restricted awareness of fantasy (especially hostile/aggressive), and transformation of countertransference hate to countertransference love.

Practitioners should use these risk factors to introspect and determine if or when they may be vulnerable to engaging in sexual boundary violations with a patient. Chapter 15 presents a measure derived from an empirically controlled study. This measure can be used for periodic risk assessment throughout a professional's career. Knowledge of the ethical code has not been found to be preventative. Further, it is dangerous for clinicians to ignore these risk factors in the belief that those who engage in sexual boundary violations are fundamentally different from ordinary practitioners or from ourselves (Gabbard, 1996; Celenza & Gabbard, 2003). The data suggest that we all may be vulnerable to boundary transgressions at some point in our professional lives and it is important to be aware of how and when this might occur.

ENDNOTES

This chapter is largely derived from a previously published paper (2005) A. Celenza, "Sexual boundary violations: How do They Happen?" *Directions in Psychiatry, 25*(2): 141–49.

1. For ease of discussion, I will use the therapist-patient relationship as a template for a relationship that contains a structured power imbalance. All of the discussions that follow can be applied in a general way to academic and mental health professionals, including psychologists, psychiatrists, social workers, psychoanalysts, psychiatric nurses, mental health counselors, teachers, and clergy. While there are important differences in these relationships, they all rest on a basic and structured power imbalance that renders sexual relations unethical.

2. An often cited prevalence study (Holroyd & Brodsky, 1977) has unfortunately contributed to confusion regarding the prevalence of one-time versus multiple transgressors by failing to distinguish between multiple contacts with the same patient versus multiple offenses with different patients. That study, as well as Tillinghast and Cournos (2000), made use of the term *recidivism* in an idiosyncratic way to denote multiple occasions rather than multiple patients.

3. For ease of discussion, I will often refer to the transgressor as "he" or "the therapist" and the patient as "she" or "the patient," because this is the most frequent gender pairing.

2

THIS COULDN'T HAPPEN TO ME

The [therapist] knows that he is working with highly explosive forces and that he needs to proceed with as much caution and conscientiousness as a chemist.

—S. Freud (1915, p. 170)

I have learned to beware the phrase "I would never do that." It has been a hard lesson to learn, however, since I have heard it uttered by both friends and colleagues, years before an eventual revelation of a complaint against them. It is also true that many other friends and colleagues, with no eventual charges or transgressions, have said the same, or other phrases such as "This could never happen to me," "You just don't do that," or "I always suspected he...." (We are so wise in retrospect.) Best to keep in mind the epigraph printed above; the treatment context is an intensely emotional and involving relationship. Either member of the dyad may be in a desperate state. It can be scary; it can explode.

In this chapter, I present a composite case derived from my experience with over seventy therapists, psychoanalysts, and clergy who have engaged in sexual boundary violations. It is also a distillation of the characteristics most commonly found in these cases and is offered to anchor in reality the more conceptual issues that will be discussed in later chapters. Though the case is a composite, none of the material is fabricated.

In what follows, I emphasize and elaborate the internal experience of the therapist, since the primary purpose of this book is to identify pitfalls, vulnerabilities, stress points, and warning signs for all mental health professionals, academics, and clergy. In addition, I do not mean to discount, in any way, the experience of the victim and the ways in which she is harmed. This imbalanced focus of attention is unavoidable, however, in the effort to enhance our training and our preventative armamentarium.

It also must be emphasized that the case illustration that follows is a particular kind of sexual boundary violation. Dr. Burn is a one-time transgressor whose psychology and situation are not that different from most mainstream practitioners. I have selected his case as an illustration in order to present the difficult, subtle, and more frequent type of challenge that we all face. I firmly believe that more help and understanding is needed in order to adequately address this very prevalent problem. Dr. Burn is not a psychopathic predator. He is not a person from whom we can feel a safe distance, and therefore he is not so easily dismissed. At the same time, for victims who have been exploited by the more egregious multiple transgressor—that is to say, the psychopathic predator—this case will not speak to their experiences. Since psychopathic predators are not amenable to rehabilitation, I have not focused my efforts toward them. Instead, I am putting a large measure of my efforts toward a more frequent type of sexual boundary transgression, as I see a more pressing need in this type of case.

I hope to address several common queries in this effort: first, to demonstrate how commonplace the precipitating circumstances and predisposing mental state of the transgressor are—in effect, to demonstrate how much both the circumstances and mind-set are like those in which you or I would find ourselves. It may be tempting to distance ourselves from Dr. Burn's dilemma and to convince ourselves that he is different. I am not so convinced. Further, it is important to remember that Dr. Burn was not in his usual frame of mind, nor was he at a typical time in his life. When he began treating the victim, Dr. Burn was about to turn 55, he was on the heels of a separation and divorce, and was in a dissatisfying new relationship. He was also dangerously isolated in his private practice, working too many hours, and was financially stressed. These situational stressors, often cited in the literature as the backdrop against which most sexual boundary violations occur, can facilitate the emergence of our less than optimal modes of functioning and states of mind.

Second, I hope to show how the road to ruin is most often paved with good intentions. At least on a conscious level, there are a great variety of rationalizations that serve to justify, for the therapist and sometimes for the patient as well, the seemingly harmless boundary crossings, even as these become closer to frank violations. They are always viewed with some sort of belief that the patient will benefit, will be healed, or will at least feel better in the short run. Sometimes this is indeed true, especially if the boundary crossings are the kind we all face. Accepting a gift, hugging at termination, or attending a wedding are not anathema to even conventional, mainstream practice. These crossings may be rare, but they need not be viewed as possibly signaling a downward trend on the so-called slippery slope—nor should they be glorified or relied upon in place of the more gritty and difficult work of everyday practice. Here, it is useful to be aware of Axel Hoffer's (personal communication, 2006) distinction between boundary crossings and boundary violations, the former being a minor departure in everyday technique and, most importantly, capable of being discussed within the treatment framework. (See Gutheil and Gabbard, 1993, for a more elaborated discussion of these differences.)

Third, I aim to show how the slippery slope is made up of small, easy-to-take, missteps along the way. Not one of these, especially at the initial part of the slide, can be taken out of context as a definitive signal that the therapeutic process is in trouble. It may be true that all sexual boundary violations begin with a slippery series of missteps, but it is also true that we are all *always on* the slippery slope and can engage in minor boundary crossings that do not eventually lead to more egregious boundary violations. The slippery slope is the terrain of everyday practice (Howard Levine, personal communication, 2001). Sexual boundary violations are not an inevitable outcome of slippery-slope missteps, however.

Simon (1995) has delineated a series of steps that can be viewed as constituting the so-called slippery slope in an effort to illustrate what the series of missteps that leads to frank boundary violations often looks like. These may start with a gradual erosion of the therapist's neutral position, for example, addressing each other by first names. Soon the therapy sessions become less clinical and more social. The patient begins to feel she is treated in a "special" way, perhaps more like a confidant. This ushers in a tendency toward therapist self-disclosures and may even include times when the therapist touches the patient (for example, a pat on the back when leaving the session). This touching then progresses to hugs and embraces, usually when the patient is upset about something distressing in her life.

What is happening on a deeper level is that the therapist is gaining some measure of control over the patient, usually by manipulating the transference, that is, using the patient's positive, idealizing, and perhaps loving feelings for the therapist in order to influence her to respond in ways he wants and needs. There may be negligence in prescribing medications or other routine aspects of the therapeutic role. Extratherapeutic contacts occur, therapy sessions are rescheduled for the end of the day, and/or therapy sessions become extended in time. Perhaps the point of no return has already been reached; however, it is certainly crossed when the therapist stops billing the patient. At this point, there is little semblance of a therapeutic process and it is not unusual for the therapist and patient to meet in an outright social manner, perhaps beginning with drinks and/or dinner after sessions. The final two steps, according to Simon, include dating and then finally sexual relations.

Although the slippery slope is never traversed in such an orderly way, these are reasonable descriptors of the ways in which steps are taken in many cases and serve as a good exemplar of what the dangerous slippery slope may look like. Davies (2000) has described her own experience on the slippery slope as more one of "a sudden awakening" where she is "perched on the tip of an inverted cone, with almost no room to maneuver and surrounded by treacherous slopes" (p. 223).

Lastly, in the illustration that follows, I aim to give a clinically contextualized picture of one therapist's traversal of the slippery slope as it occurred with a particular patient. As a colleague once asked, after hearing of a mutual colleague's transgression, "But how did he get out of his chair?" This is how.

DR. BURN

Dr. Burn, a middle-aged male therapist, sought treatment with me after his license was suspended for having become sexually involved with a patient. This therapy was mandated by the licensing board as part of a multifaceted rehabilitation plan that included restriction from independent practice, supervision, psychoeducation, and individual psychotherapy. We met once or twice weekly for eight years, though the therapy was mandated only for two. (After the two-year mandate expired, Dr. Burn was evaluated by the board members. This included an evaluation of the adequacy of all aspects of his rehabilitation program. He then was allowed to reapply for licensure. This required that he retake the licensing exam, which he successfully passed, and his license was reinstated.)

Dr. Burn was intelligent, attractive, and carefully groomed, and had an emotionally responsive nature and quick humor. He was psychodynamically trained and primarily conducted long-term treatments with adults. He was divorced, had several children from his marriage, and had been living with a girlfriend for about a year when he became involved with his patient. He was relieved to be out of his marriage but suffered greatly from the separation from his children. He also felt relatively unsupported in his new relationship.

Dr. Burn recalls feeling almost wholly isolated at the time of his involvement with his patient. His primary contact with adults, other than his girlfriend, was with his patients in his practice. Most importantly, his relationship with his girlfriend had been on a deteriorating course for several years. They were emotionally estranged and he felt little hope of regaining a more satisfying relationship. He was highly self-critical of his apparent inability to reach his girlfriend. He was attempting to engage a couple's therapist, though his girlfriend was resistant to the idea.

Dr. Burn's initial understanding of his transgression revolved around a sense that he had been in love with his patient and that he had hoped to provide for her a "corrective emotional experience" (his words) in reparation for her profound history of abuse by men. He felt compassion for her as a victim of domestic violence in her marriage and sexual abuse in her childhood history. He was aware of a strong desire, even need, to help her and relieve some of her distress.

Interestingly, the treatment with this patient had been difficult from the beginning. Dr. Burn had experienced her as hard-to-reach and withholding, with great difficulty trusting men. Previous treatments with female therapists had proved unsatisfactory to her so she contacted Dr. Burn with the hope of a different experience. She was depressed, married to an alcoholic man who was prone to violent behavior and who had hit her on several occasions.

The patient was resistant to talking about herself and spent many sessions in silence, vigilantly watching Dr. Burn as if she were afraid of him. Dr. Burn was initially respectful of her fears but was also aware of feeling frustrated at her inability to talk to him. He became more overtly reassuring to her and uncharacteristically offered to hold her hand or hug her; his conscious rationale at the time had been that he was attempting to help her feel safe. (During our work together, we learned that although this was the only patient whom he had actually physically touched, Dr. Burn tended to become reassuring or gratifying in nonphysical ways when he experienced his patients as frustrated, disappointed, or hostile.) He also had been dimly aware of feeling increasingly helpless and had begun to view the patient as *willfully withholding*. This had echoed Dr. Burn's experience of his mother, who had overtly resisted his attempts to engage yet had been hostile and critical if he had withdrawn. In an analogous manner, the patient's perception of Dr. Burn had paralleled her experience with her father, where she had felt intruded upon along with a continual pressure to prop up his self-esteem. At this time, however, she was greatly distressed and could not risk displeasing or losing Dr. Burn, so she responded to his advances.

Dr. Burn had become increasingly affectionate toward his patient, consciously attempting to help her feel safe and embracing the belief that she would be cured if she were loved in a constructive, caring way. The handholding and hugging at the end of sessions seemed to help, in the sense that she began to feel better. However, Dr. Burn overlooked the appeasing effects of his efforts (Apfel & Simon, 1985) and the manner in which these served to circumvent (at least temporarily) the patient's hate and rage, preventing their emergence in the transference, at least for a time.

The affectionate advances began to include sitting next to her on the couch. She soon would lean into him and put her head on his shoulder, coinciding with a deepening of her ability to share her distress with Dr. Burn. In one particular session, she was acutely upset, saying she would kill herself if she had to bear another moment. Dr. Burn held her until the end of that session.

In the next several sessions, the patient's suicidality became a prominent and continuing focus. She began to complain that Dr. Burn was not helping her and that the hugging was not enough to make her suicidal feelings go away. Dr. Burn was shaken, feeling he was doing all he could to help her. Besides the hugging and being physically close, he thought he was trying to help her understand her feelings and help her feel stronger so she might leave her abusive husband. The patient began to express her fear that she was unlovable, unworthy, and undesirable, evidenced by the fact that Dr. Burn could never love her fully, especially outside of a therapeutic frame. She said she was going to kill herself and that this was the only way out. At this point, Dr. Burn kissed her and they embraced passionately.

Hugging and kissing became part of each session thereafter until they were involved in a full sexual relationship. Dr. Burn terminated the therapy relationship and they continued their involvement for another year. Throughout this year, the patient had become more trusting, and had exposed more of her feelings and situation to Dr. Burn. Not surprisingly, she had fallen in love with him and wanted him to leave his girlfriend. Dr. Burn thought he was in love with her as well and they talked about being together for life.

Dr. Burn recalled that during his tumble down the slippery slope, he had felt conflicted about his actions due to his awareness that he was violating the ethical code. Yet he also remembered feeling trapped by his patient's suicidality, fearing that she might actually kill herself and he would have felt responsible for her death. He also remembered feeling excited by the fantasy that he would be the one to save her, especially where other therapists had failed. He rationalized his romantic and sexual involvement with her through the belief that she would be cured if she were loved in a constructive and caring way.

Dr. Burn was not aware of competitive feelings toward her husband or toward the other therapists whom she had seen, but he did consciously entertain fantasies of rescuing the patient from her distress and teaching her to love in nondestructive ways. He reminded himself that his training emphasized the "healing power of love," which he interpreted to mean some kind of corrective emotional experience. He told himself that she had not been helped in previous, more traditional modalities and he thought he understood her in a special and unique way that other therapists would not understand. He knew he could not describe this therapy to anyone (a supervisor or a colleague) and he asked her to keep the treatment confidential as well. They both thereby constructed a thick insulation around their relationship from this point on, a kind of "hyper-confidentiality" or treatment bubble that is typical of these kinds of sexual boundary violations.

Once they became more fully romantically and sexually intimate, the patient's behavior toward Dr. Burn changed as well. She became openly affectionate and idealizing of him. He remembers having several powerful fantasies at that time in which he felt closer to God—perhaps identified with him. He recalls a dream in which he saw himself diving from a very high place into a small bit of water, yet surviving. He recalls experiencing, in certain private moments, an oceanic feeling—a oneness fantasy in which he felt empowered by the universe and felt he could accomplish anything.

Dr. Burn and his patient constructed a narrative about their love that rivaled any involvement they had ever experienced or seen previously. They understood each other's dreams and they could communicate without talking. In short, they were soul mates. Not surprisingly, the patient began to have the fantasy that Dr. Burn would leave his girlfriend for her. She became increasingly disappointed that he did not. Over time, their bliss was tarnished by her frustration. She began to experience him as weak and passive. He felt trapped and feared she would report him to the licensing board if he left her.

One evening, the patient saw Dr. Burn at a concert with his girlfriend. Something "clicked" in her mind. She suddenly knew that he would never leave his girlfriend. In an understandable rage, she wrote a complaint to the licensing board, sending along with the complaint copies of love letters that he had written to her. She also wrote a letter to Dr. Burn informing him of the complaint and stated, "I needed to get out of this trap with you somehow and I also know you need help. I have done this to help us both." The licensing board contacted Dr. Burn several weeks later, asking him to write a response to the complaint and instructing him not to have any contact with the patient from that moment forward.

FORMULATION

The following formulation is comprised of discoveries and constructions that Dr. Burn and I arrived at during the course of his psychotherapy (see chapter 11 for an elaboration of his treatment). It is a retrospective construction of how he was feeling and what he was responding to at the time of his involvement with his patient. Many of the insights that follow were not available to him at the time of his involvement with the patient, nor were they in his awareness at the beginning of his psychotherapy with me. Rather, they emerged over time as we explored his feelings and memories, and did our best to construct a formulation of what had occurred.

As Dr. Burn recounted the sequence of events, it became clear that the gradual seduction of his patient had occurred when he had felt the therapy was reaching an *impasse,* at a time when hostile and angry feelings were beginning to emerge and be directed toward him. Of course, these should have been allowed to emerge and become articulated as the patient's negative transference to Dr. Burn that he then should have explored. However, at the time, Dr. Burn was too narcissistically fragile and situationally stressed to tolerate her criticisms of him and his own frustration with her.

In a mutual way, then, it can be seen that the impasse had a countertransference component as well since Dr. Burn was unable to explore and bear the patient's emerging hostility (later directed toward herself in the form of suicidality) because of his fragility and countertransference to her. Dr. Burn was reacting to his own emerging hostility and a fear that the patient would become angry or blaming of him because of his difficulty reaching her, helping her, and ultimately keeping her safe. Like his withholding and critical mother, Dr. Burn unconsciously experienced the patient as a cold and hostile maternal figure. This confluence of factors was intolerable to Dr. Burn at this barren and stressed time in his life. The seduction served to lure the patient away from her negative transference and reinforced a defensive idealization that both she and Dr. Burn found easier to bear.

Though unaware of his motives at the early phase of the relationship, Dr. Burn retrospectively surmised that he had been unable to tolerate his unconscious hostility toward this patient, felt in response to the patient's withholding. Because his countertransference had included unconscious and unresolved transference elements from his own past, he had felt responsible for the patient's dissatisfaction much as he had felt responsible for his mother's unhappiness. In the face of the patient's dissatisfaction, Dr. Burn's need to remain connected with a benign, accepting maternal figure and his need to escape self-blame and anger had led him to abandon the therapeutic stance.

On a conscious level, Dr. Burn had misconstrued the meanings of the therapeutic alliance and the process of empathy, confusing understanding with loving and collaboration with providing a corrective emotional experience (see chapter 14 for a fuller elaboration of these rationalizations and clinical errors). This was a confusion that could be detected in his overall therapeutic orientation, a confusion that might have been addressed had he been in a careful and attentive supervision. Unconsciously, he had allowed his needs to be admired and accepted to influence his behavior in a way that manipulated the patient's transference away from hate and rage toward admiration and love.

In addition, as the patient's behavior began to replicate a familiar but unresolved pattern from his past, he unconsciously used his sexual feelings for the patient to circumvent the recognition of his countertransference hate toward her. Thus, his "love" of his patient was being mobilized in the service of a defense against his increasing frustration, anger, and fears of abandonment by the patient as a maternal figure. In this way, his manifest "love" for the patient really had more to do with his hatred of her.

Other aspects of his relationship to his mother were replicated in this particular transference/countertransference (mis)fit as well. As elaborated in chapter 11, Dr. Burn felt that his mother had been depressed and chronically disappointed in her spouse. He had experienced his father as passive, weak, and totally controlled by his wife. Throughout childhood, he had felt his mother regarded her son as her savior, yet he had felt helpless to please her. He had developed grandiose, compensatory rescue fantasies of himself as a woman's ultimate savior that existed alongside a view of himself as helpless and weak. He had feared exposure of this imagined incompetence, and this had intensified the pressure to act in the face of perceived disappointment in the maternal figure. (For an elaborated discussion of these dynamics as they emerged in Dr. Burn's subsequent therapy, see chapter 11.)

THE ROAD TO RUIN

Many of the steps in the so-called slippery slope, if taken separately or in certain contexts, may be a part of a therapist's natural style and may not necessarily be problematic. It is not uncommon, for example, for some therapists to have patients address them by their first name. This can often be the case with patients of the same age or generation. A hug, especially at the end of treatment, may not signal a problematic boundary crossing; indeed, the absence of a hug in certain circumstances may be more problematic, such as with the tragic death of a child or other extreme events in a patient's life. Janet Malcolm, in a tragicomic novel about classical psychoanalysis, refers to an example cited by Greenson (1967) where a distraught young mother talks of her ailing baby. The analyst largely does not respond and then adds a comment about her resistance. Shocked at his lack of humaneness, she quit her analysis, stating on her way out, "You're sicker than I am" (1981, pp. 74–75).

Clearly, the constricted and often caricatured image of a psychoanalyst who cannot express any compassion or human feeling is a trend gone too far. Contemporary psychoanalysts are more likely to integrate their humanity and empathic expressiveness in their routine mode of technique. Gutheil and

Gabbard (1998) emphasize the important role of context in establishing the meaning of a particular behavior. In addition, these meanings must be examined both from the therapist's and the patient's point of view. It is not unusual for a patient to understand a gesture or statement made by the therapist in quite a different way than the therapist had intended. Similarly, behaviors (including statements) can be understood differently (by either the patient or the therapist) when recalled at a different time and context.

Many behaviors and statements made by the therapist are accompanied by rationalizations that serve to justify (in the moment) their enactment. It is only after the fact (Renik, 1999), sometimes long after or perhaps never, that the therapist becomes aware of a self-serving or defensive aspect to his or her behavior that prevented the therapist from seeing the inadvisability of the action. Many self-disclosures fall into this category. The context that is likely to provide the fodder for a defensive reaction on the therapist's part may be the patient's emerging disappointment, sometimes stated directly but often just subliminally sensed by the therapist. If the therapist is unable to explore and tolerate the patient's frustration, he or she may react with a conscious rationale to become more revealing, perhaps by disclosing some personal information with the idea that the patient will benefit from learning of some similarity between them.

There is some concern that the increased awareness about maintaining boundaries will stifle creativity (Williams, 1997) or encourage a "politically correct" constraint in the way in which therapists embody their role. I have not found this to be the case. In my experience, the increased awareness of the precursors, motivations, and consequences of sexual boundary violations has helped those involved in the profession, including consumers of mental health services. How could it be harmful to learn more of the truth? The clearer we all are about where the pitfalls in our endeavors are, the better equipped we will be to provide sound care to our patients.

In the effort to more greatly understand the terrain of our work, it has become clear to me that it is not so much the behaviors that are problematic by themselves, but rather whether they are engaged in for narcissistically driven reasons. In each moment of the treatment, it can be asked, Is this for me or for the patient? The Exploitation Index (Simon, 1999) is a measure designed to indicate the degree to which behaviors associated with the slippery slope are part of a therapist's experience, repertoire, and/or current experience with a particular patient. This is a helpful measure to signal to therapists that they may be engaging in boundary crossings or violations. However, there is also a need for therapists to introspect, to be aware of internal pressures and situational stress in order to assess their vulnerability at different times in their professional lives (see chapter 15 for a useful tool exploring these factors).

It is important here to note the larger context in which Dr. Burn's relationship with his patient occurred. Dr. Burn was engaged in his own personal therapy of several years at the time. This therapist described himself as "humanistic/eclectic" in orientation. Dr. Burn reported that his therapist was aware of Dr. Burn's involvement with his patient and, according to Dr. Burn, explicitly encouraged the misconduct. (This therapist also knew the professional ethical code against such behavior.) The rationale for this astonishing aspect of Dr. Burn's situation had to do with the therapist's view that Dr. Burn was masochistic (a description of Dr. Burn's character that was largely accurate). Given his masochism, it was the therapist's view that Dr. Burn should not "deprive himself of the pleasure his patient might give him." The therapist reasoned that if Dr. Burn were to so deprive himself—that is, if Dr. Burn were to ethically maintain the treatment frame and *not* become sexually involved with his patient—the therapist would view this as an act of neurotic self-deprivation of which Dr. Burn had a long history. When the licensing board became aware of Dr. Burn's therapist and his views, he was called before the board and reprimanded. No formal complaint was filed against him nor was he limited in his ability to practice. He was told, "We're watching you." No further information about this therapist is available.

Now, before dismissing this entire case based on the larger context of Dr. Burn's clearly misguided personal therapy, it is important to note that in most cases the transgressing therapist is wholly isolated in his practice, discussing the case with no therapist, peer, or supervisor. In these cases, the therapist loses his way on his own and with no externawl encouragement. Another very common larger context is where the transgressing therapist does meet regularly with a supervisor, trusted colleagues, and/or a peer supervisory group. In none of these venues does the case with the victim/patient get discussed, however. Thus, a facilitating context is not always in the form of direct encouragement. It may take the form of an *absence* of input and the failure of a third or outside perspective (see chapter 13 for more discussion of the role of consultation and outside observers).

Context, countertransference, conscious and unconscious defensive tendencies—all of these issues must be taken into account when considering a departure from standard technique. Still, there is no guarantee that any behavior or statement will be understood with the meaning that the therapist, at least consciously, intends. The crucial factor in all treatments is the extent to which interactions and events within the treatment can be verbalized and discussed as grist for the mill. In this way, boundary crossings become part of and contained by the therapeutic process (Gutheil & Gabbard, 1993). This is, in the final analysis, the purpose of the treatment in the first place—to render conscious and verbal that which was beyond words and outside of one's control.

In an effort to aid practitioners in this effort, I have derived a measure, presented in chapter 15, that quantifies several of the characteristics found to be precursors of sexual boundary violations. This is a measure derived from an empirically controlled study of transgressors (subjects who had been involved in at least one sexual relationship with a patient). These subjects were given a series of questionnaires designed to assess those factors that clinical experience has indicated are problematic features of sexual boundary transgressions. The scores on these measures were then compared and contrasted with therapists who had not been involved in sexual boundary violations at any point in their career. (See appendix A for an elaborated discussion of this study.)

Chapter 15 presents the Boundary Violation Vulnerability Index (BVVI), a 45-item questionnaire that practitioners may use to indicate whether or not they have the characteristics associated with boundary violation vulnerability. This is not a predictive measure but one designed to signal potential problematic areas. While these characteristics are those that distinguish boundary violators from nonviolators, there is also some overlap between these two groups. No studies to date have been performed that prospectively predict boundary violations; thus the measure is not designed to be predictive of future problematic behavior.

3

PRECURSORS TO THERAPIST
SEXUAL MISCONDUCT

> The therapist must recognize that the patient's falling in love is
> induced by the analytic situation and is not to be confused with
> the charms of his person; so that he has no grounds whatever for
> being proud of such a "conquest," as it would be called outside
> of analysis.
>
> —S. Freud (1915, pp. 160–161)

There is an undeniable curiosity about what may lead an analyst or therapist
to engage in sexual relations with a patient. The fantasy that one might
desire another person profoundly enough to risk one's entire professional career
is at once horrifying and intriguing. While most analysts and therapists would
acknowledge having been sexually attracted to a patient at one time or another,
the ability to tolerate such feelings and resist the temptation to act is not usually
compromised, even when intense affects, fantasies, and impulses are aroused.

What leads some therapists to translate such feelings into action? Is it the
intensity of the feelings, an unusual and specific affective state itself, something inherent in a particular dyad, or special vulnerabilities in the therapist?
In an attempt to answer these questions, this chapter presents data on a group
of therapists who had engaged in sexual relations with a patient.

The data for the present chapter come from therapies, evaluations, or
supervisions of 17 offenders—14 male and 3 female. (This sample is a subset
of over 100 mental health professionals who have engaged in sexualized dual
relationships of various types. Only those mental health professionals who
are *therapists* are included in this subset; the findings have been corroborated
in the larger sample.) All male offenders' transgressions involved one or more
heterosexual relationships. All female offenders transgressed in one homosexual relationship. Some therapists were sexually involved with a patient

only briefly, while others sustained a longer term relationship. A few were involved with more than one patient, either simultaneously or over time.

The therapists were referred to me in a variety of ways. Two sought treatment and two others sought supervision after the suspension of their license. One female therapist sought treatment during her involvement with her patient. Two were involved in a patient-initiated consultation. Of the remaining ten, three referred themselves, and seven were referred by an overseeing professional organization or licensing board for a comprehensive evaluation after their licenses had been suspended. (Other therapists have sought treatment as a preventative measure in response to anxiety that they might become involved with a patient. These cases are not included in the present discussion, but illustrate the need for a less punitive atmosphere within the profession so that therapists feel free to seek consultation when they feel the need.)

The evaluations included extensive interviews, a full psychological test battery, and, whenever possible, consultation with the therapist's supervisors, colleagues, spouse, and therapist, as well as the patient/victim. None of the offending therapists were psychoanalysts, although two had had personal analyses. All were psychodynamically trained and conducted intensive psychodynamic psychotherapy. All saw themselves as competent, experienced, and sensitive to transference/countertransference enactments.

Characteristics that were reflected in 73% or more of the cases are included in this discussion. (More than half of the characteristics were present in 88% or more of the cases, see table 3.1.) These characteristics, derived from the convergence of test data (especially Rorschach scores and Thematic Apperception Test [TAT] themes), background information, and clinical observation, may represent precursors to therapist sexual misconduct.

It is important to note at the outset that the findings presented here are not the result of a controlled study or a prospective study. At this point, it cannot be concluded that the findings predict therapist sexual misconduct or that

Table 3.1.   Common Characteristics

Characteristic	1	2	3	4	5	6	7
% Endorsed	94	73	80	85	93	100	88
# Endorsed	16	11	12	11	14	17	14
# Not Endorsed	1	4	3	3	1	0	2
Missing Data	0	2	2	3	2	0	1
Total Assessed	17	15	15	13	15	17	16

Characteristics: 1 = Low self-esteem; 2 = Childhood history of emotional deprivation and sexualized overstimulation; 3 = Restricted awareness of fantasy; 4 = Family history of boundary transgressions; 5 = Anger toward authority figures; 6 = Intolerance of negative transference; 7 = Defensive transformation of countertransference hate to countertransference love.

the predisposing factors are characteristic of therapists who engage in sexual misconduct as opposed to those who do not. Because this is not a report on a prospective study or a study that included a control group, these findings are presented as preliminary and represent a starting point for future research. Subsequent to the performance of this study, a controlled empirical project was performed comparing these and other characteristics in therapists who had engaged in sexual boundary violations to therapists who had never transgressed sexual boundaries. The findings of this subsequent study corroborate these precursors and are reported in appendix A.

From the data under discussion, it appears that the motivation for the sexual transgression(s) most often involved unconscious, denied, or compartmentalized[1] conflicts about which the therapist had little insight. These issues were usually related to personal conflicts in the character of the therapist, rendering him vulnerable to enactments when intolerable helplessness, loss of self-esteem, or intense frustration were evoked. In almost all of the cases, this formulation was based on interpretations of the data that the therapist confirmed over time. Many of these precursors were not possible to glean at the outset or without an intensive evaluation or therapy.

CLINICAL FINDINGS

There are eight risk factors that have been identified that may represent precursors to sexual boundary violations (see table 1.1). The first involves long-standing and unresolved narcissistic neediness and lifelong struggles with low self-esteem and depression. Almost all therapists reported a lifelong struggle with a sense of unworthiness, inadequacy, or outright feelings of failure. The therapists have been described as lovesick (Twemlow & Gabbard, 1989) or narcissistic (Gonsiorek & Schoener, 1987). I have referred to them as narcissistically needy. One therapist reported always feeling "empty and needy, like I was lacking in something." He related these feelings to the punitive and shaming atmosphere in his home. He believes he had become a high achiever but could not derive satisfaction from his accomplishments. Another therapist described his mother as a "devastating critic" who was unrelenting and unpredictable in her hostility toward him. He believes he had internalized chronic feelings of self-doubt and "a sense of inner badness" with which he has struggled all his life. Still another therapist reported a "frightening feeling of bottomless need."

Consistent with these reports were Rorschach indicators of characterologically based emotional neediness and interpersonal longing, noted in 75%

of the cases. For example, texture scores occurred at a frequency of more than three standard deviations greater than the normative mean (Celenza & Hilsenroth, 1997). There was also an abundance of percepts described as "damaged," "wounded," "chewed," "broken," or "killed." Content scores reflected a preoccupation with body integrity, feelings of damage and vulnerability demonstrated in the preponderance of percepts involving anatomy, x-ray, and morbid content (Celenza & Hilsenroth, 1997; for a more extended description of the findings of this study, see appendix B).

In all cases, the therapists acknowledged these feelings as long-standing. In the therapy during which he or she had transgressed, the treatment purpose was typically subverted so that the therapist's needs had become the central focus. This may have begun in a subtle manner where the therapist begins disclosing personal information. This was then rationalized by the therapist as educating or guiding the patient or as an attempt to reduce a power imbalance by sharing personal information. It can be speculated, however, that underlying the technical rationale was a need for sympathy, soothing, and/or a muted plea for rescue.

The patients often reported a perception of the therapist as highly powerful (at least initially) and were consequently unable or reluctant to deny the therapist's needs for attention. Of the therapists studied, however, 94% reported a paradoxical *subjective feeling of powerlessness*, especially in relation to the patient with whom he or she transgressed. From a review of their practices and therapeutic styles, it was clear that these therapists tended to rely on their patients to meet their narcissistic needs and required that their patients always hold them in positive esteem. Many patients reported a sense that angry or disappointed feelings toward the therapist or the treatment were taboo.

These therapists do not appear to be overtly arrogant or grandiose (unlike the charismatic psychopathic predator); rather, they display *a covert and denied grandiosity* (the second precursor) that is apparent in their fantasies and ideals. Observation usually reveals a mild-mannered, self-effacing, and humble exterior that hides underlying (and unchallenged) beliefs in powers of rescue and omnipotence. It is not unusual to find the therapist engaging in rationalizing boundary crossings because both therapist and patient view themselves as "exceptions" to the usual ethical practices (Epstein & Simon, 1990; Gabbard & Lester, 1995a; Notman & Nadelson, 1999).

Upon close examination of their clinical practices, there are usually many slippery-slope boundary crossings with unusually challenging patients. Indeed, these therapists often pride themselves in being able to treat the untreatable and to do so in unconventional ways. It is important to note, however, that these boundary crossings are not warning signs in and of themselves since challenging patients are often difficult to engage and may require unusual methods by any therapist. The so-called slippery slope is one where we all find ourselves; whether the boundary crossings will eventuate in later sexual boundary violations is not indicated by the boundary crossings themselves. However, it is also the case that many seemingly benign boundary crossings can be misconstrued by the patient and/or be portrayed in a worse light in retrospect (Gutheil & Gabbard, 1993). Examples of such boundary crossings include hand-holding during the session, extra or longer sessions, a hug viewed by the therapist as an attempt to soothe, and a variety of self-disclosures rationalized as joining or sharing oneself with the patient.

The third precursor is described as an *intolerance of negative transference* in these therapists. For some transgressors, this risk factor is not particular to the therapist-patient dyad in which the exploitation occurred but is characteristic of his treatment style in general. Most likely due to the fragility in self-esteem, this group of transgressors has great difficulty tolerating and exploring disappointments, frustrations, and/or criticisms that the patient may have about the treatment. Other transgressors, however, do not show a particular fragility in this area; they conduct thorough explorations of negative transference with a large majority of their patients but are highly sensitive to criticism from the patients with whom they eventually transgress. This again points to the issue of the particular dynamic in the therapist-patient dyad (a question more extensively explored in chapters 2 and 4).

With some exceptions, it can be said that these therapists tended to rely on their patients to meet their narcissistic needs and required that their patients always view them in positive ways. When patients were consulted, many reported a sense that angry or disappointed feelings toward the therapist or the treatment were unwelcome. One therapist, who was psychodynamically trained, was asked how he deals with the hostile or devaluing projections of his patients. He replied, "None of my patients feel negatively toward me. I have had no complaints."

Six of the therapists in this sample were pastoral counselors who by training are placed in multiple roles with respect to their patients (e.g., performing religious ceremonies, counseling, educating, home visiting). For pastoral counselors, the ability to alternate among these multiple roles is seen as a virtue, and their education and training typically does not address the impact of these practices on the transference. One therapist routinely hugged or affectionately (from his point of view) touched parishioners as they exited church. Many of these parishioners were also his therapy patients. His stance in therapy could be described as a kind of "naive goodness" where he attempted to effect positive change by offering acceptance, nurturance, and insight. He divulged personal experiences to clients, gave them books to read, and informed them of workshops he would be attending, all in a conscious attempt to teach or guide. When a parishioner or patient expressed disappointment or frustration in him or in the therapy, he would suggest a consultation or transfer the patient to another therapist. He even referred one patient for psychological testing, as though the patient's anger was a sign of a cognitive deficit!

The fourth precursor is comprised of two separate but related characteristics in the childhood history of the transgressor. These therapists report *a sexualization in their relationship with the primary caregiver* (usually the mother). The data here do not refer to outright sexual abuse, but rather an overstimulation of the child in a sexualized manner. This was reported by the therapists in a way that indicated no conscious awareness of having been overstimulated as a child. Only one therapist in this sample reported having been the victim of outright sexual abuse. (In a national, randomly drawn sample of 323 mental health practitioners, Jackson and Nuttall [2001] found that although childhood sexual abuse was not prevalent per se, the severity of childhood sexual abuse increased the likelihood of engaging in subsequent sexual misconduct with clients.) In my sample, however, it was more typical for the childhood sexualization to take the form of covert seductiveness and overstimulation that, most importantly, occurred against a background of *emotional deprivation and neglect*. Their childhood is described as one where early needs for recognition, affirmation, attention, and affection were not met, leaving the child hungry for any kind of contact or attention. The maternal figure demonstrates a contradictory style in this regard where she, usually the authoritarian, dominant parent, tends to be prohibiting and depriving yet unwittingly seductive. This results in a lack of differentiation between tender and lustful feelings wherein soothing, understanding, and holding inevitably stir up sexual longing.

For example, one therapist who was raised in a conservative and highly religious family reported early memories of his mother undressing, not in an intentionally seductive way but in an asexual manner, seemingly unaware of the stimulating potential of her body. Another therapist described his mother as highly intolerant of physical touch, prohibiting her three young sons from hugging her or even holding her hand. He commented, "The more I tried to get close to her, the more frightened she became." This mother, however, enjoyed a vicarious titillation from hearing of her sons' multiple sexual exploits when they were older. This therapist stated, "My mother always enjoyed lusty sons."

Another therapist considered his mother a powerful matriarch who could be warm and loving toward his nine sisters but was unaffectionate and unpredictable toward him, her only son. He felt he could not please her and that he was often punished, seemingly solely because he was a boy. This same therapist's father was described as a man who "enjoyed his manhood." His father built cars, raced hot rods, and brandished a "rape whistle" about which he would joke, "If you want it, blow it."

Yet another therapist described his parents as "Edwardian, very formal, unaffectionate, and repressive." His parents slept in separate bedrooms, had little contact with each other, and maintained an austere family atmosphere in the home. This therapist recalls being slapped on the hand in response to naughty behavior and longed to be slapped again since this was the only physical contact he remembered with either of his parents. At the same time, his father had homosexual lovers who would visit the home in the afternoons and with whom he would shower. Though all members of his family were aware of these affairs, they were never openly acknowledged.

One therapist's Rorschach imagery expressed this dilemma poignantly. On Card VII of the Rorschach (a card that typically evokes imagery associated with femininity or maternal figures), he perceived, "Two female puppets— you can put your hand in through the bottom and make them move whatever way you want." This therapist's projective testing reflected a perception of women as emotionally unresponsive except through sexual manipulation (see appendix B for a further elaboration of Rorschach indices).

As other authors have noted (Gabbard, 1994a, 1994b; Twemlow & Gabbard, 1989), this childhood experience can result in unresolved needs that are then enacted in the therapeutic dyad on a part-self- and object-representational level. Intimate relationships are characterized by intense longings for understanding, acceptance, and acknowledgment of one's goodness while oedipal-level issues of jealousy, rivalry, and whole-object relatedness are relatively absent. Consistent with this were sexual content responses on the Rorschach (Celenza & Hilsenroth, 1997; see appendix B), wherein 77% were perceived as isolated body parts (as opposed to integrated aspects of whole human responses). These responses were often associated with primitive, morbid, or aggressive content (e.g., "a bleeding vagina, it looks like it's splashing, ejecting with some force"; "a penis that's not fully developed"; "a scrotum with just testicles, no sack"). It is often possible to interpret the sexualization of the therapy process as actualizing an underlying "therapeutic copulation fantasy" (Searles, 1979; Gabbard & Lester, 1995a), that is, the belief that sex will cure the patient's ills.

Fifth, there is usually precedence in the family history of *boundary transgressions by parental figures.* This occurs against a background of high moralism and represents a denied hypocrisy. Family members may be aware of this hypocrisy. Wishes were simultaneously prohibited yet covertly permitted in a denied, unintegrated way. Examples might include infidelity or financial misdeeds. Many of the therapists reported having been aware as a child of parental extramarital affairs. For example, one therapist reported that his mother had had multiple affairs while his stepfather was away on work-related trips. While the stepfather apparently never knew of the mother's extramarital involvements, the son (now therapist) knew her secrets and felt forced to keep them from his stepfather. This occurred in a context of otherwise rigid adherence to moral guidelines.

Another therapist viewed his parents as strict, prohibitive, and sexually naive though he acknowledged his father's reputation as a "Romeo." When asked if he thought his father had been unfaithful to his mother, this therapist responded, "That's out of the question. He was too straight-laced. . . . Though now that I think about it, he was frequently away at night." This therapist then offered the belief that "people don't do what they actually do." Yet another therapist reported that his mother's first husband was his father's brother.

The boundary transgressions are not always played out in the sexual arena. One therapist reported that his parents asked him for a financial loan when he was a freshman in college. A few years later, they asked him to cosign a bank loan in order to secure it. Here the boundary transgression is generational, where the son is treated as the responsible parent. This same therapist reports an event in childhood that has always remained ambiguous: His father was suddenly out of work, with no explanation, and remained so for almost a year. Presently, this therapist has wondered if his father were fired for some kind of sexual impropriety since he also remembers, as a teenager, discovering his father's pornography collection.

It is easy to see how such a family situation may set the stage for the internalization of *vertically split superego structures* (one aspect of which is based on an identification with the transgressing parent), which *prohibits overt need gratification yet permits the gratification of wishes in secret and forbidden contexts.* The child develops a dual mode of moral functioning (or a split in superego structures) based on an identification with both levels of functioning in the parent(s). Thus, reality consists of two levels: one that is moral and consensual but restrictive and depriving while another is secret, compartmentalized, and immoral. It is in this latter reality where forbidden needs may be gratified. This dynamic may mirror the patient's wish to reenact a sexual relationship with a forbidden object with which the therapist then colludes (Gabbard, 1994b). The therapeutic dyad presents a context where these dynamics may be enacted; it is both sexually stimulating and forbidden. For some therapists, there may be an enactment of childhood incestuous wishes involving masochistic self-sacrifice as well as a courting of punishment for forbidden pleasures (Gabbard & Lester, 1995a).

The part of the therapist that is identified with the transgressing parent is a serious risk factor that may explain why these therapists permit themselves to violate boundaries against their conscious judgment and ethics. The emotional deprivation experienced during childhood results in fragile self-esteem and displaced needs for acceptance and love. Finally, the identification with the transgressing parent includes permitting the gratification of wishes in secret, forbidden contexts. The therapeutic setting is one such context.

Sixth, there was usually intense and unconscious *unresolved anger toward authority figures*. This factor is evident in their histories as well as in current preoccupations. Though they often can present themselves as highly remorseful (which is genuine), the exploitation itself represents a rebellion against the authority of their profession and an underlying desire to break the rules. Derived from unresolved anger toward the authoritarian parent (again, usually the maternal figure), the licensing board, ethics committees, and/or professional organization can come to represent these authority figures.

In one case, after several months of intensive psychotherapy, it became apparent that the therapist had the fantasy that he and I were in secret collusion against the licensing board to reverse the suspension of his license. This fantasy paralleled an unresolved oedipal dynamic in which his mother had prohibited gratification while his father secretly had colluded with him (Celenza, 1991; see chapter 11 for an elaboration of this dynamic). Another therapist (a minister and pastoral counselor) experienced his involvement with his patient as an attempt to "fuck God and fuck the church at the same time."

Yet another therapist told a revealing story on the second card of the TAT. On this particular card, the therapist was asked to tell a story in response to a picture of a man raking a field, a pregnant woman leaning against a tree, and a young woman in the foreground:

> There's . . . a dark side of it—a flirtation—not dark, maybe ambiguous. . . . There's sexual tension between the man and his niece, because of her freshness, her openness. . . . That sets up a triangle. That newness catches his eye, catches his soul. I don't think anything [happens]. But there might have been, if that doggone pregnant woman weren't keepin' such a close eye. I think he'd probably like to.

It is not insignificant that I was eight months pregnant when I had evaluated this therapist! At the time, he displayed no awareness that he had revealed both his need for and hostility toward me as an authority figure.

In my consultations, it has generally turned out that the maternal figure was the authoritarian parent who was experienced as seductive yet prohibitive and rejecting. The unresolved authority issues are re-experienced in the negative maternal transference and may be projected onto the overseeing board or the professional organization. Among psychoanalysts who have transgressed, Gabbard (1994a) and Gabbard and Lester (1995a) have found evidence of unresolved anger or resentment at the institute or training analyst with a concomitant fantasy of embarrassing these authority figures by disgracing oneself.

Seventh, *restricted awareness of fantasy* was observed in a majority of the therapists, especially in those who presented with genuine guilt and self-reproach. This restriction is evident in both sexual and aggressive realms where the therapist is unable to admit to or access hateful or desirous wishes except in conventional or muted ways. Since a restriction in the ability to use fantasy impedes symbolic thinking, transference, countertransference, and defensive feelings are taken at face value. There is a loss of the "as if" nature of the therapeutic relationship and, in general, a loss of the ability to explore multiple meanings. In particular, these therapists had great difficulty perceiving aggression in themselves or others.

This is often related to unresolved unconscious guilt over hostile feelings (toward the patient and/or toward any person). These therapists describe sanitized images of interpersonal relationships where people interact without envy or competitive and hostile feelings. This restriction is consistent with the highly moralistic ways in which these therapists were raised; however, it also plays a part in the therapists' limitation in understanding more severely disturbed patients who are often overrun with hostility, envy, and other intensely felt feelings. It is not that the therapists react to such patients with moralism or judgmentalism; rather, they tend to seriously underestimate the patient's pathology and have difficulty recognizing the patient's hostility and desire to corrupt the therapeutic process (Gutheil & Gabbard, 1993).

Notably, most also had great difficulty acknowledging the transgressions as inherently hostile. Not surprisingly, these therapists were exceedingly moralistic toward themselves. Conscious fantasy lacked aggressive play and other impulses considered by them to be immoral or repugnant, representing, as Gabbard (1994c) has also observed, an impairment in fantasy functions. This accords with Freud's (1911) early discovery that consciousness plays a central role in the capacity to delay—that it is those unconscious impulses that are most likely to be acted out.

One therapist stated that he considered it his "job to eliminate anger" and reported being unable to "sustain anger" in relation to his own past. Another therapist reported having had a panic attack at the memorial service of a coach who had excluded him from the high school basketball team. This therapist subsequently developed an anxiety disorder with periodic dizziness and fainting spells in situations where he felt disappointed or frustrated. Later in life, with the help of his personal psychoanalysis, he formulated that he had unconsciously held the belief that his anger and frustration at his coach had somehow played a part in the coach's death. (This therapist also had a conflicted relationship with his domineering mother who was often in ill health.) Another therapist discovered in the course of his therapy that he had a "seething rage underneath a placid and good exterior" so as to hide his aggression from everyone, including himself.

With therapists who presented with little or no remorse, there appeared to be a more pervasive restriction in internal experience with minimal capacity to identify motivations or feelings that may have led to the transgressions. These therapists tended to externalize responsibility and had minimal insight into how their behavior was associated with past experience. They usually had had more conflictual relationships with parental figures, resulting in intense anger at authority figures. Though clearly identified with an aggressive parent, the self-representations associated with such conflicted identifications were defensively disowned, as if occupying a space outside the boundaries of the self. One therapist recounted the seduction of his patient wholly in terms of *being seduced by her*, even to the point of disclaiming responsibility for his body's physiological sexual response. When asked why he did not simply leave the room when he felt unable to prevent his patient's sexual advances, he responded, "My body responded, I did not."

For other therapists in this subgroup, libidinized aggressive fantasies were acted out in a compartmentalized way—that is, the boundaries demarcating a hated or feared "other self" were conscious and actions associated with this "other self" became permissible in special, usually taboo, contexts where the usual superego prohibitions did not apply. These representations were conscious but were not sufficiently integrated within the self-structure; the therapists were able to recognize their behavior as motivated from within but were unable to accept it as part of their usual character or self-image. These therapists might report "being in a fog" or giving in to impulses they otherwise would struggle to keep under control, with little understanding of their dynamic origins. One therapist reported, "I did with my ethics what I did with others' needs whom I violated: I simply set them aside."

The last factor involves a *circumventing of unconscious countertransference hate through the misuse of conscious countertransference "love."* This is a defensive process triggered in part by the therapist's intolerance of his or her own aggression. As mentioned, many of these therapists had great difficulty viewing themselves as potentially aggressive, and there was a striking absence of exploration of such feelings in their personal therapies. One therapist, who had been in psychoanalysis prior to his acting out, reported that he "had never said a negative thing" to his analyst. He also reported that he rarely was aware of negative feelings toward his analyst and when he was, he never discussed them.

The defensive circumventing of countertransference hate was particularly related to the therapist's inability to view himself or herself as depriving or non-nurturant. These therapists tended to emphasize supportive and guiding views of therapy, overrelying on the so-called corrective emotional experience. The therapeutic orientation can be characterized as overly gratifying, suggestive, or even manipulative. One therapist, who sexually exploited a patient with multiple personality disorder, reported being drawn to "the alter who was open and accepting of me. She was demanding, upset, and angry in her other states."

On a conscious level, there were numerous rationalizations that reflected an overvaluing of countertransference "love" with an underlying intolerance of countertransference hate. These therapists always needed to be viewed as caring and giving. This issue calls to mind a familiar quote of Winnicott (1971), where he refers to the mother-infant dyad analogously to the therapy relationship:

> If all goes well, the infant can actually come to gain from the experience of frustration since *incomplete adaptation to need makes objects real, that is to say, hated as well as loved* . . . exact adaption resembles magic and the object that behaves perfectly becomes no better than an hallucination. (p. 11, italics added)

Consistent with the moralism with which they were raised, these therapists harbor the unrealistic belief that they should love every patient (everyone) and be able to treat every patient (everyone) at all times (Celenza, 1995). The hateful or angry patient inevitably challenges this belief, upon which their self-esteem rests. Norris, Gutheil, and Strasburger (2003) identified three risk factors that dovetail with this precursor: a tendency to idealize a "special" patient, an inability to set limits, and a denial about the possibility of boundary problems.

THE BIG PICTURE

The seduction of the patient frequently occurred when the therapist felt the treatment was at an impasse (Celenza, 1991), that is, in response to frustration of his or her efforts to help the patient or when the patient had begun to express anger or disappointment in the therapist. As mentioned, the patient with whom the therapist transgressed was usually experienced by the therapist as particularly difficult and hostile. From the therapist's point of view, the seduction seemed to represent a desperate attempt to connect with the patient in a way that protected the therapist's fragile self-esteem. One therapist reported, "I was reaching the end of my rope. I didn't know how to help her. So I seduced her because I knew how to do that." This therapist's conscious experience was of overwhelming helplessness. He used his sexuality to ward off unconscious hostility toward the patient and wrest control of the process. Similarly, Jung wrote to Freud of his involvement with Sabina Spielrein, "When the situation had become so tense that the continued preservation of the relationship could be rounded out only by sexual acts, I defended myself in a manner that cannot be justified morally" (McGuire, 1988, p. 236).

In a moment of clarity, Ferenczi wrote to Freud in 1912,

> I know, of course, that by far the greatest part of her love for me was father transference, which easily takes another as an object. You will hardly be surprised that under these circumstances I, too, can hardly consider myself a bridegroom any longer (quoted in Brabant et al., 1994, p. 331). (Gabbard & Lester, 1995a, p. 75)

[Despite this momentary recognition of the patient's transference, Ferenczi struggled with his love for Elma as well as her mother, Gizella (also his patient), whom he eventually married.]

In general, the transference/countertransference scenarios may be described as grandiose rescue and reparenting enactments (Simon, 1999) derived from unresolved childhood wishes and frustrations. The transgressor usually has a history of being the "parentified" child selected to repair his mother's depression and put his own needs aside. The therapy relationship mirrors this frustrating and overstimulating context from childhood.

CONCLUSION

One inescapable conclusion that emerges from this study is the continuous need for therapists to monitor their level of personal need and fulfillment in their lives. The study of sexual boundary violations teaches us that it is not only inappropriate and unethical to look to one's patients or clients for personal gratification, it is downright dangerous. We cannot approach our professional lives in a state of personal deficit or unfulfillment. The work itself requires a high degree of emotional self-deprivation and this is only exacerbated if the caregiver is already in a state of emotional need.

On a more theoretical level, the question of what accounts for the breakdown of controls can only be answered in the context of a particular case. For any one individual, risk factors may increase the internal pressure to act, but these are not predictive if viewed outside the context of the individual's particular psychic organization. Although vulnerabilities may be observed, these factors do not necessarily outstrip the capacity for containment or control.

The degree to which affects and impulses are integrated within a coherent self-structure delimits the capacity for containment. An individual's psychic organization, considered from a *one-person* perspective, must be coherent and integrated in order to be capable of affect containment, a prerequisite for mutual, *two-person* engagement. Fantasies associated with conflicted identifications, for example, may be defensively disowned and thereby occupy a space outside the conscious boundaries of the self. Or intolerable affects and impulses might be compartmentalized where the boundaries demarcate a hated or feared "other self" enacted only in certain forbidden contexts. Thus, the capacity to tolerate the full range of affects is inherently connected to the coherence and integration of self-structure.

For therapists and analysts, such integration is necessary to maintain a background of containment and holding while bringing into focus the transference and countertransference elements that arise from each person's past. Simultaneously, the therapist or analyst and patient are involved in the "intersubjective creation of a new reality," an ordinary relationship, and the mode of relating framed by the therapeutic endeavor (Modell, 1991). The therapist or analyst strives to maintain an awareness of these simultaneous yet irreducible levels of reality as neither mutually exclusive nor more or less real (Jonathan Slavin, personal communication, 1997).

Tolerating the irreducible tension among these levels allows for the greatest openness to the patient's experience. In the cases discussed, however, the therapy relationship was most often experienced by the therapist as replicating an intolerable childhood scenario involving early unmet needs and anticipated hostility. This stimulated a sadomasochistic solution in the therapist because of his need to dominate the relationship, a solution that evoked self- and object-representations that were essentially outside the boundaries of a conscious and coherent self-structure. In this way, the therapist was disconnected from his past and lost the awareness of the transference and countertransference influences as such. The repetition of the past was mistaken for a created new reality, one that required the therapist's overt participation in order for him to maintain control of the relationship. It was, in essence, a sadomasochistic relation in that it involved the annihilation of the patient's subjectivity and required her submission to the therapist's needs (Benjamin, 1988).

Unfortunately, when therapists are at risk for engaging in sexual intimacies, they are least likely to get consultation. This is presumably related to their fear of exposing inappropriate feelings and their shame at losing the capacity to maintain the boundaries of the therapeutic frame. In some cases, the resistance to obtaining consultation may also be related to an anticipation of being told to end the relationship (Gabbard, personal communication, 1994). The inherent difficulty sustaining the irreducible tension among the multiple levels of the therapist-patient dyad (Modell, 1991) should be more openly acknowledged. This would encourage therapists to view periodic consultation as an expectable need for all involved in intensive and mutually absorbing engagement with their patients. More elaborated discussions regarding prevention are presented in chapters 13 and 14.

ENDNOTES

This chapter is largely derived from a previously published paper (1998), A. Celenza, "Precursors to Therapist-Patient Sexual Misconduct: Preliminary Findings," *Psychoanalytic Psychology, 15*(3), 378–395. Since the publication of this study, more data has been collected that further corroborates these findings.

1. Compartmentalization is used here to denote the conscious coexistence of a nonintegrated, often contradictory experience of the self. Perhaps through the mechanism of a "vertical split," the unintegrated experience of the self may include instinctual, affective, ego, and superego elements.

4

WHEN IS A COUCH JUST A COUCH?

Thus far, I have focused on the psychological and dynamic factors that play a role in sexual boundary violations. There are also concrete and tangible aspects of the therapeutic context that may take on symbolic value. What role do these aspects—the props, so to speak—of the therapeutic setting play in setting the stage for sexual boundary violations? In the analytic play space, the only concrete behavior permitted between patient and analyst is talking and we are accustomed to viewing talking as not doing. When doing becomes the mode of relating, polarizing these two truncates the play space in the sense that meanings are telescoped, at least in terms of what is being explored or elaborated. This is an essential characteristic of perversions and the use of a fetish, in that play is constrained, repetitive, and objectified (Stoller, 1979, 1985; Coen, 1992; Bach, 1994). Many perverse sexual acts hinge on the use of some concrete thing or ritual for sexual pleasure.

In the therapeutic context, sexual boundary violations have such a character of perversion. The doing gets going, the talking stops, meanings are enacted and not explored. There can be the use of a concrete aspect of the setting, such as the couch, as part of this drama. In this mode, the play space has collapsed and the analytic couch becomes just a couch. This can be described as the collapse of the symbolized and the symbol. What is symbolized is what the analytic couch represents, that is, the potential space and play between analyst and patient. The symbol is the couch itself.

In psychoanalysis, the talking is often about love and sex. In turn, the language of love and the language of sexual longing constitute what we mean by desire—the desire to be close, literally (i.e., physically) and intimately (on an intersubjective level). This desire carries with it the desire to possess and to transgress, that is, to be inside the other or to take in, devour, and have the other inside you. The treatment situation aims to symbolize all of these longings in verbal form. But this very talking presents an inherent challenge that is part of what can sexualize the treatment situation itself (Celenza, in press).

43

This challenge is the performative nature of sexual language—the fact that the language of sexuality is, in and of itself, erotic and arousing (see, for example, J. Davies, quoted in Slavin, Oxenhandler, Seligman, Stein, & Davies, 2004; Havens, 1997). Here's where the polarization of talking and doing, seeing them as distinct and even opposite, breaks down.

So, the treatment situation can get very hot, rippled with unmet longings and frustrated desire. How to keep the action at the level of discourse and symbol, metaphor and play? When do the concrete aspects of the setting lose their power to evoke layered images, multiple, perhaps infinite, potential modes of relating and become instead co-opted into some degraded, concretized scenario?

THE FETISHIZED COUCH

Consider the case of a Christian minister, Father C. He became involved with a female parishioner whom he had been counseling for many months. Each session ended with a ritual—they would move to the chapel and join hands in prayer. One thing led to another and then they would have sex under the altar. The altar, this icon of worship, was inextricably bound up in creating the context for desecration and corruption. In Father C's words, "This was a way to fuck God and fuck the church at the same time." The desecration of a holy symbol was, for him, a way to corrupt love, a sacred act, and to blasphemize the church. (I am reminded here of the scene in Ken Russell's *The Devils* where Sister Jeanne, played by Vanessa Redgrave, masturbates with a crucifix.)

What is the function of the prop, the altar? Did it matter that the deed was done in a chapel under the altar? I would say, yes, it mattered very much. Would it have happened anyway, were a chapel not nearby? Yes and no. Yes, it would happen anywhere because the boundaries, or lack thereof, are, in the end, internal. Without an altar, however, it might not have happened in just this way. Still, we can use the visual-spatial arrangements in the external setting to help elucidate the unconscious drama that is being played out (Celenza, 2005) since they play a crucial role in the mind of the transgressor whether they are physically present or not.

In a psychoanalytic context, the analogous object to the altar, undeniably, is the couch. So, we may ask, when and how does a psychoanalytic process, along with its setting, become degraded, as in sexualized boundary violations? Or, when is a couch just a couch? I would say that in psychoanalysis, a couch is never just a couch, but there is a way in which we can say that the play space—that sacred, multilevel, expansive area of the mind and intersubjective space—can collapse such that the couch becomes a concretized object, that is, just a couch, functioning much like a fetish. It is this couch that plays a part in the staging for sexual boundary violations in psychoanalysis.

But to refer to the couch in the psychoanalytic setting is already to refer to a fetishized object. The phrase "Are you on the couch?" has been shorthand for "Are you in analysis?" I say "has been" because I know that today there is a greater appreciation for psychoanalysis according to its intrinsic features— that is, as an intrapsychic and intersubjective process that cannot be simply defined by extrinsic criteria such as frequency of meetings or where one sits or lies down (Gill, 1984). Still, historically the couch has symbolized psycho-analysis and, in that sense, remains an icon.[1]

So to ask "Are you on the couch?" is to conjure up a set of images, at-titudes, and feelings associated with psychoanalysis. If this same question is asked in reference to sexual boundary violations, "Are you on the couch?" really means "Which couch are you lying on?" There are two couches that are relevant in sexualized boundary violations: the degraded icon of psycho-analysis (that is, the fetishized object) and the furniture. This couch, in both of these functions, is not the couch of the analytic play space. The psychoanalytic couch functions in multiple domains, containing the potential for multiple relational configurations, as in parent/child, analyst/analysand, man/woman, friend/lover, and perhaps colleague too. Obviously, not all of these potential modes of relating are cultivated or developed (Mitchell, 1993; Modell, 1990), but they remain potentials in the room. The couch of sexual boundary viola-tions is one where the collapse of the symbol and symbolized has occurred; it is a concrete couch that functions solely in two domains—a place for both analyst and analysand to physically lie down (that is, to have sex) and a place to desecrate and degrade. When the analytic couch is concretized, it retains its symbolic function as a degraded icon.

DIRECT AND DISPLACED OBJECT SCENARIOS

When psychoanalysis is the stage on which this drama is played out, it also is important to ask, Who is being degraded in this use of the couch as a fetish? We can approach this question on a visual-spatial level as well, by asking whether the drama is a *direct* one or essentially a *displaced* scenario incorporating a third object in the mind of the transgressor.

The direct perverse scenario is an example of a classic perversion where the perverse act is focused directly on the other. In classic perverse fantasies, there is usually an attempt to degrade the other in an attempt to manage, control, and reduce (that is, objectify) the other's potentially dangerous subjectivity. This is essentially a direct unconscious scenario in that the drama revolves around the other who is objectified, thereby reduced from a separate subject to an object, and then sadomasochistically controlled. Most sexual boundary violations have this structure.

However, some sexual boundary violations, perhaps the most notorious type, make use of a displacement object and thereby are more accurately referred to as a displaced perverse scenario. In these cases of sexual boundary violations, the effort to degrade is not primarily directed to the other but is directed to the profession, the body or figure that oversees the dyad—hence the use of the symbol of the couch, the icon of psychoanalysis, as a place to enact this perverse scenario. In this sense, the couch represents a third object[2] and in this way, symbolizes psychoanalysis. *The patient is a displacement object*—a stand-in, so to speak—for an aspect of the setting or context.

The question of who is being degraded and whether the unconscious drama is essentially direct or displaced depends on the type of sexual boundary violation. As has been discussed in previous chapters, it is possible to broadly categorize the different types of sexual boundary violations into two types (Gabbard & Lester, 1995a; Celenza & Gabbard, 2003). One includes the egregious, notorious cases that have attracted statewide and sometimes national attention. These usually involve a therapist or analyst who is a psychopathic predator and who has sexually exploited multiple patients multiple times over many years. Though this is probably the best-known type, largely due to the extensive media attention such cases typically attract, fortunately these predatory actions are not representative of the most prevalent type of sexual boundary violations.

For the psychopathic predator, the unconscious drama that is being played out is best characterized as a displaced degradation. It is largely the profession that is being degraded, though, of course, the patient, in the way she is used, objectified, and even minimized in dynamic importance, is degraded along the way. In the main, however, she plays a relatively small role in the unconscious psychic drama of the transgressor, and by this I don't mean to downplay the traumatic effects such an experience can have on her. But in the mind of the transgressor, she is usually replaceable by multiple others who may or may not be involved contemporaneously. The externalization of the drama extends as well to the staging and props, including here and perhaps especially so, to the couch. Analogously, Father C was not fucking his patient but was using her to fuck God and the church, symbolized by the altar.

So, in this way, the perversion of the psychoanalytic process—largely aimed at corrupting the profession itself—is brought about by using the very means of healing in order to exploit and harm rather than help, and to do so in a sometimes flagrant manner. We all know the cases that have involved chairs of ethics committees, the most trusted "analyst of analysts," or the couple's therapist who, while treating the couple, has sex with the wife between sessions. These are, invariably, displaced dynamic scenarios and, even when these psychodynamics are understood, it is difficult to put ourselves in the transgressor's shoes.

DIRECT PERVERSE SCENARIOS

As I have described in previous chapters, the other and most prevalent type of sexual boundary violation involves a heterosexual male analyst or therapist who becomes sexually involved with only one of his patients. Gabbard (1994a) refers to this type of offender as lovesick; I have called him narcissistically needy (Celenza, 1998). As described in chapter 1, the analyst or therapist of this type is usually midcareer, isolated in his practice, and is treating a difficult patient in a highly stressful time in his life. The "love" relationship that ensues is an intensely absorbing love affair (at the time). It may last for several years and the couple may feel that they have found "true love," at least initially. Sometimes the therapy relationship is terminated while the sexual relationship continues. If the relationship is brought to an end by the therapist, this is the time when a complaint is most likely to be filed by the patient.

When we think of this type of sexual boundary violation, it is tempting to think that it's about love or even sex. But in my work with these cases, I have not found love in the air. This type of sexual boundary violation usually occurs because there is danger in the air. From the analyst's perspective, something is dangerous and it has to be managed. More than love, or even sexual attraction, this type of sexual boundary violation happens when a narcissistically fragile analyst or therapist feels that the treatment process is threatening his own delicate narcissistic equilibrium. He feels threatened by the patient, by the instability of the treatment, and is in a subjectively helpless, desperate state. A related point, it is important to note, is that acute suicidality in the patient is a major feature in over half of these cases (Celenza, 1998; Celenza & Gabbard, 2003). This is not an intersubjective engagement, as in subject/subject, but one better characterized as subject/object or doer/done to (Benjamin, 2004).

Here, I believe, the degradation, though unconscious, is primarily aimed at the patient (as opposed to a third object). It is a sadomasochistic relation, focused on the other who is objectified and reduced from subject to object. This is an example of a classic perverse scenario where the dangerous subjectivity of the other is controlled and reduced through objectification (for other examples of sadomasochistic perversion, see Stoller, 1979, 1985; Bach, 1994; and its relation to pathological dependency, Coen, 1992). I say this because in this type of sexual boundary violation, the seduction occurs when the therapist believes that the therapy is at an impasse, a time of threat, acute suicidality, or some other type of critical juncture (Celenza, 1991, 1998). The sexualization serves to shift the process from one of enormous frustration and challenge to one of seduction and sexual gratification. It also manages to transform the patient's emerging negative transference toward the analyst or therapist to a positive idealizing transference, a much more comfortable mode of relating for such a narcissistically fragile analyst or therapist. This is not the mutual surrender of healthy loving (Ghent, 1990; Maroda, 1998) but a perverse submission because it occurs in the context of threat and turns a setting of healing into one of domination and control.

Thus, the degradation in this type of sexual boundary violation is primarily focused on the felt danger in the patient. It is a direct, unconscious scenario in the mind of the transgressor and here, the couch or the setting is a less important prop on the stage. In my experience with this type of boundary violation, the sexual act is at least as likely to occur in the patient's home as in the office, home office, or hotel. In other words, the official props of the setting are less important; the transgression occurs more in and between the minds of the two.

THE DANGER IN THE ANALYST

The felt danger charging the atmosphere in most cases of sexual boundary violations comes not only from the *patient's* subjectivity, however. There is also the danger that the patient may feel in the *analyst's* subjectivity. In this sense, the danger is mutual. The potential dangers for the patient inherent in psychoanalysis are illustrated in any number of *New Yorker* cartoons: the analyst's lack of caring (as in clipping his toenails, sleeping); the analyst's aggression (poised with a dagger, about to strangle); or the analyst's judging or shaming response (shaking his head or laughing). All of these revolve around fundamental questions: Do you like me? Am I safe? Will you hurt me? And again, Why can't we be lovers?

Liking is one of many aspects of our subjectivity that forms the basis of the alliance, the background of safety (Sandler, 1960) that makes it possible for the analysand to reveal herself. But liking is only meaningful if "not liking" is also a possibility. This brings me back to the couch and to aspects of the patient's motivation to get the analyst on the couch with her. The *New Yorker* cartoons are humorous because they depict as real our worst fears—that behind our back, the analyst is laughing or sleeping (I'll leave out the one with the dagger). Whether or not we like our patients (and this is just the precursor to the question, Why can't we be lovers?) can become a matter of life or death for some patients. Again, it is worth reminding ourselves that acute suicidality in the patient is a major feature in over half of cases of sexual boundary violations. When the patient's desire is focused on the analyst, the refusal to engage in a sexual/love relationship can become a life or death struggle between them.

An analysand of mine has gone from total asexuality to hiring prostitutes. I'll respectfully call him Randy. He says in comparison, my fees are low because my services are limited. He tells me there's a benefit you can sometimes get where she will "do the girlfriend thing." This means she will pretend that she likes you. Some charge extra for this; others throw it in as a freebie.

This was just the beginning of Randy's emerging erotic transference toward me. He began with a hint that he needed to know that I liked him. The implications of what he gets from prostitutes and what he does not get from me loomed large in the room. Soon, he more directly revealed a desire that we have sex, run off together, and live happily ever after. When I refused to return his desire in the ways he wanted, he felt devastated and then a humiliated fury emerged. He called my Hippocratic Oath "my Hypocritical Oath" and said he felt trapped, depressed, and wanted to kill himself. This eventually took the form of a fantasy to stab me with a knife (see Celenza, 2006, for a more elaborated discussion of this case).

What would it have taken to get me to respond in the way analysts and therapists do when they sexually violate boundaries? Fortunately, I do not have now (and hopefully never will) the characteristic features of those transgressors. I was able to withstand the danger, bear it, seek consultation (a lot of it), and remain in a terrifying but affectively healing relational position with Randy. Had I been in a different mental state, perhaps at a different time of my life, and under extreme situational stress, I might have needed to manage this danger in a different way. Perhaps in desperation, sexualization might have seemed an option.

So, the motive to love and be sexual on the couch (or anywhere) is a mutual desire in this type of transgression. Here, I do not mean to shift responsibility in the direction of the patient, just to describe the transference/countertransference pressures that are part of the unconscious drama and to emphasize that it is a two-person act, though only one bears the responsibility of maintaining boundaries. I also do not mean to excuse the transgressor, just to explain what I have learned.

It is tempting to think that words might suffice in this context. Why not just tell Randy I like him? Or love him, especially since I do? But as Randy has often put it, "*Octa non verba*"—Latin for "Action, not words" (or so he tells me). Words are thin and have an excruciatingly short lifespan. (In effect, you just said you love me, but what about *now?*) The only lasting truths are those we feel, the ones that are informed by our guts, our ability to intuit, feel, and recognize as real what is already in the atmosphere between us. These are the skills I try to help Randy and all of my patients hone, to pay attention to what they know because they can *feel* it. Knowing from that level is more reliable compared to what anyone might say. (After all, people lie.) In this sense, analysts and analysands who engage in sexualized boundary violations, especially of the direct type, are trying to make real—that is, feel—by doing rather than saying. The need to make real by physical touch is, at times, an attempt to make the body feel where emotions are mistrusted or too weakly recognized. Words increase in power only as they resonate with a recognized internally felt state.

ANGER IN THE AIR

In all cases of sexual boundary violations, whether two or three are represented in the unconscious dynamic scenario, it can be difficult to empathize with the position of the analyst. The question comes up, How does one cross that boundary between talking and doing, loving and actually having sex?

To understand how this may come about, it is necessary to appreciate the complexity of the feelings the analyst is trying to express or control. It is never simply love or sexual attraction. In all cases of sexual boundary violations, it is common to find a vast reservoir of *unresolved anger toward authority*. This factor is evident in the transgressor's history as well as in current preoccupations. Though they often can present themselves as highly remorseful (which is genuine), the exploitation itself represents a rebellion against the authority of the profession and an underlying desire to break the rules (see also Fogel [2006] for an insightful account of resentment and defiance as these relate to sexual boundary violations).

In the displaced scenarios of the psychopathic predator, I have found that the expression of unresolved anger toward the profession is primary and is rooted in an unconscious, unresolved aggression-laden drama toward an abusive parent. Like Father C, the hostility is aimed at the figure of the third, the overseer of the dyad, as in God and the church. Why did he do it? The triumphant response is, because he could! Derived from unresolved anger toward an authoritarian parent, the licensing board, ethics committee, and/or professional organization can take on this aspect of the transference. This is a crucial phase of the subsequent treatments of transgressors (see chapter 11).

For the one-time transgressor, this hostility is expressed within the dyad, directed toward the patient and directed inwardly, in an unconscious self-destructive move that usually results in the expulsion from his profession.

Sexualization and concretization (or objectification) are defenses employed by the analyst who commits a sexual boundary violation. These defenses serve to transform the meaning of the analytic play space from one of expansion and potentiation to one of constriction, objectification, and degradation. Whether the unconscious dynamic scenario is direct or displaced, someone or something is being degraded. As mentioned, the degradation of the profession, the third object in the displaced perverse scenario, is effected largely through concretization—a transformation of the icon to its base function. In the direct perverse scenario, the other is objectified, the harm is in being dehumanized and dominated. In other words, sexual boundary violations turn a couch into mere furniture, thereby enacting a perverse ritual that degrades a place of healing, and turns the setting into its opposite, a place of exploitation and betrayal of trust, the very opposite of what the symbol was meant to represent. This is my preferred meaning of perversion, to use the tools of a healing process in the service of an opposite aim, to harm.

WHY CAN'T WE BE LOVERS?

So, why can't we be lovers? Isn't this the fundamental question we *all* have of each other?[3] Most answers dodge it: That's not our purpose, we didn't agree to that, it's not our contract. "But things change!" is the reasonable response. Or, You didn't know me then. Haven't I made myself irresistible? Don't I have that power? And finally, Some analysts do it!

One response gets closer: We can't because of transference. If this were all there was to it, however, no marriages could be condoned. So, the question "Why can't we be lovers?" is only satisfactorily answered by referencing the immutable and undeniable structure of the psychoanalytic setting itself (see chapter 5). By virtue of the fact that it is the structure of the psychoanalytic setting that inherently embeds transferences, the imbalances organized by this structure are thereby rendered unresolvable. In the psychoanalytic setting, *transference is structuralized,* that is, it is embedded in the structure of the setting, and thereby rendered immutable.

Here again are ways in which the concrete aspects of the setting may be used to symbolically represent efforts to equalize the various power imbalances in order to deny the immutability of the psychoanalytic structure. For example, an analyst may believe that lying on the couch with the patient creates equality between them. This, however, is an empty gesture, and usually effects a denial only in the mind of the analyst. The transferences developed when roles and expectancies were assigned. Lying on the couch together does not transform the analysand into an adult; she becomes a parentified child.

It is also true that there are multiple potentials that exist in any interpersonal relationship, lovers being one example. In the psychoanalytic setting, many potentials are purposefully not cultivated (Mitchell, 1993) or developed when the treatment contract is agreed upon. While it can be said that in most relationships, the undeveloped potentials remain as real potentials by choice, the psychoanalytic situation and the structure that defines it limit the extent to which such choices remain unencumbered. This is why sexualized boundary violations are deemed unethical, even when the patient is an adult. It is not simply by virtue of being under the influence of transference, however, but also for the fact that the transferences are structuralized and therefore immutably constraining.

In contemporary theory, it is generally recognized that transferences always organize the various ways of experiencing self and other in relationships. Even Freud recognized that it was impossible to distinguish between transference love and love in real life (Freud, 1915). It is not that "true" or "real" love has no transference in it, but that loving in real life (i.e., outside the psychoanalytic setting and structure) is negotiable (theoretically, at least) and thereby accessible to new experience. The structure of the psychoanalytic situation is designed to evoke those ways of experiencing that unconsciously foreclose new experience, thereby rendering loving in the psychoanalytic situation constrained by old patterns of relating.

ENDNOTES

This paper is derived from a 2006 paper by A. Celenza, "Sexual boundary violations in the office: When is a couch just a couch?" *Psychoanalytic Dialogues, 16*(1), 113–28.

1. The first-year candidates engage in constant questioning about who has bought a couch, where you get one, what type, and so forth. Buying your couch is a ritual that symbolizes the indoctrination into the analytic community. One candidate analogized it to losing her virginity, where who did it first becomes pertinent. (I am indebted to Ellen Golding, Ph.D., for these thoughts and anecdote.)

2. The term "third object" as used here is differentiated from some of the ways in which the concept of the third is used in contemporary theory (see Benjamin, 2004;

Britton, 2004; Hanly, 2004, for helpful reviews). In the present discussion, the use of the third object is to be rigorously distinguished from the intersubjective third or symbolic third in that there is no recognition of a separate subjectivity in the mind of the transgressor. Rather, the third is used as in Benjamin's (2004) "negative third" in complementarity or doer/done to relations, as Ogden's subjugating third (1994), or the way in which Aron (1999), Greenberg (1999), and Spezzano (1998) use the concept, as representative of the analytic community.

3. I am indebted to Lew Aron for encouraging me to admit this universal truth.

5

THE THERAPEUTIC CONTEXT

Can the love which is manifested in analytic treatment not truly
be called real? . . . The love consists of new editions of old traces
. . . but this is the essential character of every love.

—S. Freud (1915, p. 176)

As introduced in chapter 1, it can be said that the fundamental question a patient has of his or her therapist is "Why can't we be lovers?" This question
can become the organizing crucible around which all other themes revolve. Its
frank expression can signal a surfacing of deep longings or unresolved problems in loving that either underlie other struggles in life or capture some difficulty in the relational sphere. At times, the patient may seem obsessed, stuck,
"erotomanically preoccupied," or totally disinvested in his or her outside life
to a destructive degree. For some dyads, the pressure to act in response to this
question proves irresistible and the treatment is irretrievably destroyed.

In a myriad of ways, the question "Why can't we be lovers?" is put to
the therapist with intensifying pressure as the treatment evolves. Expressed in
highly individual ways, each patient formulates and places before his or her
therapist the unresolved and traumatically internalized ways he or she loves and
has been loved. One person's need might be to know the strength of his "mag-
netic appeal" while another needs to see and feel her therapist's desire despite all
efforts to push him away. Whatever the form, it is the nature of the therapeutic
process, by virtue of its structure, to stir up fundamental desires that unconsciously dominate the way our most intimate relationships are experienced.

What is it about the structure of the therapeutic setting that brings these
desires so urgently to the foreground? The answer lies in the structure of the
therapeutic setup itself and the way in which the special combination of mutual, personal engagement along with an asymmetric distribution of attention (Aron, 1996) is experienced. This unusual structure creates a universally

55

wished-for context—a context in which one's needs and wishes are continuously placed in the foreground despite one's best (conscious and unconscious)
efforts to keep them buried, unexpressed, or denied. This offer of unconditional commitment constitutes the therapist's discipline and responsibility to
the patient. It is the therapist's role, his or her professional ethic, that has its
forerunner in the infant-mother dyad. Though a universal and tenaciously
held lifelong wish, it is rarely replicated in other relationships. It can be found
at moments between lovers, but still only periodically even in the healthiest
intimacies. On a practical level, it is a necessary structure that is defining of the
therapeutic context. On an experiential level, however, it is highly seductive.
Most are unprepared for the intensity of feeling that can be stirred up.

THE SEDUCTION OF BEING IN IT TOGETHER

By virtue of the two defining dimensions of the treatment setting, mutuality
and asymmetry, an important dialectic is established that greatly intensifies
the experience and longing for intimate, sexual union in the psychotherapeutic context. First, there is the background experience of mutual, authentic
engagement. This dimension is bidirectional in the sense that there are two
persons committed to working together and withstanding whatever emerges.
As already mentioned, this commitment holds out the hope for and promise
of continued acceptance and understanding for the patient of even the most
loathsome aspects of the self. Since the patient is invited and encouraged to
reveal areas of self-contempt and self-hatred, the promise of continued engagement in the face of these aspects of the self is simultaneously dangerous
and seductive. The danger is inherent in the risk of rejection or withdrawal,
despite the (sometimes overt) promise of sustained commitment. The seductive aspect coincides with the universal wish to be loved totally, without judgment or merit. Though rarely actualized, the wish to be loved totally without
having to give anything in return remains a lifelong wish (see, for example,
Smith's [1977] discussion of "The Golden Fantasy"). These longings are never
given up but can be set aside as life fails to fulfill them.
    The seductiveness of unconditional acceptance and commitment is fu-
eled and intensified by other fundamental and universal wishes as well. These
include: (a) the desire for *unity* (to be loved totally and without separateness),
(b) the desire for *purity* (to be loved without hate and unreservedly), (c) the
desire for *reciprocity* (to love and be loved in return), and finally, (d) the desire
for *omnipotence* (to be so powerful that one is loved by everyone everywhere at
all times). All of these universals figure prominently in fantasies of romantic

perfection and are stimulated in the treatment setting since the treatment contract partly institutes their gratification. It can be said that the treatment frame both stimulates and frustrates these universal wishes, which will be freighted with the patient's historical meanings and unresolved developmental trauma.

A male patient with a history of subjugation to his single mother says, "I want to flow with my emotions for you, but it's a trap. I can flow, but I don't want to because I'm always reminded that this is not life. I want to believe it is real between us and be able to say, 'She really cares about me.' I ask myself, do I feel something personal between you and me? I would like to believe there's something flowing from you to me, but I don't trust it. Is it our purpose? Why is it relevant? Is it unprofessional? It's not our work, it's not your job. If I want to believe you care for me personally, then I'm in the therapy trap."

ASYMMETRY FOR THERAPIST AND PATIENT

The second dimension of the treatment context is defined by the asymmetric distribution of attention that comprises the therapist's professional and disciplined commitment to the patient. This axis of asymmetry is hierarchical in that it is constituted by several power relations, yet these are not straightforward or simple. It is an asymmetry that frames several power imbalances at once, each of which is ambivalently held by both patient and therapist. On the one hand, the patient is positioned as special (and thereby of elevated status) and at the same time, in a desiring or needful state (thereby vulnerable and disempowered). The therapist, by contrast, is relatively contained in his need of the patient (thereby empowered) yet also discounted in terms of the distribution of attention paid (and thereby dismissed, in terms of his personal needs). This asymmetry deepens and is concretized as the treatment progresses in the sense that the therapist continues to learn more about the patient while the reverse (relatively speaking) is not true.

These two axes, mutuality and asymmetry, function in dialectical relation. For example, the asymmetry deepens the patient's need for mutual, affective engagement as a way to ameliorate the humiliating, disempowering aspects of being the continuous focus of attention. In this way, it is the facilitation and encouragement of the patient's openness and vulnerability that makes the therapist's love and acceptance all the more important (Hoffman, 1998) and intensely felt. Likewise, it is the extent to which the patient reveals herself, especially areas of self-hatred and self-loathing, that intensifies the therapist's power in relation to the patient. In other words, it is the patient's self-revelations that empower the therapist and intensify the desire for a mutual, authentic engagement (deriving from the patient's disempowerment).

As the epigraph displays, Freud (1915) raised many crucial questions about the nature of analytic love and its similarities to love in "real" or outside life. Love is an experience more abnormal than normal; however, it is always in some great measure a repetition of earlier loves, for good or ill. Analytic love or love experienced in the therapeutic context cannot be decontextualized and is, thereby, inherently structured by this context. It therefore is an intensification of the types of love that mirror this imbalanced structure, especially with regard to power imbalances and nonreciprocal modes of relating. As Freud noted, "It is to a high degree lacking in regard for reality, is less sensible, less concerned about consequences, more blind in its estimation of the person loved" (1915, p. 177).

In these ways, the treatment setting is a complex structure that uniquely instantiates several contradictions. Especially interesting is the way in which the treatment setting combines these two contradictory axes: the axis of equality and mutuality (a "we're in this together" type of experience) along with the contradictory and imbalanced focus on the patient (a "you are in this alone" type of experience). The treatment setting is the point at which these two axes converge, creating the paradox of a simultaneous feeling of mutuality and asymmetry, of intimacy and aloneness, and of equality and hierarchy. These are tensions that the patient is persistently moved to resolve, to disequilibrate or level the hierarchy, so to speak, and to make contact with the authentic person behind the professional role.

It can be said that psychotherapy and psychoanalysis are processes by which the patient attempts to both empower and disempower the therapist (and vice versa) in an ongoing and increasingly more urgent way. By virtue of the special combination of mutuality and asymmetry, a tension is established that the patient both desires and hates. This necessarily will reconstruct and recapitulate the patient's relationship to authority and power in general. The psychotherapeutic context and the patient's experience with the therapist, given the power structures within it, is a particularly intense instantiation of this relation. Not surprisingly, in those for whom parental experiences are freighted with trauma and hypocritical or exploitative uses of power, the therapeutic process will be experienced with great mistrust and skepticism.

A male patient recently revealed that when we began our treatment a few years ago, he was simultaneously seeing four other therapists for almost a year. He explained that he had done so because he believed he was such a complicated person that a single therapist would not likely be much help. He reasoned that one therapist would see the tail of the elephant, another would see the trunk, another the leg, and so on. He, himself, would do the integration—that is, discern what kind of animal he was—and thereby be helped. He soon realized, however, that each therapist described a different part of a different animal. One saw the tail of a giraffe, another saw the head of a baboon, and so on. He became hopelessly confused and terminated with all but one because "You saw the most parts of the same animal." When I suggested that perhaps his initial desire to have five therapists reflected some anxiety about being involved with only one, he responded, "In the past, I've had only one therapist be dominant." I remarked at the interesting choice of words. He then remembered a female therapist whom he saw as a child and who would periodically speak with his mother. His mother, a domineering, reprimanding type, would use the therapist's insights to justify time-outs.

He went on, "Therapy is like government. It has the power to coerce. At some point, you no longer have a choice. That's when your heart is involved. Like with love. *The power to love is the power to destroy.* I always want to make a woman addicted to me. Like a slave. If she became my slave, I would be committed to her and I couldn't hurt her. But what does it mean to have that power? To be on top? You could hurt me because my heart is involved. You have the power to exploit me."

THE AUTHORITY AS BAD OBJECT

The therapist must continually withstand the pressure to level the hierarchy as well, from both within and without, that is, from within himself and from the patient. From the outside, as mentioned, the therapist must withstand (by holding the tension) the patient's pressure to disempower him. This is the pressure derived from the asymmetric distribution of attention and the patient's attempts to ameliorate the humiliating consequences of it. In this regard, it is important that the therapist not feel undue guilt about the power inherent in the structured asymmetry of the therapeutic relationship. In contemporary Western culture, it is popular to disclaim the desire for power. To want power, or to even be comfortable with it, is one kind of new bad object, a politically incorrect, non-egalitarian object. Our patients do and don't want to experience their therapist as an authority and we, as therapists, are similarly ambivalent about being imbued with authority. But today, there is an extra layer of taboo associated with wanting power. It is difficult enough to be the patient's bad object, but it is even less appealing to be our own bad object (see, for example, Davies, 2004).

Despite the admirable ring to this morality, egalitarianism denies the inherent asymmetry in the psychotherapeutic structure. It may not be surprising that egalitarianism is an often expressed value that functions to rationalize sexual boundary violations. Along with other factors that have gone awry in such treatments, the therapist's collusion with the patient's press to level the hierarchy between him and her is often a more conscious part of the sexualized enactment.

A therapist whose license was suspended for sexual involvement with a patient states that he has always disliked "the authoritarian tone of the therapy role." He dislikes placing himself above others and to signify this, he never wore a jacket or tie when he conducted his sessions. He also had his patients address him by his first name. He stated emphatically, "People listen to each other better if you level the playing field." Gabbard (1996) describes a female therapist who shared many of her problems with her patients, rationalizing her "egalitarian approach" as a way to "equalize things." This therapist was sexually abused as a child and would share this aspect of her history with her patients as well.

The problem is made more complex by virtue of the fact that many behaviors, such as hugging, dining with, self-disclosing, and making house calls, are among behaviors that are consistent with the ethical practice of humanistic, behavioral, and pastoral psychotherapies. Clergy routinely hug parishioners as they exit church and it is considered a spiritually enriching experience to have a pastor for dinner. Likewise, behavioral modalities necessarily include graduated exposure techniques that require confrontation with the anxiety-arousing stimulus, such as riding in elevators, walking around the block, or taking an airplane ride. All of these frequently occur in the presence of the therapist.

Williams (1997) cautions that innovative practice might be stifled by risk-management concerns, especially for these modalities. Training in the maintenance of clear boundaries and roles when treatment might occur outside the office or in social contexts can be confusing for both the practitioner and the patient. Many practitioners address this problem only halfway by asking, "Am I clear about my intent here? Do I feel a hint of seduction in myself?" Answering these questions solely from the point of view of the practitioner, however, leaves out the most crucial aspect of the problem, that being the way interventions are or might be experienced *by the patient*. The crucial focus in maintaining boundaries does not revolve around the awareness of one's own intent (which may be clouded by unconscious motivations and conscious rationalizations) but revolves around the potential meanings the behavior might have for the patient. Therefore, the most important questions to ask are, How might the patient perceive my actions? Can my motives be misconstrued? Most of the time, the answer to these latter questions is an affirmative "yes."

Gutheil and Gabbard (1998) emphasize the importance of considering the context in which interventions might occur in differentiating sound ethical practice from unethical boundary violations. For example, it is crucial to distinguish between conscious and unconscious intent, love used to defend against aggression versus the loving component of the alliance, and hugging at termination versus part of a seduction.

The problem is that training, conventional practices, and even necessary protocol (such as graduated exposure techniques for agorophobics that may include taking walks, home visits, and so forth) all include complex challenges in cognitive-behavioral, pastoral, and humanistic modalities. The inherent blurring of boundaries as contexts overlap may seem, at first glance, insurmountable. It is important here to remind ourselves that psychodynamic therapists have a lower prevalence of sexual misconduct (Borys & Pope, 1989). It is speculated that this derives from greater awareness of the importance of clear, nonexploitative, and therapeutically oriented roles, boundaries, and responsibilities, such as maintaining the frame, the holding environment, and appreciation for transference. If an awareness of these remains in the forefront of our minds as practitioners and we continually take into account and discuss with our patients how they are experiencing the relationship, the effort to maintain clear boundaries will be largely surmounted, even as contexts overlap.

Awareness of one's own motives, defensive proclivities, and current stressors are also necessary issues to continually monitor. As mentioned, cultural factors may also come into play, such as the current trend toward egalitarianism. This egalitarian attitude can contain a genuine attempt to empower others in order to engage in a constructive dialogue; however, it is also simplistic and limited in scope. For one, it is an assertion made solely from the therapist's conscious point of view, essentially sidestepping the perception and experience of the therapist's power from the patient's point of view. Since the power imbalance in the therapeutic context is inherent and irreducible, such attempts to "level the playing field" can only involve superficial symbols of disempowerment (e.g., informal clothing, being called by one's first name). These gestures are ultimately ineffective.

Undeniable and inescapable, the therapist's power is contextualized in the structure of the therapeutic setting. Because it is embedded in the structure of the therapy itself, it is definitional and is thereby irreducible. Gestures that symbolize humility or equality are empty and false in this context; they appeal to the therapist's self-ideal as a humble, power-rejecting individual, yet they bring neither about. This is not to suggest that the therapists in the above examples were consciously lying or intentionally deceiving their patients, but that they did not grasp the complexity of the problem and context, that is, the power inherent in their role, especially from outside their own points of view. Paradoxically, these attitudes inadvertently encourage the patient's dependency on the therapist through the valorization of the therapist in an effort to ingratiate the patient. (If there is no desire for power, why the need to disclaim it? These therapists took pains to minimize or disclaim the power they insisted they did not have or want.)

The pressure to level the hierarchy arises in another way as well. The therapist's responsibility to maintain the treatment frame (especially the asymmetric distribution of attention) comprises a constant frustration of the therapist's needs and wishes that he or she is continually pushed to indulge. The therapist must resist his or her own temptation to level the hierarchy from within, so to speak, since it is this aspect of the asymmetry that disempowers the therapist. (This also represents a stress point and risk for sexual boundary transgressions, especially in times of personal crisis in the therapist's life.) It is here that the therapist's commitment to his or her professional role is most sorely tested.

Urges to level the hierarchy, prompted either by the therapist or the patient, are most frequently activated in relation to the limitations imposed by the therapeutic frame. This is why boundary transgressions most often occur "at the edges" of treatment, so to speak (e.g., when the hour is at its end, at the moment of greeting in the waiting room, or outside the office). It is during these transitional times, when the proscription for professional role behavior (on the therapist's part) is ambiguous, and thereby are moments when the patient has greatest hope for mutual and authentic contact. Indeed, it might be said that these moments of trespass (Hoffman, 1998), transition (Gutheil & Simon, 1995), or disregulation (Stechler, 2003) signal a reversal of role wherein, for a moment at least, the therapist and patient need each other equally and the imbalanced nature of the therapeutic structure is momentarily equilibrated.

This contact, urgently sought, can easily become sexualized, since "Eros always involves an element of transgression" (Slavin et al., 2004), the overflowing of ordinary boundaries (Slavin et al., 2004), the illusion of continuity between self and other (Bataille, 1986), contacting the Other (Dimen, 2003), and the potential to omnipotently transcend realistic limits.

A male patient says, "I have a conflict—you're a good therapist. You strive to help me. But you will not reveal anything about your personal life. Like a blind man develops a heightened sense of hearing or touch, I read you. I'm imagining you watching me. I have a fantasy about you. We have sex, it's mutual, loving. We each leave our spouses and live together forever. I want that."

In this example, it is possible to see how the asymmetric aspect of the therapeutic setting stirs up the patient's longing (to know the therapist). This, then, is experienced as love that, in turn, becomes sexualized (a desire to know the therapist in the biblical sense, so to speak).

These are the special features that define the structure of the therapeutic context. It is easy to see how the love, experienced in this context, is borne out of a power struggle and inherently limited by this struggle. Multiple levels of reality exist simultaneously within the therapy-patient relationship (Modell, 1991). There is a dimension of ordinariness, where two people are interacting; there is a man/woman dimension; role assignments determine another dimension (as in doctor/patient); and there are transferences that imbue all of these at the same time. Some of these modes of relating are embedded within the structure of the treatment contract, specifically the role assignment and the power imbalance associated with it. This aspect of the relationship is not accessible to negotiation, making the transferences that develop within it elusive and unchangeable.

When a therapist tells his patient that she is special, he becomes the oedipal father to his adoring daughter. When he tells her she is an equal, he speaks to her adult self and cultivates a parentified daughter, likely repeating a way in which she was treated as a child. He also gives up the opportunity to help her resolve the oedipal dilemma that likely brought her to treatment in the first place. Margaret Mahler discussed her reaction to August Aichorn's advances in just this way. Aichorn was her analyst and Mahler writes that when he treated her as special, he "only buttressed my self-image as an 'exception.' . . . I became a sort of Cinderella, the love object of a beautiful prince (Aichorn) . . . my analytic treatment with him simply recapitulated my oedipal situation all over again" (Stepansky, 1988, p. 68, quoted in Gabbard & Lester, 1995a).

Thus, there is a profound responsibility associated with the power imbalance that inherently structures the therapeutic situation. While it may be immutable, it must be acknowledged and managed. This is no less the case, in a basic way, in supervisory and academic contexts. In the next chapter, the similarities and differences between academic and supervisory contexts compared to the therapeutic context are discussed at length. However, the basic power imbalance remains in all. The student or supervisee is inextricably bound to a more disempowered role as long as these structures (i.e., role assignments) are in place.

ENDNOTE

This chapter is in part derived from A. Celenza, "Analytic Love: Responsible Responsivity," *Psychological Inquiry*. Forthcoming.

6

ACADEMIC AND SUPERVISORY CONTEXTS

The voice of the intellect is a soft one.

—S. Freud (1927, p. 53)

What are the circumstances under which two adults may be considered consenting, relatively free of transference-based pressures and structured power imbalances? How are these aspects of the supervisory relationship reconciled with the fact that a teacher and student are devoted to the same profession, thereby reflecting inherent similarities of interest and inclinations? Don't these similarities make sexual and/or romantic appeal more likely? The academic and supervisory contexts do not exactly replicate the many potentially exploitative aspects associated with the therapeutic relationship. However, there is a hierarchy and potential for exploitation embedded in the structure of academic and supervisory relationships that must be taken into account. As long as these structural features are in place, the student/supervisee cannot be considered free to consent and the relationship must be viewed within a context that is bound by professional ethics.

In general, the features associated with the potential for exploitation in the educator-student (including supervisor-supervisee) relationship revolve around the learning needs of the student and the power inherent in the educator/supervisory role. These features are easily seen when the educator/supervisor has evaluative, training, and/or employment placement functions. The student/supervisee comes to the educator/supervisor with learning needs, and these establish certain structures and expectations that must be honored. The learning needs are tied to aspects of the educator's role: the promise to impart knowledge in a way that is amenable to learning, the often necessary function of evaluation of the student/supervisee's performance, and other role-imbued advantages that may be accessed by the student/supervisee, such as job placement, advancements, awards, and the like.

As compared to the therapeutic relationship, however, academic and supervisory contexts are more reciprocal than the therapeutic relationship. Though the primary purpose of the educative/supervisory relationship revolves around the learning needs of the student/supervisee, the method of imparting knowledge does not include as marked an asymmetry as in the therapeutic relationship. For example, it is acceptable and even desirable for the educator/supervisor to disclose aspects of his personal history details of his professional experience to exemplify and model various aspects of technique, and so forth. Further, the imbalance does not deepen and become entrenched over time since each member of the dyad is reciprocally exposed to a variety of aspects of each other's lives.

In this chapter, the similarities and differences of the educative/supervisory relationship compared with the therapeutic relationship will be delineated. In addition, the boundaries of ethical care are discussed in conducting educative and supervisory relationships. The manner in which careful reassignment of all educative and supervisory duties may make a romantic and sexual relationship between an educator and student or supervisor and supervisee fall within ethical bounds, *as long as certain conditions are met.* These conditions are delineated below.

DEFINITION AND PREVALENCE

Much of the literature on sexual boundary transgressions in academic and supervisory relationships appears in psychology journals addressing supervisory concerns. Whenever possible, studies of educator-student sexual boundary transgressions will be cited and referenced as such. In any case, the academic context is directly analogous to the supervisory context and the data is applicable to both contexts. Therefore, in the discussion that follows, I will most often use the terms supervisor and supervisee to refer to both educator/supervisor and student/supervisee.

Sexual involvement between supervisor and supervisee constitutes a violation of the letter and intent of existing ethical principles in every mental health discipline (Conroe et al., 1989). There are several reasons why this must be the case. The supervisory contract revolves around an agreement to learn clinical technique, but when a romantic and sexual involvement occurs, these contractual learning needs become subservient to romantic and sexual ones. Further, the supervisory contract includes a mission to impart ethically based practice to the supervisee in various ways: direct teaching, modeling, role-playing, identification, and so on. Engaging in a sexual or sexualized transgression with a supervisee is a perversion of this aspect of the supervisory contract since what is being modeled is unethical, the opposite of the purpose and design of the mission and context.

Despite this clear prohibition, prevalence studies have revealed a higher incidence of sexual transgressions between educators/supervisors and students/supervisees than is found in the studies of therapist-patient sexual misconduct. Three national studies have obtained data on educator-student misconduct, all in the field of psychology (Pope et al., 1979; Robinson & Reid, 1985; Glaser & Thorpe, 1986). All of these surveys are based on anonymous, self-report questionnaires; thus, it is likely that these prevalence rates are an underrepresentation of the true prevalence rate.

Pope et al. (1979) found an average of 9.4% of student/supervisee respondents reported overt sexual contact with educators (16.5% women; 3% men). Educator/supervisor respondents reported 13% overt sexual contact with students/supervisees (8% women; 19% men). Robinson and Reid (1985) found 13.6% respondents reported having sexual contact with an educator (all subjects in their study were women). Glaser and Thorpe (1986) found 17% of the respondents reported engaging in intimate sexual contact with psychology educators (including clinical supervisors).

These studies also reflect a gender difference in prevalence much like that found in sexual intimacies between therapists and patients. The most common case is a male educator/supervisor with a female student/supervisee; the opposite gendered pairing may also occur, but at a lower incidence rate (Pope et al., 1979; Rozsnafszky, 1979). Also similar to the findings in the literature on therapy relationships, female students/supervisees are more likely to be involved with their educators/supervisors than are male students/supervisees. Pope et al. (1979), for example, found only a 3% prevalence in male trainees while 16.5% of female trainees reported sexual contact with their educators/supervisors.

Since gender differences play an important role in boundary transgressions, especially as they refer to power hierarchies, it is not useful to consider this data without differentiating the genders for either the educator/supervisor or student/supervisee. When the genders are analyzed separately, female students and supervisees are disproportionately represented (on average, 15.7% as compared to 3% of male students and supervisees) as having engaged in sexual relations as students/supervisees with their educators/supervisors. Little data is available as yet differentiating opposite-gendered versus same-gendered pairs. Brodsky (1986) reported a lower incidence of same-sex involvements in supervisory relationships.

Along with these averages, it is interesting to note that the gender and power dynamics are consistent with therapist-patient sexual misconduct (though, as mentioned, the prevalence rates are higher) where the most frequent pattern involves a (structurally) empowered male who exploits a disempowered female. In a similarly consistent pattern and again, reflecting higher prevalence rates, 19% of the male educators/supervisors acknowledged having engaged in sexual relations with students/supervisees. In contrast, only 8% of the female educators/supervisors acknowledged having engaged in sexual relations with students/supervisees (Pope, 1989c). The prevalence rates are also higher for educator-student relationships as compared to clinical supervisor-supervisee relationships. One study showed an increase of the overall rate of educator-student sexual activity over time (Pope et al., 1979). Most of these relationships were educator-student relationships (as compared to clinical supervisor-supervisee).

It is not surprising that the overall prevalence rates of sexual misconduct are higher for academic and supervisory contexts as compared to therapist-patient sexual misconduct, since the imbalance and the transgression in the context of a therapy relationship is more extreme and more pointedly taboo. However, in Pope et al.'s (1979) study of educator-student misconduct, only 2% of the respondents endorsed the statement "I believe that sexual relationships between students and their psychology teachers, administrators, or clinical supervisors can be beneficial to both parties." It appears that the rational, reasonable, and moral mind-set is widely divergent from the self under the sway of romantic and/or sexual desire.

ETIOLOGIES

Since the great majority of educators and students acknowledge sexual misconduct in academic and supervisory contexts to be unethical, the causes of the high prevalence rate must be explained with reference to factors that motivate professionals to violate their overtly stated ethics. These causes are likely to be multidetermined. The etiology in any one particular case may include personal risk factors, situational stress, and/or lack of knowledge. At a different level of analysis, these factors may be related to theoretical orientation, cultural and modality factors in the training context, and/or programmatic or systemic deficiencies related to prior training.

Some insight may be gained by looking at data from the psychotherapy literature since some factors are analogous to the educator/supervisory realm. With regard to personal risk factors, clinical lore holds that at least in the therapeutic arena, therapists who engage in sexual boundary violations have themselves been violated at some point in their lives. This makes good psychological sense since practitioners know well the tendency to repeat old patterns, either by seeking to master the victim role or become a perpetrator oneself in order to feel the power of being in control. A history of childhood incest in therapist/transgressors, however, is not the rule (Celenza, 1998), and it has been demonstrated (see chapter 3) that the risk factors are more subtle and complex than having been victimized or violated oneself.

There is also clinical lore regarding the transmission of exploitation and abuse from the supervisory or educative context to the therapeutic context. In other words, there is a suspicion that those who were exploited as supervisees or students are more likely to transmit that abuse to a therapy patient. The lore contends that therapist/transgressors were themselves abused in the supervisory context, and thus betrayed by a trusted supervisor at some point in their training. Only one study has measured the prevalence of prior supervisory exploitation in later therapist/transgressors (Pope et al., 1979). This study indicates that those who, as students, engaged in sexual intimacies with their educators are indeed at significantly higher risk, as therapists, to engage in sexual intimacies with patients. However, the fact that female professionals are overrepresented in the exploited student/supervisee group, yet are underrepresented in the therapist/transgressor category contradicts this inference. There is no doubt, however, that the dynamics making one vulnerable either to the transmission of exploitation or the vulnerability of being exploited follow certain patterns (Pope, 1989a). These must be examined within subgroups and may not have overall explanatory power.

Hamilton and Spruill (1999) believe that despite personal risk factors in particular trainees, boundary transgressions are more strongly related to systemic, programmatic, and pedagogic characteristics of the environments in which students train. This is a factor that I have observed in my experience through several consultations of trainees who had engaged in sexualized transgressions with their patients. In some cases, supervisors openly encouraged trainees to disclose personal history, reveal their attachment to their patients in overly demonstrative ways, or "befriend" patients in ways that blur boundaries and confused the participants, that is, both trainee and patient alike. This is a particular problem on in-patient units where therapists may meet with their patients in their bedrooms or have casual interactions with them in the hallway throughout the day. Both the setting and the supervisory practices may facilitate the blurring of roles and boundaries that make learning proper boundary maintenance difficult.

Theoretical orientation is likely a factor that explains why some mental health professionals have higher prevalence rates of misconduct. As Borys and Pope's (1989) study reflected, psychodynamic and psychoanalytically oriented therapists have lower prevalence rates of misconduct than therapists of other therapeutic orientations. This, no doubt, is related to the greater appreciation of and skill in handling transference and countertransference pressures. Psychodynamic and psychoanalytic training entails the development of a greater awareness of defensive processes as well, both in terms of transference manifestations and countertransference responses. This is especially important in the extent to which erotic transferences and countertransferences may defend against intolerable hostility and angry feelings in the therapy relationship. The problem is made more complex in the treatment of patients with severe psychopathology.

Still, there is not nearly enough support and guidance for students and supervisees with highly challenging patients, even in psychodynamic and psychoanalytic settings. When difficult patients present with complicated defense-driven dynamics, the potential for boundary blurrings is made more acute for students and supervisees whose theoretical orientations do not prepare them adequately. When an educator or supervisor overlooks or neglects the power imbalance within the educator-student relationship (even if the dynamics are not wholly analogous), this sets an unacceptable precedent and is particularly dangerous for those trainees whose theoretical orientation inadequately prepares them for handling difficult and more intensely involving cases.

Thus, the vulnerability to boundary transgression is exacerbated if trainees are not educated to appreciate transference and countertransference feelings or do not have models within their professional milieu that demonstrate appropriate and skillful handling of transference and countertransference feelings. Woolley (1988) and Hamilton and Spruill (1999) note the pervasive tendency of supervisors to become inordinately anxious about how to help their supervisees with erotic feelings and other anxiety-arousing countertransference responses toward their patients. There is a common tendency for supervisors to refer the supervisee to their personal therapists to discuss these complicated feelings rather than to directly help them understand, tolerate, and appropriately handle these feelings. While this is, in part, an appropriate suggestion so that the trainee may examine the more personal and deeply rooted origins of his or her own responses to the patient, such a suggestion is not all that the trainee needs in these moments.

It is in the supervisory context where trainees should obtain concrete advice about how to handle both the patient's and their own feelings, that is, how to understand them, what to say, and what to do or not do in relation to a particular patient. There is an absence of this level of guidance in one's personal therapy, so that even if trainees faithfully report and examine their own erotic feelings toward patients in their personal therapy, the need for more concrete instruction and guidance in their work with a particular patient remains. The supervisory context is the appropriate place for them to gain this level of knowledge and skill. Supervisees need direct and concrete help in learning how to manage and therapeutically use these feelings with their patients.

Theoretical orientation within the supervisory context also makes an important difference in the extent to which supervision allows for an extensive and intrapsychically deep discussion. One cognitive-behavioral therapist, who referred herself for treatment when she became sexually involved with a patient, reported that she had been talking about her treatment of this patient with two supervisors before she had become sexually involved with her patient. She believes she had attempted to be as open and revealing about her feelings as possible; however, she also felt that the supervisory discussions lacked depth. She reported that they revolved too much around how to manage and control the patient's feelings and how to change the beliefs associated with them. This therapist remained isolated with the feelings she herself was experiencing and helpless in the face of the patient's increasing demands. Unfortunately, she ended up seducing her patient. After a number of months in a psychoanalytic psychotherapy as well as engaging a psychoanalytic supervisor, this therapist reported, "I feel so much more equipped. I have so much more competency around dealing with hostility and my own temptation to sexualize when I'm afraid of being abandoned."

From a contrasting view, Williams (1997) notes that many behaviors consistent with the ethical practice of humanistic and behavioral psychotherapies, as well as eclectic approaches deriving from those schools, are now being viewed as boundary violations. Such behaviors include hugging, dining with, self-disclosing to, or making house calls to patients. (Clergy face a similar problem where many standard practices of pastoral care would be viewed as transgressing the boundaries of ethical practice within psychodynamic and psychoanalytic frameworks.) Williams cautions that innovative practice might be stifled by risk-management concerns if engaging in such behaviors is viewed solely through the lens of boundary crossings or violations.

One way out of this dilemma emphasizes the importance of considering the context in which these behaviors might occur in differentiating sound ethical practice from unethical boundary violations. For example, it is crucial to distinguish between conscious and unconscious intent, love used to defend against aggression versus the loving component of the alliance (Celenza, 1995, see chapter 14), and hugging at termination versus part of a seduction (Gutheil & Gabbard, 1998). In short, the careful consideration of meaning, derived from contextual and personal factors, must be taken into account.

PREVENTION IN ACADEMIC AND SUPERVISORY CONTEXTS

The first caveat in helping students and supervisees prevent sexual boundary transgressions is to model ethical behavior oneself. Careful attention to boundaries, respectful appreciation of the disempowered position of trainees, and scrupulous attention to the learning needs of the student should all be at the forefront of the educator's mind at all times. Here it is wise to remember that "the elephant does not feel the bird under its feet," and it is remarkably easy to forget the power one has in relation to students and supervisees. As in the therapeutic context, the crucial question is not the extent to which the supervisor or educator feels his or her own power, but the way in which the student or supervisee is disempowered by virtue of the structure of the setting.

We are trained to use our own experience to reference the experience of the other (one facet of the empathic capacity), yet in so doing, we may miss the ways in which our trainees are hierarchically at a disadvantage. In my experience, it is especially difficult to maintain one's awareness of the power differential with supervisees and students for whom we feel a special affinity, whom we like and would want to befriend. Perceived similarity is a powerful attractor in this regard. This is one of the elements that causes female therapists to blur boundaries with their female patients, since overidentification is the primary factor that causes them to lose their therapeutic stance.

Role assignment and the responsibilities associated with that role are the hallmarks of the educator's position in relation to the student/supervisee. The educator/supervisor must be accountable for the responsibilities he or she has undertaken in this context. It is wise to remember that the phenomenal (i.e., subjective, at conscious and unconscious levels) experience of each member of the dyad differs markedly, especially with regard to the power dimension of the relationship. This is especially true with regard to feelings of empowerment, so that gestures of egalitarianism, designed to equalize the roles or experiences of each member, will not change the way the trainee subjectively experiences the relationship.

The way the student/trainee experiences the educative or supervisory relationship is not the same as the way the educator/supervisor experiences it. For teachers/supervisors to use their own internal barometer as a guide as to whether socializing might feel or be appropriate is not adequate or even useful. Many therapy transgressors make this same mistake and later report, "But I didn't feel more powerful than she and besides, I asked her if she was comfortable." The power that the educator/supervisor has is embedded in the structure and role; it is thereby not necessarily part of the educator's subjective experience. Simply asking the student/trainee if she feels comfortable is also fallacious since, being in a less powerful position, she is not truly free to say "No, I'm not comfortable with that."

Pope (1989a) outlines several recommendations for educators and supervisors in addressing the problem of educator/student sexual intimacies. These include: (1) maintaining the student's interests as primary; (2) remaining aware of the deleterious effects of boundary transgressions on a student's training needs; (3) appreciating the effects of educator-student intimacies on the safety and openness in the learning environment; (4) appreciating the potential compromise of the evaluative function; (5) appreciating the potential exploitation of the power differential, especially with regard to future job placement, recommendations, fellowship placements, and so forth; and (6) appreciating the vulnerability of the training program to class action lawsuits or misconduct complaints. All of these factors need to be kept in the forefront of the educator/supervisor's mind.

CAN EDUCATORS OR SUPERVISORS EVER DATE A TRAINEE?

It is a difficult line to draw, especially given that students frequently rate their best mentors and their best supervisors as those with whom they have socialized and with whom they have developed a close personal relationship (Schoener, 2005). Besides, who *wants* to draw this line? Aren't we behaving a bit prudishly to say these boundaries can never be crossed when our professional lives and social circles will inevitably and even preferably overlap? This highlights a basic truth about the helping professions in general: the foundation rests on a relationship of love and nurturing. Love is the fertilizer of the student's growth and healing potential. It is impossible to conceive of this relationship outside of the context of what the supervisor or educator desires, both for and with the supervisee or student. These qualities, in turn, are what the supervisor/educator wants for himself as well.

The structured power imbalance in the educative and supervisory context is more easily transformed than is the structure defining the therapeutic relationship. The roles and functions that the supervisor serves can be transferred to others in ways that can render the structured power imbalance accessible to renegotiation. When the functions and roles associated with education and training are dissolved, the structured power imbalance is also (relatively) dissolved. What may linger are unresolved idealizations that were established when the relationship initially began; however, these will be amenable to transformation since the relationship no longer contains a structured (and thereby inaccessible) power imbalance.

Age differences may contribute to power imbalances that refer more to differences in development and maturation, but these are private negotiations that are not the concern of professional ethics. Similarly, there will be transferences (as there are in any relationship); however, as long as the educative or supervisory functions have been transferred, removed, or have otherwise ended, these transferences will not be embedded in inaccessible structures that cannot be renegotiated or resolved. Further, in academic and supervisory contexts, the transferences that may be in place have not been enhanced or intensified by virtue of the training functions. This is a marked difference between academic/supervisory contexts as compared to therapeutic contexts. In academic/supervisory contexts, the relationship should not have included disclosures of personal and professional experiences in a one-way fashion. In this way, educative and supervisory relationships are more reciprocal, or at least potentially so.

Once the evaluative and educative functions of the academic/supervisory relationship are dissolved, the relationship is essentially the same as with colleagues and peers because the supervisee is no more vulnerable or exposed than is the supervisor. In short, by virtue of the greater reciprocity in disclosure in supervisory relationships, there is a difference in both quality and degree of the power imbalance (asymmetry) as compared to a therapeutic relationship. The differences will be more markedly apparent over time as well.

Since the power imbalance in the context of educator-student is structuralized but not necessarily deepened over time, it is easier to address and redress the potentially destructive or exploitative elements so that sexual intimacies may be ethically engaged. This is especially relevant for the clinical supervisory context since these roles are usually assigned for a relatively short time duration (e.g., one year, as compared to four to five years in the academic context). If a supervisor and supervisee want to engage in a romantic and sexual relationship, it may be ethical to do so if the supervisee's educational and supervisory needs are reassigned to other supervisory relationships. In short, the supervision must be terminated and the supervisee's training needs must be attended to elsewhere. It is necessary for the supervisee to obtain alternative supervision, for example, and all coincident evaluative responsibilities must be reassigned as well.

The same does *not* hold true for directors of training, chiefs of staff, chairs of programs or departments on academic faculties, and the like. By virtue of the overarching authority of these positions, as long as the student or supervisee is in the academic or training program, these roles cannot be reassigned. Therefore, romantic and sexual relations with students/trainees for the duration of the student's training program should be considered unethical unless the trainee's learning needs can be arranged in some independent manner.

7

SEXUAL MISCONDUCT IN THE CLERGY

The argument that sexual misconduct is really about power and not about sex is so familiar as to become cliché. However, this is an even more obvious truth in the clerical context. To begin with, the pastoral relationship is structured around a power imbalance in many of the same ways that structure the therapy relationship. Additional issues that intensify this imbalance refer to the spiritual realm where the idealization of the pastor or priest elevates him to godlike status. The layperson imbues the priest with godlike qualities derived from the belief that the priest is more closely associated with God and, for some, is the human embodiment of God. This may be true for rabbis as well, despite the fact that the defining role of the rabbi is one of a teacher or interpreter of the Torah, not as divine or as a conduit to the deity.

The professional relationship between clergy and parishioner may be formal, as between a pastoral counselor and a counselee, or less formal, as in priest and parishioner (Fortune, 1989). Prevalence data suggest that sexual misconduct is a more extensive and deeper problem in clergy as compared to other mental health professions (see Schoener, 2005, for a thorough historical review as well as Frawley-O'Dea, 2007, and Frawley-O'Dea & Goldner, 2007). Blackmon (1984) surveyed 300 clergy in southern California from four denominations—Assembly of God, Episcopal, Presbyterian, and United Methodist. Results reflected a 13% prevalence rate of sexual intercourse with a parishioner (Schoener et al., 1989). However, in the same study, 39% acknowledged sexual contact with a congregant. In a 1987 survey of *Christianity Today*, 23% respondents indicated inappropriate sexual behavior after having entered ministry. In the past 50 years, there have been 4,500 documented cases of sexual abuse by 1,100 Catholic priests, representing about 5% of the Catholic priesthood during that era (Frawley-O'Dea, 2005). Similarly, Lothstein (2004) reports 3–6% of the 45,000 Catholic priests in the United States have been identified as having serious sexual pathology with minors.

Though the response to sexual misconduct has varied over time, there is a general improvement in accountability on both individual and organizational levels. Marie Fortune's (1989) book and others (see, for example, Kochansky and Herrmann, 2004; Robison, 2004) have challenged the religious community to deal more effectively with sexual misconduct in the church. Frawley-O'Dea (2005) reviews themes of dominance/sadism and submission/masochism that rely on the valorization of suffering to justify power structures and relational approaches directly implicated in the sexual abuse crisis. She reports that some priests hold the attitude that sex abuse survivors have been given the opportunity to share the cross with Jesus and should graciously shoulder their burdens rather than aggressively seek redress.

The effect of sexual misconduct on the parishioner or counselee is profound and has its equivalent in the psychotherapy victim. Again, however, there is a spiritual dimension to the priest-parishioner relationship, thereby adding a deeper dimension to the traumatic sequellae associated with misconduct. Especially in a pastoral counseling relationship, the pastor has access to the spiritual core of a person's being, thereby potentially damaging the parishioner's relationship to her spiritual self and her relationship to God (Fortune, 1989). Worse, if the church responds inadequately or destructively to the victim's call for help, she may have a crisis of faith and lose not only her counselor and pastor but her religion and trust in God as well.

The training of ministers and priests in general is not comprehensive with regard to the understanding and handling of psychological issues. Most priests have a limited understanding of transference and countertransference processes. In addition, the blurring of boundaries is inherent in many aspects of pastoral training, where spiritual meetings and counseling sessions may take place in a variety of places, including the parishioner's home, the church, a hospital room, or at a retreat.

While many religious professionals take vows of chastity or celibacy, those who do not still regard adultery and sexual contact outside of marriage as sinful and a violation of sacred vows. Some male priests have been known to rationalize their involvement with male minors as residing "outside" the prohibition of adultery since it is not categorized (in their mind) as sex with another woman. The same holds true for their vow of chastity: sex with male minors does not count as sex and therefore does not violate their sacred vows. It is important to note that this is not a conscious or acknowledged rationale in any ongoing way, but may be used to justify the abuse at the time.

As with psychotherapists, problems in narcissism have been identified among clergy and pastoral counselors (Kochansky & Cohen, 2005; Kochansky, 2005; Kochansky & Herrmann, 2004; Lothstein, 2004). Bradshaw

(1977) conducted a study of clergy evaluated at the Menninger Clinic and found 39 out of 140 were considered narcissistic personalities. Another parallel to therapist-patient sexual misconduct resides in the categorization of the different types of exploitation. Like therapist-patient sexual misconduct, the varieties can be, in broad strokes, described in one of two ways: cluster sexual abuse (akin to the multiple transgressor) or the narcissistically needy minister at a stressful time of life (akin to the one-time transgressor).

Cluster sexual abuse is defined as the sexual abuse of multiple victims by an authority figure in an organization or church (Bera, 1995). This is the category of pedophile priests, although technically, most are "ephebophiles" who are attracted to pubescent or teenage victims as opposed to prepubescent children (Lothstein, 2004; Kochansky & Cohen, 2005). Most of these ministers are charismatic, are highly esteemed in their church, "groom" their victims in a gradual way, and molest multiple victims over many years (Bera, 1995). Like the psychopathic predator, there is much doubt about rehabilitation potential for these ministers if and when they are discovered.

Controversy also abounds in reference to whether cluster sexual abuse is perpetrated largely by homosexual or heterosexual priests (Allen, 1991). There is general agreement that the majority are ephebophiles who sexually molest pubescent or postpubescent males (Kochansky & Cohen, 2005; Lothstein, 2004). Though there is no single clinical profile that characterizes these priests, there are common psychological variables, including: (1) confusion about sexual orientation, (2) childish interests and behavior, (3) lack of peer relationships, (4) extremes in developmental sexual experiences, (5) personal history of sexual abuse or deviant sexual experiences (such as sexual abuse by a priest as a minor), and (6) an excessively passive, dependent, conforming personality (Rosetti, 1990). These characteristics are consistent with Bryant's descriptive analysis highlighting dependent and narcissistic personality disorders (2002).

Lothstein (2004) emphasizes the importance of differentiating between *fixated* pedophiles who are exclusively sexually attracted to children or adolescents and *regressed* pedophiles whose sexual relationships with minors are reactive to stress and stand in contrast to their more characteristic higher level of psychosexual organization. Findings based on a variety of clinical data including psychological tests revealed a predominance of Cluster C and Cluster B personality disorders.[1] Cluster C, the most frequent type, includes individuals with dependent, avoidant, or obsessive-compulsive personality disorders. Cluster B includes more primitive personality organizations such as antisocial, narcissistic, borderline, and histrionic personality disorders (Lothstein, 2004).

The damage to the victims of clergy sexual misconduct is profound and shares many similarities with the consequences of incest and therapist-patient

sexual misconduct. However, as mentioned above, in clergy sexual misconduct, there is the added dimension of spiritual betrayal that causes a crisis of
faith as well. Since the trusted minister was the representative of God and the
church to the victim, it is often difficult or may be impossible for the victim to
regain a sense of faith in any such institution again.

The congregation and organization of the church itself is traumatized
along with the victim(s) and recovery is likely to take years. Systemwide educational and therapeutic efforts aimed at raising awareness and increasing
compassion for victims are helpful in the healing process (Bera, 1995). Any
member of the congregation who had engaged in a meaningful religious ritual
with the offending priest will have some sort of crisis, casting doubt on the
sacraments performed by this priest, some of which were quite personal (e.g.,
baptisms, marriages, last rites). Just as other patients of a transgressing therapist
will wonder about the adequacy or legitimacy of their own therapy with him,
members of the congregation may wonder if the sacraments performed by the
offending priest were or are holy or blessed as they had originally thought.
Some members of the church will never accept the allegations as true; others
will feel the need to leave the congregation and either join another church or
lose their faith entirely.

A second type of clergy abuse occurs frequently and is akin to the most
frequent type of therapist-patient sexual misconduct (Hulme, 1989). This is
the most prevalent type of sexual misconduct among all mental health practitioners, including clergy (priests, ministers, and pastoral counselors). For the
issues that are the focus of this section, I have found no substantive differences
between clergy who are pastoral counselors and those who are not. Therefore,
for the sake of simplicity, I will refer to all clergy as priests and to the parishioners or counselees as victims. My discussion will focus on Christianity in
general and, at times, Catholicism, celibacy, and the hierarchy of the Catholic
Church in particular. I believe that the unconscious fit between these priests
and some of the teachings of Christianity, Catholicism, and the attendant organizations may render priests particularly susceptible to this type of sexual
misconduct.

The problem of sexual misconduct in these contexts involves a priest
who becomes sexually intimate with one adult victim. Because the victim is
either a member of the priest's parish and/or a counselee, the relationship is
inherently structured around a power imbalance. This renders consent moot,
even if the victim believes she or he desires the relationship, since it is freighted
with transferences to the structurally imbued authority. Such relationships, in
my experience, are most likely to be heterosexual, between a male priest and
a female victim.

A COMPOSITE ILLUSTRATION

The following is a composite case that illustrates the most frequent characteristics of clergy sexual misconduct. Some elements are situational; others are
features of the priest's personality organization or typical behavioral patterns.

Reverend X, a married Christian priest, has devoted his adult life to his
ministry. In fact, there is no boundary between his identity as a priest and his
person, nor is there a functional distinction between his work life and his home
life. Ordination marked a change in external status and formal responsibility,
but he has always felt called to the priesthood and sees it as his special mission
and talent to help others on their spiritual journey and in their relationship to
God. He feels it is his duty to put his own emotional, physical, and sexual needs
aside in order to minister to the needs of others. Often enough the needs of parishioners take precedence over family duties, as his pull toward family confuses
him. He feels anxious and guilty when not serving the church more directly.

Reverend X worked tirelessly for many years in this way. Long hours often take him away from his wife and children in order to minister to the needs
of his parishioners. His family is largely supportive and forgiving of the many
times he is not with them. They join him for services and other activities in
the church. As can be predicted, self-induced burnout gradually and inevitably
sneaks up on him.

It was after a service that he noticed Ann, a recently divorced, childless
woman who had seemed to be attending services with greater frequency in the
past few months. On this particular day, Ann looked on the verge of tears and
when he hugged her (an accepted practice upon leaving a service), she asked if
she could meet with him privately. She stated that she needed some guidance and
support. They agreed to meet that afternoon in his office. During this meeting,
she poignantly described her struggle to get back on her feet, both financially
and emotionally, after her husband left. She told Rev. X that her husband had
been unavailable and emotionally abusive. She told Rev. X that she had been a
victim of incest as a child. Reverend X was intensely moved by her suffering
and felt a need to be generous with his time, compassion, and kindness.

They met several times a week over the next several months, and alongside this pastoral-counseling relationship, there developed a more intimate
interest in each other, an intriguing feeling of specialness to each other that
was unmistakably sexually tinged. Though Rev. X believed that he was only
trying to help Ann cope with her loneliness, hurt, and confusion about her
recent divorce, he was also dimly aware that she held a particular fascination
for him. She was, perhaps, a female version of himself, an unpotentiated self
he had not lived out, a freer, secular spirit that he had never allowed, even in

his own imagination. He particularly loved *her* passion for *him*, her wish *to own* him that was at first unstated but experienced, then later was enacted through intense arguments over her jealousy of his wife and family. He sometimes felt afraid of her, even trapped in the relationship, yet he could not stop thinking about her and felt throughout that he had found his soul mate.

Their sexual relationship lasted over a year when, after increasingly escalating arguments over Rev. X's inability to leave his family, Ann wrote a complaint to the bishop.

This is a composite picture of the most common type of sexual misconduct among all mental health professionals, including clergy of all denominations. Even celibate Catholic priests can break their vows in a manner that fits this composite. Though clinicians typically associate sexual misconduct with therapeutic relationships, any structured power imbalance will elevate and encourage the idealization of the professional in the eyes of the victim (see, e.g., Schwartz & Olds, 2002). This imbalance can then be exploited. (For a detailed description of a psychotherapy of an offending priest [a composite illustration], see Celenza, 2007.)

SEXUALITY AND POWER: THE CHRISTIAN SOLUTION

Sexuality and one's relationship to God reflect the ways in which an individual has come to terms with two bodily imperatives: the challenges to one's omnipotence and the press of sexual needs. In this chapter, I discuss how pathological relations to sexuality and power reflect a narcissistic refusal of certain existential conditions rather than a transcendence of them. Though celibacy can reflect *a transcendence* of bodily appetites, it can also be used self-deceptively *to disavow* the pleasures of the body, in order to establish a temporary means of (self) control. Likewise, a spiritual relationship to God can express an enlightened awareness of the mysterious nature of being and of the human condition. However, for narcissistically vulnerable priests, it may also serve an unconscious omnipotent desire to elevate and empower an enfeebled self.

There appear to be at least two reasons why this type of misconduct occurs with great frequency among Christian clergy. First, there are specific vulnerabilities in the character of *some* individuals who are attracted to clerical life. Many of these coincide with the personality characteristics that are precursors to sexual misconduct. These typically include: (a) the absence of a father figure (in fact) and/or the presence of a degraded father figure either in actuality or in the mind of the mother; (b) a tendency toward concrete thinking or a restricted fantasy awareness; (c) extensive, unresolved narcissistic needs (i.e., needs for recognition, mirroring, pride); and finally, (d) a great fear of and anxiety around the felt experience of anger and expression of aggression in general (Schoener, 1995; Celenza, 1998; Celenza & Gabbard, 2003). All of these vulnerabilities stand in some relation to power and sexuality; all are considered to be precursors to sexual misconduct (Gabbard, 1994a; Gabbard & Lester, 1995a; Celenza, 1998).

A second reason why this type of misconduct occurs with great frequency among clergy may have to do with the teachings of Christianity and Catholicism in particular, both of which may offer vulnerable individuals partially adaptive, compensatory strategies to cope with and manage (but not resolve or transcend) their vulnerabilities.

> Thou art the same, and Thy years shall have no end.
>
> —Psalm 102:27

> World without end, Amen.
>
> —Ephesians 3:21

One common childhood experience of vulnerable clergy is the absence of a positive father figure in the experience of the family.[2] This is true whether the father was present or not, since it refers to the felt experience by the child of the absence of the actual father, or the presence of a degraded male figure in actuality or in the mind of the mother. Under optimal circumstances, the child psychically represents the father in his fantasy, combining his mother's image of the father and his actual experience of him. He identifies with this image in some ways and contrasts himself to it in others, all in an effort to experiment with and construct for himself the man he wants to become.

In cases where the father is absent, the son must rely primarily upon the mother-son dyad as the matrix within which to find and potentiate his masculine identity. When the "father-in-the-mother" is absent or degraded, there can be a denial of difference between the son and his mother. The son may feel that sameness (to his mother) is the only acceptable mode of relating with her, and that exploring their differences (e.g., being male) is not. With the absence of a third figure or position, the mother's psychic burdens become absorbed by the son. This can eventuate in the omnipotent fantasy of his being wholly responsible for (and perhaps having to sacrifice his life to) the mother's well-being. While such a fantasy supports the child's grandiosity, it also binds the child to his mother via the illusion of rescue, which in turn creates the experience of omnipotent oedipal triumph, as well as the earlier experience of pre-oedipal guilt around the child's desire for separation and differentiation.

The early childhood constellation described above accords with Benjamin's (2002) notion of the absence of "the outward vector," "the second other," or a positively toned "identificatory love object." Likewise, Parsons (2000) refers to the impossibility of structure building in the absence of triangulation, leaving the child capable only of degrees of closeness and distance within the maternal-child dyad. The importance of a third presence (internally) is prerequisite to symbolic capacity (as the child represents or symbolizes the relationship between mother and father, a relation in which he himself does not participate).

Catholicism can hold special appeal for priests with these early psychic conditions and psychic organization. This is because its beliefs and practices can be said to foster the conflation of the literal and the metaphoric, especially for those who lack a fully realized symbolic capacity. This is particularly true with regard to the sacraments, many of which are meant to transcend the symbolic.[3] Symbols do not *represent* a holy act, they *perform* the act, as in the transubstantiation of bread and wine into the body and blood of Christ. Likewise, Catholic fundamentalism takes Mary's immaculate conception not as a metaphor of her virgin birth but as a concrete reality.

Thus, the spiritual culture of Catholicism, which collapses the tension between the metaphoric and the symbolic (the "as if" becoming the "is") can also support concreteness in the work of some pastoral counselors. When engaging in sexual misconduct, transgressing priests collapse the symbolic register of the transference into the actuality of the relationship. One vulnerable priest reported that he felt responsible for his female patients' pain, as if he had caused it, with an urgency that led him to feel he must *do something* to alleviate it. The urgency to act, for this priest, reflected a loss of symbolic capacity, an inability to maintain or regain emotional and cognitive distance in the face of his patient's distress.

This conflation of metaphor and actuality operates in other dimensions of Catholic theology that are also problematic for priests with a vulnerable psychic structure. By making the third vector in the mother-child dyad an omniscient and omnipotent figure (i.e., God), ordinary paternal power can never be tested or impacted. When the father figure is real (i.e., human), the son can play with and test his potency against the father's, the son can compete with it, aggress against it, compare himself to it, and even diminish the father's power (see Herzog, 2001). But God's power is never diminished and his limits are never felt. The Catholic priest is destined to submit his authority and power to the magisterium and the ways in which the hierarchy already permits. (This may be one way, as well, that the hierarchy of the church coincides with and encourages the internalization of anger and the tendency toward masochistic action, discussed below.)

To the extent that the third represents the "outward vector" or the representation of the outside world, the maternal-child dyad without a viable positively toned vector can become a closed system. The son may feel there is no acceptable alternative outside the mother, either in another woman or, alternatively, in a man if, for example, the degraded image is of a retaliatory, aggressive male. One Catholic priest, who broke his celibacy vow in a romantic and sexual relationship with a female parishioner, expressed, "I was afraid to devote myself to a woman for fear I would lose her. This felt inevitable because she might leave me or she would eventually die. I believed God might kill her because he was angry with me for betraying him. . . . I decided to make God my primary love object. . . . He is always there. I am never alone."

For this priest, the fear of retaliation by the father still persisted after this psychic shift and was sometimes transferred to his superiors. He longs to be accepted by a father figure, yet never achieves it in a lasting way: "Everyone is called father, never dad. There is no intimacy. I spend a lot of psychic energy trying to please father figures from this distance. I'm always saying to myself, 'I hope I'm doing this the way they want. . . . I hope this won't displease.' My sexual acting out, in part, was a way to free myself. But something was going on between me and God that I sought this woman out in the first place. I was running away from God."

When the mother is narcissistically fragile herself, merger fantasies in the son may threaten annihilation as the child's fragile identity suffers from a lack of mirroring, recognition, and acknowledgment of separateness and difference. Often, the experience of the child self is dissociated as the child precociously adopts a mirroring stance toward the mother in order to make contact with her and find relief from isolation. This dissociated self may be revived later in an overidentification with the victim. This is especially common in the female priest/female victim pairs I have examined. One female priest described her lover (the victim) as "the child I was." Another reported, "I couldn't stand the pain in her. I understood it. It was the same I have known but never expressed."

> Cease from anger and forsake wrath.
>
> —Psalm 37:8

In the case of a degraded male identificatory figure, either in the mind of the mother or in the child's actual experience of the father, the priest may inhibit the capacity for aggression in a defensive attempt to disidentify himself with this image of men. One priest described his father as always holding back his temper. He sensed in his father a powerful and violent presence that required constant monitoring. On several occasions during childhood, his father lost his temper and released a tirade of verbal and physical abuse. Although there were only a few occasions upon which his father lost control, the son felt that his father's anger was a constant presence. This priest stated, "I consider it my job to eliminate anger."

The inhibition of aggression represented, for this priest, a disidentification with the aggressor, his father. But he was also unable to differentiate himself from his mother because differentiation in the context of psychic merger is experienced as a psychologically aggressive act.

When males are degraded in the mind of the mother and/or fathers are experienced as unacceptable in actuality, the son cannot use the father or his image as a pathway to his own masculinity. The son may turn to the church for alternative pathways that devalue aggression and power. Sexuality may be interpreted as an aggressive act as well. One priest considered his mother an autocratic matriarch who could be warm and loving toward his nine sisters but was unaffectionate and unpredictable toward him, her only son. He felt he could not please her and that he was often punished solely because he was a boy. Alongside this maternal degradation of masculinity was his experience of his father as a man whose sexuality was perversely aggressive. He had the sense his father may have been inappropriately sexual with women in the neighborhood as well.

On a conscious level, reconciliation can be found in the Christian ideal of nonviolence, often masking a prohibition against assertion and separation. Merger fantasies with Christ or God (the acceptable masculine ideals) are ritualized and can offer a triumph over oedipal rivalry without competition or aggression. For example, in the Eucharist celebration (prior to Vatican II), Christ in the form of a host is taken in *without chewing*; the boundaries melt, as it were.

All hierarchies may conjure up unresolved oedipal struggles, but the hierarchy of the Catholic Church is particularly rigidified. At least on a conscious level, most priests do not seek promotion within it or believe promotion is possible. Climbing up the ladder requires a self-acknowledgment of ambition, competition, and other narcissistic needs that are deemed unacceptable, forbidden desires. In this way, the Catholic priest's attraction to the church hierarchy can be viewed as a search for the oedipal father (the third) who cannot be dethroned or displeased.

Likewise, in cases of therapist/analyst sexual misconduct, there is almost always the absence of a third presence, as in a consultant, supervisor, or peer supervisor. The enactment can be viewed as an actualization of the internal dyadically structured configuration. Transgressing priests (and therapists and analysts alike) describe the relationship with the victim as feeling as if they were in an insulated bubble. The transgressors report feeling isolated and totally dominated by the need to manage and control the relationship *on their own*. Though there is an undeniable grandiosity underlying this attitude, it is very common for the transgressor to feel overwhelmed and helpless in the face of the felt responsibility to rescue the victim. Not only is there no help in the outside world, but there is also the absence of a third within.

> That all may be one, father, as you are in me and I am in you.
>
> —John 17:22–23

A patient of mine (a Catholic priest) stated, "Celebrating the Eucharist is about being present to the eternal. Being one with God. . . . In eating the host, we become Christ. When you and I have him in us, and we are one with him, we become one with each other. There is a mystery inherent in this act: *we accomplish this unity without losing our individuality and without Christ being divisible*" (italics added). In this way, merger fantasies in the priesthood can represent a uniquely compromised solution. As in all fantasies of merger, the boundaries of time and space are dissolved, presenting the priest with a symbolic solution to difference and separation in return for the security of the maternal womb, without aggression or loss. In this way and through the Holy Spirit, the third vector of the Trinity, the priest becomes one with Christ and God without separating from the maternal object and without diminishing the power of the father. Thus, a defensive use of priesthood as a difference marker (Goldner, 2002) can solve the separation crisis by, in Benjamin's terms, "inventing a magical solution to the profound human crisis of interdependence: a strategy for separating without feelings of loss" (Goldner, 2002, p. 76).

Similarly, the identity of priest (as a feminine kind of male) can be used to solve the crisis of impotence in relation to a domineering mother and an absent or unacceptable father. The priest takes in a masculine figure that dominates the maternal object without aggression by elevating himself above her. He also takes in a masculine ideal without dethroning (i.e., losing or provoking) him. An avowed Jesuit priest described it this way:

> The Catholic Church is a very castrating [his word] hierarchy. Bishops to priests [and] the pope to bishops. It removes the opportunity for initiative. Ordination is *it*. Usually there is little opportunity for promotion. Everybody becomes a pastor and that's it. [For the vowed religious priests] there are three vows: chastity, in Latin is *castitas*, which means "to be made impotent," obedience, submit your will; and poverty, surrender ownership.

Similarly, Christ himself can be viewed as an anti-oedipal figure, in total identification with the father's will (Vitz & Gartner, 1984).

Lead us not into temptation

—The Lord's Prayer, Matthew 6:9–13

As this part of the Lord's Prayer conveys, we are not the authors of our own desire, but are tempted by others to be led into sin. Like Eve offering Adam the apple, ownership of desire is already one step removed. Many clergy who choose celibacy as a way of life seek out the priesthood as a haven from bodily desire. In this way, they hope to find a solution for conflicted or dissociated desire by substituting disavowal for transcendence. Transcending the satisfactions of the material (bodily) world from this position is not viable since one cannot give up what one refuses to own or legitimize. Actions that afford bodily pleasure and violate the priest's vows are relegated to a disowned self. Such a psychic cleavage is a common finding in cases of sexual misconduct and may represent a precursor to it (Celenza, 1998, chapter 3), to keep apart the "me that wants" from the "me that sacrifices for others."

I have understood this precursor as derived from the sexualization of preoedipal (pregenital) needs. In the early childhood histories of vulnerable priests, it is common to find such sexualization, usually taking the form of covert maternal seductiveness and overstimulation (though outright sexual abuse is unusual). Most importantly, this occurs in the context of an emotionally depriving relationship with the maternal figure.

For some priests, the church takes on aspects of the maternal transference and serves to provide a way for the priest to reenact his pathological relationship to his mother while finding the father at the same time. In this self-object configuration, he remains secure within the mother's domineering orbit while being exempt from the responsibility of authorizing his own desire. Cozzens (2000) describes the way in which the church and the bishop fall psychically into place:

> This maternal Church, while supportive and pointing to his dignity as a priest, is also demanding and controlling. His sexuality is restrained, his dress is determined, his residence assigned. This mother wants him for herself. The defining decisions most men make as they claim their personal ground as men are denied. At the same time, the ecclesial mother in partnership with his father-bishop provides identity, status and security. (p. 57)

Thus, the priest finds the maternal holding through merger (with *her*, the church) while taking in and becoming one with a masculine and omnipotent ideal (with *him*, Christ and God).

Moreover, the experience of maternal holding through the institution of the church combines with the narcissistic elevation that accrues to the role of the priest in reality, providing a pseudo-solution to the painful mother-son bond. Cozzens (2000) describes the social status conveyed to mothers of priests in Catholic circles. Narcissistic and oedipal needs (for both mother and son) coalesce around the experience of, "[M]y son the Messiah. . . . Aware of his human neediness and his special dignity as a priest, he becomes her special prize" (p. 64). In this way, the son's omnipotence is inadvertently supported by the church.

> Cultivate humility. To be exalted is to be in danger. Pride is . . .
> sin because it warps our existence. It establishes our lives on a
> false foundation. Not to want praise, not to be proud, . . . to
> distrust one's own will.
>
> —*The Rule of St. Benedict* (McQuiston, 1996, pp. 31–37)

The cultivation of humility in a manner that denies needs for recognition, assertion, and pride is a form of deprivation, specifically in the narcissistic realm. Yet the church also tempts narcissistic needs, especially as these are represented in paternal symbols. As a Catholic priest remarked,

> I sometimes doubt my own motives for enjoying the celebration of public mass. I know everyone is watching me. I wear special robes. I can do something nobody else can do. The church has made me special. I perform the sacrament of the Eucharist. Only I can change the bread and wine into the body and blood of Christ! It may be good psychology but it is bad theology.

I asked him to explain more about this distinction and he continued, "It is not me that changes the bread and wine. Only God can do that, through our faith, all of ours, not just mine. But sometimes the idea sneaks up on me that it is I who has that power."

Under a thin cloak of humility, symbolically enacted in many rituals and sacraments, there is also a placement of the priest in a position closer to God, viewed by parishioners and priest alike as a conduit to the holy, a step closer to the sacred than ordinary beings. In this way, the hierarchy of the church tempts and may support omnipotence rather than challenging it, while at the same time offering a vehicle for its disavowal. As Cozzens (2000) describes, the elevation to bishop (much like being chosen or "tapped" to be a training analyst) can be constructed in the mind of the chosen as evidence, "*that he is not like other men*" (p. 49; italics in original). Moreover, "ordination . . . constellates a fresh Oedipal configuration . . . bishop-father, Church-mother, and priest-brothers. . . . By God's grace, the bishop is clearly a man of the Church, a shepherd of the Church, an icon of Christ . . . as a bishop he is anointed to be a kind of martyr" (p. 54–61). Thus omnipotence and grandiosity are paradoxically tied into the stance of humility, and together they can mask envy, jealousy, rage, and competitiveness, while compensating for the denial of pride, sexuality, and other relational needs.

As Cozzens (2000) describes, "This oedipal desire to be the center of the world, to be loved and admired as no one else, to be first among one's siblings and peers, to possess all power and knowledge, to be *special*, is from the psychoanalytic perspective, *the* original sin" (p. 52; italics in original). Martyrdom, self-sacrifice, and humility can perform a psychological undoing of consciously disavowed omnipotence.

> Forgive us our trespasses.
>
> —The Lord's Prayer, Matthew 6:9–13

> To find the peace without want without seeking it for ourselves, and when we fail, to begin again each day. We humble ourselves. . . . We keep silence.
>
> —*The Rule of St. Benedict* (McQuiston, 1996, pp. 22, 74)

The public is aghast at the Catholic Church's response to the current crisis, especially in its apparent unwillingness to take responsibility for the horrific transgressions of pedophile priests. The silence, lack of apology, and worst of all, inaction in the face of repetitive acts of exploitation are shocking. However, the Christian faith is founded, in part, on turning the other cheek, forgiving through prayer, confessing, and performing acts of contrition in private conference with God. What looks to the public as inaction, silence, denial, and arrogance may be rationalized and dismissed by some transgressing priests as symbolic acts of forgiveness for one's frailty, weakness, and inevitable humanity. This is another example of a preemptive solution: the privileging of forgiveness in a context of disavowal is nothing more than an immoral evasion of accountability.

> Wrath killeth the foolish man, and envy slayeth the silly one.
>
> —Job 5:2

The pervasive denial of aggression in the culture and psyche of priests includes a denial of anger toward authority figures. For vulnerable priests, the church or overseeing professional organization can take on this aspect of the transference. One patient, a Protestant minister and therapist, revealed the fantasy that he and I were in secret collusion against the licensing board to reverse the suspension of his license. This fantasy paralleled an unresolved oedipal dynamic in which his mother had prohibited gratification while his father secretly colluded with him to obtain gratification without the mother's knowledge (Celenza, 1991, see chapter 11).

It is typically the maternal figure who was the authoritarian parent in the childhood of these priests and who was experienced by the child as seductive yet prohibitive and rejecting. The unresolved authority issues are usually re-experienced in the negative maternal transference and are easily projected onto the church. Among analysts who have transgressed, Gabbard (1994a) has found evidence of unresolved anger or resentment at the institute or training analysts with a concomitant fantasy of embarrassing these authority figures by disgracing oneself.

On a more positive note, there can be poignant moments of redemption as transgressors seek to rehabilitate themselves. In a consultation with a priest who presented as genuinely contrite, if not self-punitive, I noted his ability to take responsibility for his misconduct. He discounted this empathic understanding from me. His style was not off-putting but appeared as an earnest effort to do the morally correct thing without asking anything for himself. He made a striking point in response to my query about his current relationship to God. He said, "I don't feel anger toward God. I have too much guilt. I don't feel God violated his part of the bargain. When I was feeling desolate and alone, it was because I had left, not because he did. Can I be forgiven? I have so violated my position of trust as one of his servants. I'll just have to see." Then, apparently realizing I might misinterpret his statement as depending on the outcome of this evaluation, he added, "This is not a contemporary question. This is an eternal one."

ENDNOTES

Parts of this chapter were previously published in 2004 as A. Celenza, "Sexual Misconduct in the Clergy: The Search for the Father," *Studies in Gender and Sexuality, 5*(2), 213–232.

1. In this context, "cluster" refers to the DSM IV categorization of Axis II personality disorders. It is distinguished from the less formal usage previously noted in "cluster sexual abuse" that denotes multiple victims.

2. All quotes from the bible are taken from Rev. P. J. Bradley, *The Holy Bible: Catholic Action Edition* (Gastonia, NC: Good Will Publishers, 1953).

3. I thank Mary Gail Frawley for her helpful comments on these ideas.

Part II

REPORTING, FALLOUT, AND RECOVERY

8

REPORTING AND OTHER ETHICAL
RESPONSIBILITIES

> If I fulfill this oath and do not violate it, may it be granted to me
> to enjoy life and art, being honored with fame among all men
> for all time to come; if I transgress it and swear falsely, may the
> opposite of all this be my lot.
>
> —Oath of Hippocrates, ca. 3rd–2nd century B.C.E.

Historically, the problem of sexual boundary violations was notorious for its ubiquity and for the equally widespread taboo against discussing it. Taking steps to address the unethical behavior (either legally or professionally) was beyond the pale for most practitioners since the issue was largely undiscussable in the first place. Several decades ago, discussions of the problem began to take place publicly, both in the professional literature and through presentations at professional conferences. One focus was the failure of psychotherapists to report colleagues who engaged in sexual misconduct with clients or patients (Davidson, 1977; Stone, 1983). The decades following these reports were characterized by a fluctuating but overall increasing interest in the problem. Along with the lifting of the taboo came a small rise in the reporting of the problem. However, three studies performed in the mid-1980s reflected that practitioners from the three major psychotherapy professions (psychiatry, psychology, and social work) were still unlikely to file a complaint against a colleague and that a large number were even unlikely to assist a patient in filing a complaint (Gartrell, Herman, Olarte, Feldstein, & Localio, 1987; Noel, 1986; Russell, 1984).

It appears that this problem still lingers, although the awareness of, teaching about, and general openness to discussing the problem have gradually shifted. It has always been the case that the single most important factor influencing whether or not a case of misconduct will be addressed is whether or not the victim has sufficient support (see, for example, Vinson, 1984). Aside from changes within the profession regarding greater awareness of the prevalence of the problem, the Internet has also offered multiple avenues for victims to access support for this and other problems of misconduct, causing a sharp increase in the number of cases that have become either professionally or legally adjudicated.

Gartrell et al. (1987) reported findings from a national survey where 87% of respondents viewed sexual misconduct as harmful, yet only 8% reported the abuse. Despite this, the majority favored mandatory reporting. Schoener and colleagues (1989) have identified six issues that figure prominently in the reluctance to report a colleague engaged in sexual boundary violation: (1) lack of belief in the investigative and hearing mechanisms; (2) lack of knowledge about complaint alternatives; (3) concern about the negative impact on the therapy; (4) uncertainty of professional boundaries or the advocacy role; (5) worry that the allegations are not true, may be exaggerated, or that the complaint may destroy the career of the subject of the complaint; and (6) fear of retaliation by the alleged transgressor. The following is an effort to elucidate some or all of the issues identified above, especially regarding the extent and scope of the practitioner's responsibility and liability.

In my experience, three of these factors figure most prominently in the decision not to report a colleague: the desire not to be destructive toward a colleague, fear of retaliation, and confusion about to what, how, and where to act. It is also reasonable to assume that unconscious factors prevent reporting, such as the taboo against revealing incest within the family (profession) and/or the prohibition and guilt associated with the exposure to the "primal scene." It is as if we are all guilty witnesses, since the transgressor is part of our family. We simultaneously identify with him and are ashamed that our family can be so perverse or destructive. Finally, sexual transgressions by colleagues are, at some level, aimed at degrading the profession and, in that sense, are directed at all of us. This can arouse a kind of paralysis in all of us, much like the paralysis that some victims feel, as we become victims ourselves of our colleague's actions. We may fear retaliation, become confused as to whose responsibility lies where, or feel inordinate guilt at the competitive pleasure of a colleague's demise. A common reaction is to do nothing and wish the problem would go away.

TO REPORT OR NOT TO REPORT

Learning of a sexual boundary violation by a colleague places a practitioner in an immediate dilemma made up of several cross-currents: conflicting loyalties, ethical contradictions, and fears of retaliation or countersuits. One aspect of this dilemma, for example, is how to maintain one's commitment to promoting psychological well-being while also maintaining one's bond, loyalty, collegiality, and perhaps even friendship, to a colleague. The complexity in this dilemma goes beyond one's relationship to the victim and transgressor, however. There are usually multiple players and the path to integrity may have many forks and dead ends.

The basic question is: What is the scope and limit of a practitioner's responsibility toward the multiple players involved: the patient, the alleged transgressor, the institution (if there is one involved), and the profession as a whole? When the responsibilities toward each of these players conflict, there is often not an easy resolution. However, the practitioner is expected to behave in ways that show and maximize a good faith effort to abide by his or her various ethical codes as best as possible. Conflicting loyalties and ethical obligations are sometimes not resolvable, especially in the short run, and this has to be tolerated. It may be necessary to confront or report a friend who is engaging in a sexual relationship with a patient, thereby sacrificing the friendship in order to maintain one's commitment to patient welfare.

It must also be said that it is not always clear or straightforward what the most helpful response is at any one time. The proper immediate response may be harmful to the patient if she is not ready to acknowledge the harm or exploitation in the relationship. The practitioner should keep his or her eye on the long-term welfare of all those involved. What may create upset and pain in the short run may prevent further harm in the long run. There is a succinct caveat to keep in mind with regard to transgressors: In the long run, it is always best for the transgressor to be stopped from further harming a patient, even when this means complete narcissistic mortification in the immediate and short run. It is best for the patient and even for the transgressor himself who will, over time, find a way to come to terms with his actions. In the ideal case, he will be amenable to rehabilitation and will become a better practitioner for it. It is also best for the profession as a whole to be able to trust that its members act with integrity and that we can be trusted to "police ourselves" (Gabbard, 1996).

It is common to be confused about what the scope and limit of one's responsibilities are when learning of ethical wrongdoing. Brushing up on one's disciplinary ethical code is often not much help, since real relationships and human behavior do not often conform to the ways in which ethical guidelines organize them. Many states have disciplinary-specific ethics committees associated with their professional organizations whose task it is to interpret the professional ethical code and help practitioners determine the proper response. It is never as clear cut as a yes or no response, as in whether to report or not. The collision of different ethical commitments is more the rule—as, for example, the mandate to resolve ethical violations and the need to maintain confidentiality.

There is a necessary series of steps that any practitioner must go through in order to maintain his own sense of integrity, keep patient welfare at the forefront, as well as determine and ultimately follow the ethical guidelines of his discipline. At the very least, these steps must also be taken to prevent future liability. As mentioned, the path may not be simple or straightforward; conflicting ethical mandates may place the practitioner in an unresolvable dilemma that must be navigated to the best of his ability.

Professionals adopt ethical codes of conduct in part to help define the proper response to wrongdoing. There are multiple codes to which each professional must attend, however, and these refer to different but overlapping domains. These are disciplinary (i.e., psychiatry, psychology, social work, or occupational therapy, to name a few); statutory (state licensing board regulations); institutional (mental health facilities and training institutions often have their own expectations and guidelines regarding ethical behavior), and legal courts of law (criminal and civil). I recommend conceiving of these as a group of multiple commitments, each encompassing its own sphere with specific standards that overlap or may conflict with the other commitments. Though most areas will overlap, there are also contradictory mandates that must be negotiated.

The practitioner is obligated to maintain her commitments in each of these domains and is liable to charges of ethical violations by each overarching regulatory body according to its specific ethical code. Thus, conflicts among the ethical codes can present serious dilemmas in how to proceed. Liberal use of consultation (legal, professional, and institutional) is recommended, with written documentation in each instance. Most disciplines state emphatically and clearly that sexual boundary violations are unacceptable and represent a severe violation of ethics. (An exception is sex therapy, where surrogates are used, which obviously must define sexual activity within the confines of its purposes in a more refined manner.) However, this standard, by itself, does not instruct the practitioner about how to proceed when other mandates are taken into account, such as confidentiality, duty to protect, obligation to resolve, and so on.

The first domain to consider is one's professional discipline. Standards of care vary somewhat depending first and foremost on discipline; the psychiatric organizations, for example, have different expectations for how their practitioners should address wrongdoing than does the psychology profession. Similarly, social work organizations, psychiatric nursing, and marriage/family counseling regulatory agencies all have their own codes of ethics. It is the practitioner's own discipline that is relevant, not the discipline of the transgressor or victim. In one case, a consultant who is a psychologist learned from her consultee that she (the consultee) was currently in a romantic relationship with her therapist. The consultee was a social worker and the transgressor was a psychiatrist. The relevant discipline in determining the proper response for the consultant is psychology since that is the professional organization that oversees and guides the practitioner's behavior.

For psychologists, the ethics code adopted by the national professional organization (American Psychological Association) makes explicit that confidentiality is a primary obligation and must be maintained with few exceptions (e.g., danger to self or others, child abuse reporting); however, a sexual boundary violation is not one of these exceptions. The same is true for the fields of social work and psychiatry, neither of which has a reporting mandate for sexual misconduct that supersedes confidentiality. The regulations under HIPPA also do not provide an exception for such reporting.

Another level of responsibility is statutory. Since most mental health disciplines are licensed by state or provincial (Canada) governments, there may be statutory regulations and state-specific ethical guidelines that must be considered. Some statutes adopt the same code of ethics of a national association (e.g., APA, NASW, AAMFT) as the disciplinary ethical code; others amend or adopt a separate code of ethics which is often called a "Code of Conduct." These may be complementary or there may be areas of contradiction. The general rule is that the stricter requirement is the one followed. Normally, if there is a difference, it is the state's code of conduct that has the stricter rule. For example, for nearly a decade the Psychology Practice Act in Florida held that for a psychologist, sex with a former patient was never okay, no matter how much time had elapsed since termination. During that same time period, the American Psychological Association code had a two-year post-termination threshold.

The same is true in Canada, where each of the provinces has its own regulatory standards. Only in the Province of Ontario, since 1994, has there been a uniform standard across professions. In that province, all 24 regulated health professions are required to report sexual misconduct by other health professions to the regulatory board or professional college (e.g., College of Physicians and Surgeons in the case of psychiatry, College of Psychologists for psychologists). This standard overrides privacy so that a professional seeking help in Ontario whose problem involves sexual contact with patients cannot get help without being reported.

There may be no uniformity between professions within the same state or province. For example, in the State of Minnesota licensed physicians (including psychiatrists), nurses, social workers, and marriage and family counselors all have mandatory reporting of unprofessional conduct, including all sexual boundary violations. Psychologists are required only to report psychologist-patient sex, and there is an exception if information is learned from the offending psychologist in the context of a professional relationship. Only psychologists have to report psychologists. In all cases, the reporting duty supersedes the professional's commitment to confidentiality. One advantage of statute-mandated reporting is that it protects the reporter against suits or licensure complaints when the report is made in good faith (Schoener et al., 1989). A person making such a report should always cite the statute.

By contrast, in Wisconsin, therapists are required to ask a patient who has had sex with a prior therapist for permission to report. If the patient refuses permission, they can report but without identifying the patient. In California the therapist is required to hand a victim of therapist-patient sex a brochure that is produced by the state about reporting.

Many states have a putative mandated reporting but do not specifically authorize an override of the commitment to patient confidentiality. In these states, it remains for the practitioner to resolve this vagueness and thus, these states are not considered to have mandated reporting in the true sense. In the final analysis, all practitioners must determine, in their own jurisdictions, what reporting duties apply to them (Gary Schoener, personal communication, November 28, 2005).

In the legal arena, there are usually few laws that bear on professional behavior since most professional ethical codes prohibit criminal wrongdoing. Complaints brought before the various overseeing courts and agencies may refer to one of four categories of laws enacted by states: criminal, civil, reporting, and injunctive relief (Haspel, Jorgenson, Wince, & Parsons, 1997). In the case of sexual boundary violations, there are 23 states that have specifically criminalized sexual misconduct in some fashion, although the standards and scope of these laws vary dramatically (for arguments pro and con, see Strasburger, 1999). As of January 2007, these states include: Alaska, Arizona, California, Colorado, Connecticut, Delaware, Florida, Georgia, Idaho, Iowa, Kansas, Maine, Michigan, Minnesota, Mississippi, New Hampshire, New Mexico, North Dakota, South Dakota, Texas, Utah, Washington, and Wisconsin. For more information regarding the legal aspects of criminalization, the reader is referred to Haspel et al. (1997) and Bisbing, Jorgenson, and Sutherland (1995). The reader may also find useful information on the Internet at www.advocateweb.org, where it is possible to view the civil and criminal codes for each state.

In terms of civil liability, only a few states have specific statutes that apply. As a general rule, an employer or anyone who carries the title "supervisor" is often held potentially liable under a theory of *respondeat superiori*—also termed *vicarious liability*. The general standard for such responsibility requires that the therapist is acting within the scope of employment, providing a service that benefits the employer, and is under the direction of the employer or supervisor. Even though it might seem that having sex with a patient is not within such scope, the reality is that those in authority are typically held liable, even if they have not ever heard about the case. There are cases where the supervisor had no knowledge of a case and yet was held liable for the sexual misconduct by a supervisee (Bisbing et al., 1995; Schoener, 2005; Schoener et al., 1989).

The issue of direct liability is more complicated. This pertains to whether the supervisor knew or should have known what was taking place, and whether he or she should have acted differently. This relates to what the standard of care for a supervisor is determined to be in a given case—that is, what a "reasonable and prudent supervisor faced with the same or similar circumstances" would have done. Examples of supervisory failures would be where the supervisee has a personal problem that is evident and has not been addressed, where countertransference was not addressed, where the case is not reviewed, where patient complaints are ignored, and so forth (Bisbing et al., 1995; Schoener et al., 1989).

Case consultation—where the consultee voluntarily brings to the consultant cases he or she needs input on—does not carry significant liability unless it is called "supervision." Unfortunately, the psychotherapy fields have a tradition of purchasing "supervision" or joining "supervision" groups where the arrangement is not in fact true supervision but rather case consultation. By calling this "supervision," one takes on the full duties and responsibility of a supervisor. A variant on this sort of error is when a group of practitioners share office expenses and space but do *not* clarify that they are in fact independent practitioners sharing space and that they do not supervise each other. Unless one does this orally and in writing, the patient may presume that it is a clinic and may in fact make the "reasonable person" assumption that it is a clinic and those who practice there are under supervision (Bisbing et al., 1995; Gary Schoener, personal communication, February 11, 2007).

Professional licenses are privileges, not rights. Therefore, the argument that a professional ethical standard violates an individual's civil rights (e.g., the right to have a romantic relationship with an adult) is arguable. When an individual applies for licensure in his or her particular discipline, he or she is voluntarily giving up certain rights in order to maintain the integrity of the profession. This usually means making a commitment to constrain one's behavior to a greater extent than is expected of the general public. Thus, the civil sphere, in terms of constraints on rights, encompasses the behavior of the professional whose privilege is defined by a greater constraint on behavior.

Finally, the ethical codes of various mental health institutions are usually duplicates of the various professional disciplinary ethical codes. When disciplinary and statutory ethical codes contradict, there may be guidelines about how to resolve them. For example, there may be a hierarchy of responsibilities, guidance on which level of responsibility takes precedence, or specific instructions within the differing ethical codes about how to go about attempting to resolve these conflicts. Consultation with associated ethics committees is always a good way to proceed in order to sort out the conflicting demands. Again, any instances of consultation should be documented.

Once the practitioner has determined his or her mandate in professional, statutory, legal, and institutional domains, the proper response may be clear. If a state and professional organization both require the mental health practitioner to report sexual misconduct, the proper response is to do so. Most often, however, there are conflicting commitments, either within one ethical code or among professional, organizational, and statutory codes. When this is the case, it is advised to seek consultation from the various conflicting organizations, document the advised responses, and seek to resolve the conflicts in ways that permit the fullest adherence to one's professional's code of ethics and personal sense of integrity.

The following example is illustrative. (Although this case involves two psychologists, one would use whatever ethical code is appropriate to the supervisor's discipline in fettering out the appropriate response.) A psychologist supervisor is affiliated with a training institution where he supervises licensed psychologists seeking advanced training. One such supervisee tells his supervisor that he is currently sexually involved with a former patient from another clinic where the supervisee was previously employed. The supervisee is careful to add that the therapy was terminated the day they became sexually involved but that he has no intention of ending the relationship. The psychologist and former patient are now living together. The supervisor is shocked and tells the supervisee that he is committing a serious violation of his professional ethical code. The supervisee says that he is aware of that, but does not agree with the ethical code in this case. He further reminds his supervisor that this case is not one for which the supervisor currently or in the past has or had any responsibility (i.e., the supervisor never supervised this case). The supervisee also reminds the supervisor that he revealed the details of his relationship in the confidential context of the supervisory relationship. The supervisee then states that he expects that obligation of confidentiality to be maintained.

What is the supervisor's responsibility? The supervisor, a psychologist affiliated and supervising for a training program, has the following domains to consider: disciplinary, institutional, and statutory. Because both the supervisor and supervisee are psychologists, the APA Ethical Code (2002, effective date June 1, 2003) is the first relevant code to consult and on this subject, it is explicit and clear:

> *Standard 10.08:* Psychologists do not engage in sexual intimacies with former clients/patients for at least two years after cessation or termination of therapy.

> *Standard 1.04:* When psychologists believe that there may have been an ethical violation by another psychologist, they attempt to resolve the issue by bringing it to the attention of that individual, if an informal resolution appears appropriate and the intervention does not violate any confidentiality rights that may be involved.

> *Standard 1.05:* If an apparent ethical violation has substantially harmed or is likely to substantially harm a person or organization and is not appropriate for informal resolution under Standard 1.04 . . . psychologists take further action appropriate to the situation. . . . This standard does not apply when an intervention would violate confidentiality rights or when psychologists have been retained to review the work of another psychologist whose professional conduct is in question.

> *Standard 4.06:* When consulting with colleagues, (1) psychologists do not disclose confidential information that reasonably could lead to the identification of a client/patient . . . unless they have obtained prior consent.

As can be seen, at least two ethical standards intersect and could potentially paralyze the supervisor from taking action. These standards are the prohibition against sexual intimacies with former clients or patients and the primary obligation to confidentiality rights (in this case, of both the supervisee and the client/patient with whom he is sexually involved). Presumably, the obligation to maintain confidentiality is placed above almost any other standard in order to foster greatest access to services (including consultation and supervision) as well as maintain the safety of these contexts for psychologists who may be in trouble. Thus, direct reporting of the violation of Standard 10.08 does not supersede the primary obligation of confidentiality (Standard 4.06).

Also, at the statutory level, the supervisor knows that, for psychologists, there is no mandate to report sexual intimacies with patients in his state. However, the APA Ethical Code also states explicitly that psychologists should "take further action appropriate to the situation" (Standard 1.05). An attempt at an informal resolution would include the supervisor's confrontation of the supervisee and the supervisor's explicit statement that the supervisee is engaging in a serious ethical violation. This informal attempt, however, did not eventuate in a resolution of the violation. In addition, it can be argued that sexual boundary violations are by definition a serious ethical violation and therefore warrant formal resolution in any case. Here, it is the psychologist's responsibility to take further action to resolve the situation while maintaining his primary obligation of confidentiality to the supervisee.

Finally, the supervisor has, by some verbal or nonverbal contractual arrangement, made a commitment with the training program to supervise the work of the supervisee. Presumably this contract includes an evaluation of the supervisee's performance that will be reported to a training director periodically or at some point. Thus, he is *expected* to report on the supervisee's performance—that is, confidentiality in the supervisory relationship is not total. However, this case is not included in the supervisor's responsibilities since the supervisee did not treat the patient within the bounds of this training program.

Balancing these conflicting obligations, the supervisor should, as part of his duty to the training program as well, evaluate the supervisee and make clear to the training director of the training program that the supervisee is not able to maintain appropriate boundaries as prescribed by the APA Ethical Code. The supervisor may have examples of the supervisee's incompetence in the cases he has been supervising under the auspices of the training program. If this is not the case, the supervisor should state that he cannot reveal an example of the supervisee's difficulties because of the need to maintain confidentiality for all of the different parties involved.

With regard to the patient or client, there may be a duty to warn or duty to protect, especially if (as is *not* the case in this example) the services rendered to the patient or client are under the auspices of an institution, program, or agency. If the patient or client knows of the existence of a supervisor or has had interaction with the supervisor, there is a likelihood of liability for the supervisor since it can be argued that the patient relied on the supervisor as a warranty for quality care or safety (Schoener, 2005).

In general, supervisors have clinical responsibility (and thereby liability) for cases being treated by the supervisee, whether or not the supervisor has heard about a particular case. It is within the scope of the supervisor's power to compel the sharing of any and all cases, to demand review of files, and to focus the supervisory sessions in whatever manner he or she deems necessary (Schoener, 2005). It is also usual practice for the supervisor to report to an overseeing agency about the supervisee's progress.

THE LEGAL FALLOUT

A future ideal, and the one this book aims to move the helping professions toward, is an atmosphere within the profession of the highest ethical standards combined with minimal moralism. This distinction is not trivial, but it is subtle. It is a standard to which all mental health professionals strive in relation to their patients, where the absence of judgmentalism and a thoroughly open and affirming attitude is part of what the therapist offers. This does not include an absence of critical thinking or an inability to make diagnostic distinctions; however, the most appropriate and health-promoting attitude involves a deep commitment to understanding complexity with an eye toward constructive (therapeutic) intervention for all.

At the moment, the responses to sexual boundary violations are unacceptably diverse and unpredictable. The same act committed by two therapists of the same discipline in the same state may result in widely divergent outcomes. The various overseeing professional agencies, including licensing boards (see, for example, Gutheil & Gabbard, 1998) vary in rigor, flexibility, and punitiveness among the various professions within and across states. Such ineffectiveness and inconsistency make all adjudicating bodies lose credibility and create more resistance to using these bodies for redress, either on the part of the victim, the transgressors, or the professionals themselves, including those who hold administrative positions.

There is also rampant punitiveness in many members of ethics committees and licensing boards whose (sometimes volunteer) membership tends to attract people who have axes to grind or rigid and punitive agendas. Perhaps the most troubling aspect of what transgressors may potentially face is the tendency for some boards or committees to respond to the cooperative and remorseful transgressor *more punitively* than to the unrepentant psychopathic predator. This is unacceptable and illogical; however, it is explainable when the characteristics of each type of case are examined. For one, the unrepentant psychopathic predator is likely to be belligerent and obstructionist, as well as inclined to threaten countersuits. Though the adjudicating bodies usually have nothing whatever to fear (they are simply doing their jobs in good faith), the organizations they represent are often underfunded and overly concerned with the cost of legal representation should countersuits be filed (see, e.g., Gabbard, Peltz, & COPE Study Group on Boundary Violations, 2001). This can lead to a hands-off kind of response in relation to the psychopathic predator, where these cases become stalled on a technicality and remain in the files for years. One study reported a substantial increase in the number of cases left pending (from 17% to 56% over a three-year period) and cited budget constraints, lack of personnel, and delaying actions by the defendants as causes (Gottlieb, Sell, & Schoenfeld, 1988). Neither the victim, the transgressor, nor the public is well served by this outcome and it is demoralizing for the members of the organization to see a problem stagnate and remain unresolved.

In contrast, the cooperative and remorseful transgressor can be somewhat masochistic by nature, guilt-ridden in character, and genuinely remorseful in relation to his transgression. He is mild-mannered and cooperative. The board, feeling battered by previous belligerent transgressors whose cases are now pending or stalled, can easily take out their frustrations on the transgressor presently before them. He is there before them and he will not retaliate. On a more neurotic level, he may seek more punishment than is deserved and the boards may be too willing to collude with him. In one case, an alleged multiple transgressor was never adjudicated because of institutional paralysis. The next case to be presented to the training institution's ethics committee involved a single transgression best described as inappropriate sexual advances (no outright sexual activity ever took place). This transgressor, however, was permanently expelled from his training institute and underwent a three-year suspension of his license to independently practice. Both of these disciplinary actions are more typical of a case of outright sexual misconduct and it can be argued that this transgressor "took the heat" from the unadjudicated multiple transgressor. In another case, a physician's license was revoked because he gave a book and a lamp to a patient (Gutheil, personal communication, 2006). This physician had the misfortune of having his case brought forward just after the licensing board was criticized in the press for failing to discipline an egregious case involving frank sexual misconduct. Obviously, the lack of consistency and unpredictability in the way cases are judged remains a powerful disincentive for therapists to cooperate with their oversight committees or adjudicating bodies. There needs to be standard practices, rules, and procedures that are followed in disciplined, transparent, and judicious ways to both guide and to limit the exercise of idiosyncratic uses of power.

TYPES OF COMPLAINTS

A practitioner can be sued or charged with a complaint under any auspice of which he or she is a member. Overseeing professional organizations and societies (including international, national, and statutory), state licensing boards, institutional affiliations, and civil malpractice suits are all possibilities. The nature of the complaints varies somewhat under each overseeing body; however, it is often the case that the same complaint will be filed with multiple agencies. It is also common for a complainant to file successive suits. For example, a complainant may begin with a local institution (perhaps under whose auspices the violation took place), then file a complaint with the local chapter of the professional organization (through their ethics committee), and on to a civil suit (that may include a monetary award). Many malpractice insurance policies have capped the amount they are willing to spend in defending cases of sexual misconduct, so the cost of multiple hearings and processes are often borne out of personal expense.

When complaints are filed simultaneously to multiple agencies, it is not uncommon for one agency to begin its administrative, investigatory, and hearing process while the other agencies put the matter on hold in order to benefit later from the findings of the first agency. This strategy is largely designed to reduce the cost of duplicating efforts and to use the wisdom of the first agency in arriving at subsequent conclusions.

Statutes of limitation are relevant for civil and criminal statutes. These are typically set at two to three years; however, it is also generally recognized that in cases of sexual misconduct, certain exceptions to the statute of limitations may be relevant. These usually revolve around when the victim realizes that injury has occurred and that the misconduct is or was the cause of the injury. Since many victims struggle with self-blame and shame at the sexual involvement, this awareness may take longer to arrive at than the statute of limitations allows. It is not unusual for the courts to set the beginning of the time elapsed to when the victim *recognizes* harm (rather than when the misconduct and harm occurred). Another exception that is often made occurs when the alleged transgressor (i.e., the defendant) misleadingly assures the victim that the harm she experiences is not related to the misconduct. For more information on these aspects of the legal situation, see Haspel et al. (1997) and Bisbing et al. (1995). Civil statutes are primarily intended to compensate the victim. Though the ordeal of a trial and the monetary reward to the victim are hardships for the transgressor, punishing the transgressor is not the primary intent of a civil suit. There is a different way of conceiving the task at hand as well, since the burden of proof is lifted because sexual misconduct is beneath the standard of care by definition.

Criminal statutes are intended to punish the perpetrator. The task at trial is to convince a jury that the therapist breached a duty owed to the victim. The primary focus is to prevent, deter, and maintain public safety. Because criminal wrongdoing carries with it the heavy penalty of incarceration, the burden of proof is more stringent and the definition of sexual misconduct more narrow. In most states where sexual misconduct is criminalized, the definition of sexual misconduct includes sexual intercourse. This excludes a great number of victims since sexual relations in the therapist-patient context does not necessarily include intercourse and, in some cases, involves bizarre or perverse activity. It is speculated, however, that despite these difficulties, criminalization and mandated reporting statutes have raised public awareness of the problem of sexual misconduct to beneficial effect. No hard evidence, such as a decrease in prevalence, has been obtained or has been tied to the effects of these statutes as of yet. For more information on these aspects of the legal situation, see Haspel et al. (1997) and Bisbing et al. (1995).

The ethics of post-termination relationships are viewed with some variability among the different disciplines. The Ethical Principles of the American Psychological Association states explicitly that sexual relations with a former patient may be ethical after two years have elapsed (Standard 10.08a), but only in "the most unusual circumstances" and that psychologists bear the "burden of demonstrating that there has been no exploitation" (Standard 10.08b). In contrast, the American Psychiatric Association's Code of Ethics states, "Sexual activity with a current or former patient is unethical" and no exceptions to this prohibition are delineated (Section 2.1). The American Psychoanalytic Association, not surprisingly, states emphatically that "Sexual relations between psychoanalyst and patient or family member, current or former, are potentially harmful to both parties, and unethical" (Guiding General Principle VI; see Levine and Yanof, 2004, for a discussion of postanalytic contacts in psychoanalytic institutes). Somewhat like the Ethical Code for Psychologists, the National Association of Social Workers Code of Ethics states, "Social workers should not engage in sexual activities or sexual contact with former clients. . . . If social workers engage in conduct contrary to this prohibition . . . it is [they] . . . who assume the full burden of demonstrating that the former client has not been exploited, coerced, or manipulated, intentionally or unintentionally" (Standard 1.09c).

In practice, the licensing boards and ethics committees vary widely in their determination of ethical violations and disciplinary action. One reason the courts and medical licensing boards generally take a harsh view toward mental health professionals who violate the post-termination prohibition is the recognition of the possibility or even likelihood that the professional engaged in a preparatory planning to "groom" a patient for a future liaison (Epstein, 2002).

INSTITUTIONAL RESPONSES

The extreme variability and lack of standard guidelines in the way licensing boards and overseeing professional organizations respond to sexual boundary transgressions is equally true of academic, clinical training, and clinical service institutions. Once a complaint of sexual misconduct has been submitted, neither the victim nor the transgressor knows what to expect. This lack of predictability heightens anxiety for all involved. It is also common for well-intentioned and conscientious administrators, determined to conduct a fair process, to feel unappreciated and criticized, and to be treated with great hostility from all quarters during the process and after it has come to a close. It may be that the problem is so distasteful that satisfaction will always remain elusive; still, standard guidelines need to be put in place so that some semblance of order, consistency, predictability, and integrity can be relied upon.

Procedures need to be outlined that are routine and impersonal, freeing all members of an organization or training institution from loyalty binds. Victims should be treated with respect and sensitivity unless there is proof of a false accusation. For the transgressors, careful distinctions should be made regarding the viability of rehabilitation and standard modes of responding should be applied without bias (see chapter 11 for more detail on evaluation of rehabilitation potential).

At the same time, these procedures and structures should not be manipulated or stalled by either the transgressor or the victim. The response to each should be performed by different subcommittees. The transgressor and the victim have widely divergent needs, and addressing the problems of each should be handled separately. The transgressor's assessment of the victim, for example, holds no credibility despite the fact that he may have known the victim for many years in a therapeutic context. It is impossible to extricate the transgressor's response to the complaint (the anger, hostility, and fallout of the complaint process from the threat to his livelihood) from his way of perceiving the victim at this point in time. Either through malice, revenge, or self-defense, it will not be possible for the transgressor to make an unbiased assessment of the victim's character or needs.

Similarly, the transgressor should not be punished through the use of the demands of the victim since the victim is in no position to know or assess the capacities of the transgressor. This is especially true after the transgressor has been rehabilitated. Such an assessment, including the transgressor's ability to return to practice to whatever degree, should be made by an independent evaluator who has expertise in assessing sexual boundary violations. It is unacceptable to attempt to appease the victim by further punishing the transgressor out of a fear of further lawsuits. In the same vein, the victim's needs and compensation should be assessed independently of both the institution and the transgressor by a professional with expertise in the trauma associated with sexual boundary violations.

In general, every aspect of the hearing process, including decisions about compensation and disciplinary action, will be affected by each member's attitude toward rehabilitation. The attitude that transgressors are always a lost cause and that every sexual boundary violator is a psychopathic predator will inevitably translate into more punitive and dismissive measures for all. Since this is not my attitude, I think the opposite view warrants careful consideration (see, e.g., Celenza & Gabbard, 2003). Suppose there is a suspicion that a colleague is violating boundaries with a patient. The rumor includes the possibility of sexual acting out, though this is not clear. There is a great distinction to be made between approaching the colleague by stating, "Your behavior is unacceptable and you're being watched" versus "Are you all right? Do you need to talk to someone?"

In this regard, the structures that exist in many organizations designed to address impairment in practitioners can provide a relevant structure for the beginning stages of addressing the problem of sexual boundary violations. There may also be a need for the members of an organization to have a context in which their questions, thoughts, and feelings may be expressed. There is fallout for all members of an organization when ethical codes are violated since the transgressor is identified with the organization and the members within it. In fact, it may primarily be the institution itself that was the true target (albeit unconsciously) of the transgressor's hostility (see chapter 4 for an elaboration of this dynamic; Fogel, 2006). The collateral damage is great and must be addressed at multiple levels (see chapter 9 for a fuller discussion of the institutional structures involved and ways to use them).

9

COLLATERAL DAMAGE AND RECOVERY

How does one recover from a sexual boundary transgression? There are many people for whom this question is relevant, whether you are the victim, the transgressor, or a colleague, spouse, or friend of either. Perhaps he was your best friend. Perhaps she was your analyst. I have known or consulted in all of these situations. These are not easy reckonings and it is traumatic for all involved, though to different degrees and in different ways. Even at the level of a training institution or clinic, there is a recovery process that must be taken seriously and there are components of this process that will mean the difference between an opportunity for growth or an irreconcilable trauma. To this extent, the boundary violation is a collective trauma (Ross, 1995).

The anatomy of the recovery from this egregious violation greatly depends on two interrelated factors. One, and probably the more important of the two, involves the attitude of the transgressor, both toward the transgression itself and his or her openness to and capacity for rehabilitation. The other factor is the attitude each of us holds toward our own fallibility, and again, not unrelated, the possibility of rehabilitation for any transgressor. As has been written elsewhere (Celenza & Gabbard, 2003), it is tempting to believe that sexual boundary violations are the fault of a few bad psychopathic predators and that the problem will be solved when these types are weeded out of the profession. Nothing could be further from the truth.

Like anything else in life, what makes the difference in recovery hinges not primarily on the actual attitudes themselves but on *the way* these are held or expressed. In other words, the way one's beliefs are expressed will lead to and convey other relevant attitudes, especially the extent to which responsibility is partially or fully embraced. All of these aspects reflect one's ethics, that is, *where* one stands, and, equally important, *how* this position is integrated within one's own sense of integrity. Both will affect whether or not the process of recovery can occur. Does the transgressor appreciate the extent of harm he has inflicted on the victim, his colleagues, the institutional context, and finally

the profession itself? Is she open and constructively self-critical such that rehabilitation is viable? Are *you* open to such possibilities or do you believe once a
person has violated their ethics, he or she cannot be trusted ever again?

The challenge for the transgressor has been well documented and is discussed at length in other chapters (see chapters 3, 8, 11, and 12). Still, it bears
repeating that the fundamental distinction between transgressors who have
potential for rehabilitation (and reparation) versus those who do not fundamentally revolves around the transgressor's attitude toward his own behavior.
Does this practitioner locate the problem internally? This can be done even
if external factors are taken into account, such as the difficulty of the treatment or the extent of the situational stress. The crucial aspect that determines
the viability of rehabilitation is primarily a question of responsibility and curiosity about one's own dynamic vulnerabilities. (The Boundary Violation
Vulnerability Index is a measure designed to illuminate and facilitate these
attitudes well before a violation has taken place; see chapter 15.)

But it is important to keep in mind that obstructionism and lack of cooperation (even belligerence) is a common initial reaction to being sued, having
one's character impugned, and having one's livelihood threatened. This is part
of a bona fide posttraumatic stress reaction and though it may not present the
transgressor in a positive light, it may be short-lived and he or she may come
to a more responsible position as the process unfolds. Still, it can be shocking
and profoundly disappointing to see a colleague, therapist, or respected mentor
deny, blame the victim, have temper outbursts, or outright lie. Even though
such behaviors are understandable reactions to threat, one expects more from
those we have trusted, and such relationships can be the most difficult to repair.

There are special and different challenges that individuals face depending
on their relationship to the transgressor and victim. The other patients in the
practice of the transgressor, so-called analytic or therapeutic siblings, face a
unique challenge. The spouse or partner of either the victim or the transgressor is usually understandably devastated, but the qualities of this devastation
vary according to the individuals and circumstances. Colleagues, peers, and
friends are also affected. These challenges and the attendant issues involved in
the recovery process will be discussed separately below.

THE CHALLENGE FOR COLLEAGUES AND FRIENDS

Beyond shock and dismay, it is impossible not to feel tremendously disappointed and betrayed by a colleague who becomes sexually involved with a
patient. This is especially true if one's professional environment has provided

education about sexual boundary violations. Though still largely inadequate, the profession is becoming increasingly aware of the lack of curriculum in both clinical and academic contexts. In some venues, there has been a fair amount of discussion of sexual boundary violations in recent years, especially in more progressive clinical and academic contexts. However, there is no indication that prevalence rates are declining. Despite this, it is reasonable to have built up an expectation that sexual boundary violations would be *less* likely to occur in these specific settings, given that there has been more education about the problem in these particular locales. Hence, there is greater shock and disappointment when a violation comes to light. However, it can also be reasoned that more education and greater awareness in a particular setting may make the possibility of transgressions more understandable, if not expectable, and this can translate into a smoother recovery process.

I would venture to say that the more horrifying instances of multiple transgressions by a psychopathic predator are on the decline; the one-time transgressor who becomes embroiled in a transference/countertransference misfit, however, will always be with us. Most of the discussion that follows refers to the recovery process in an institution or within a network of colleagues from a one-time transgression of this latter sort (described more fully in chapters 2 and 3).

When a transgression of this kind is revealed and it turns out that the transgressor is a friend or colleague, there is a profound feeling of betrayal, as if the colleague violated the boundaries surrounding the friendship itself. In most cases, the transgression is likely to have been kept a secret for some time, so there *is* a betrayal of the friendship in that an event of significant proportions was not shared. This is made more pointedly hurtful if the friendship included meetings with a peer supervision group or collaboration on a committee where such matters (anonymously, hypothetically, or involving other colleagues) were discussed. Perhaps the transgressor served in some capacity examining similar ethical issues or impairment of other members. Thus, the feeling of betrayal is, in fact, an accurate assessment of what has occurred since the transgressor may have been in contexts where he or she had espoused certain values and yet secretly was behaving in an opposite and hypocritical manner. There is an inevitable feeling that one has been taken in and duped (Kris, 2005). This is the nature of the damage that has actually been wrought on the friendship itself. Questions are raised about whether the transgressor has lied to you (presently or in the past) or can be trusted, and the entire history of the friendship comes under scrutiny.

There is an even more pointed betrayal for colleagues and peers when the transgressor was a member of one's peer supervision group and may have given lip service to the ethical principles relevant to the maintenance of boundaries.

This may occur over a long period of time coincident with his engaging in violating the very ethics he proselytized maintaining. Shocking as it may seem, there have been cases of transgressions committed by members of ethics committees; in the logic of the unconscious, this is not as far-fetched as it may seem when one takes into account unconscious guilt, reaction formation, vertical splits, and perverse, sadomasochistic dynamics. The transgressor is drawn to the very context in which he is perversely rebelling against; this is especially tempting when the object of degradation is a displacement for the profession itself (see chapter 4).

When the transgressor is a friend or colleague, there is an unavoidable retrospective revision of the transgressor's character. This can take an extreme form, where one begins to believe that everything previously known, thought, or felt about this person was false, a lie, or terribly misguided. The loss of faith in one's own perceptions and the loss of trust in the intimacy shared with the transgressor in the past are profound. But many of these extreme revisions are part of a posttraumatic syndrome for all involved, and are not necessarily long-lasting or permanent misgivings. Again, much hinges on the ability of all of us to fully accept our own fallibility and the possibility of rehabilitation. To err is human; to fall in "love," whatever that might be made of, is especially so. None of us behaves in predictable, reasonable, or consistent ways under these conditions.

Just as the viability of rehabilitation hinges on the crucial step of the transgressor taking responsibility for his behavior, acceptance by others hinges on the very same thing. Even when the transgressions include multiple victims or occurred under outrageous circumstances (e.g., the violator being a member of the ethics committee, simultaneous involvement with patients who are comembers of a group or the like), rehabilitation, reparation, and recovery for all involved cannot occur unless there is evidence that the transgressor is remorseful and is genuinely trying to account for the perversity and destructiveness of his behavior. This includes the secrets and lies that he created or told, all the ways in which he has compromised his integrity, and the overall damage he has wrought. *There can be no reparation and no recovery (for anyone involved) if this crucial attitude is absent.* Even when colleagues and friends are open to the idea of rehabilitation, the limiting factor for everyone revolves around the transgressor's appreciation and capacity to face what he or she has done. It may be human to transgress, it may be understandable given the circumstances, but it is still egregious to transgress in this particular way, and this must be reckoned with in a fully convincing and responsible way.

At the same time, it is very common for a transgressor to go through a series of phases to eventually arrive at a more responsible position and state of mind. It is not unusual and is even expectable for the transgressor to be traumatized by the revelation of the transgression, the complaint process, the hearing, and/or a more formal adjudication process. This may cause him to behave in defensive, oppositional, angry, and retaliatory ways. These may not be representative of his usual mode of functioning or character and certainly will not present him in the best light. Friends, colleagues, and those involved in the evaluative and legal process can be helpful in facilitating the transition to a more mature level of functioning by being supportive, open to rehabilitation, but also maintaining the highest level of integrity and expectations for all involved, especially the transgressor. This last point represents an attitude of holding the transgressor accountable for his actions throughout, with the belief in his potential to earn back his integrity. Anything less would be condescending and against the values of our profession. It also recognizes the person *as one knew him before* and retains the continuity of his character with the hope and trust of a recovery process. It is not enough to suddenly, as a result of an ethical violation, radically change one's assessment of a colleague when he has been a friend and colleague for years.

There can be poignant moments of redemption as transgressors seek to rehabilitate themselves, even in the more horrifying cases of multiple transgressions that occurred over a long period of time. Here is a case of a priest who had become sexually involved with more than ten congregants over a period of 15 years. All were heterosexual, adult women and he was involved with several simultaneously, although without their knowledge of each other. At some point, complaints began to be filed. Despite the many concurring accounts from several congregants, this priest denied all of the allegations persistently. He also refused to be evaluated for several years and was summarily defrocked. After three years of living outside the priesthood, he finally requested a meeting with his bishop to discuss an evaluation. Reinstatement was a possibility, but he understood it was a long shot.

In my consultation with this priest, he now presented as genuinely remorseful, if not self-punitive, as he recounted his multiple affairs. I noted his ability to take responsibility for his misconduct and expressed this to him. He discounted this empathic understanding from me. His style was not off-putting or gratuitous, but appeared as an earnest effort to do the morally correct thing without asking anything for himself. Then, he made a striking statement in response to my query about his current relationship with God. He said, "I don't feel anger toward God. I have too much guilt. I don't feel God violated his part of the bargain. When I was feeling desolate and alone, it was because I had left, not because he did. Can I be forgiven? I have so violated my position of trust as one of his servants. I'll just have to see." Then, apparently realizing I might misinterpret his statement as depending on the outcome of this evaluation, he added, "This is not a contemporary question. This is an eternal one."

The above vignette demonstrates a striking and quite unexpected attitude from a multiple transgressor who could easily be (and was) characterized as a psychopathic predator. Unfortunately, the more usual presentation for this type of transgressor includes a litany of denials, blaming the victim(s), rationalizations about his behavior, and externalizing responsibility by blaming the institutions for inadequate training or perversely facilitating environments. No sympathy is fostered when a psychopathic predator presents in this more usual manner and no rehabilitation (or redemption) can be considered viable. This priest did present in just this way at earlier intervals. However, the process of a complaint, investigation, and hearing can and should have some effect, in that it is fundamentally a process of being held accountable. It is a reckoning; and, if done in an appropriately responsive way, it can be therapeutic in and of itself. This priest was one who was able to use such a process to turn himself around. He was not reinstated into the priesthood; however, his capacity for personal redemption should be clear.

In a more hopeful vein, the one-time transgressor often displays the qualities that bode well both for rehabilitation from the outset as well as reparation and possible reentry into his professional milieu. Dr. Burn, presented in chapters 2 and 11, had such an attitude from the start and many, if not most, of the one-time transgressors I have consulted with, display such a salutary attitude. Dr. Burn, for example, had his own desire for treatment (in addition to the board mandate) since he was traumatized by the ending of the relationship with his patient, the damage he had wrought (on her, the profession, and himself), and by the disciplinary process itself. He feared he had made a "pathetic mess" out of his life and that he had "dragged a lot of people down" as well. He was extremely remorseful and self-berating. This remorse was easy to distinguish from his mortification at how he had ruined his professional career. Such narcissistic mortification was also present alongside a genuine state of regret and a conviction that he had harmed his patient rather than helped her. He often called himself "narcissistic" and "grandiose" as he recounted the story of his involvement with his patient to me. He was tearful in the early months, appeared genuinely ashamed of his actions, and feared that I would judge him harshly or that I would be hostile.

I have had the conviction that any therapist treating Dr. Burn would be similarly impressed with his earnestness and especially his desire to be fully accountable for his actions. I fear, however, this would not often be the case since I know that many colleagues harbor intense resistance to seeing any transgressor as capable of rehabilitation. This is especially striking since we are in a field that holds out hope for quite severely disturbed persons to be effectively treated. Our profession also prides itself in understanding and treating the most deeply rooted neuroses and character disorders. We are much more patient and liberal with our patients than we are with our colleagues and ourselves. It is not that we shouldn't hold ourselves to a high standard, but what does it mean to hold ourselves above the standard of being human? I suspect there is an underlying defensiveness in this attitude that bears examining.

WHEN THE TRANSGRESSOR WAS YOUR ANALYST OR THERAPIST

There is no systematic data and very little literature on the traumatic sequellae of sexual boundary transgressions from the point of view of the transgressor's other patients and clients (see Wallace, 2007, for one account of an analytic sibling's experience). The discussion in this section is derived almost wholly from my personal and consultative background. For ease of reference, I will refer to the other patients and clients in a transgressor's practice as sibling/patients.

There are special challenges to face when your own treater turns out to have been involved with a patient. This is especially difficult if your treatment was intensely involving and long term. In that case, it is often hard enough to accept that your therapist has other patients at all, much less is sexually involved with one! Then there is the inevitable and irrational, "Why not me?" "What does she have that I don't have?" is the more common phraseology. Ancient oedipal rivalries are understandably stirred up and will no longer be resolvable for the sibling/patient directly with the transgressor himself. In the internal world of the sibling/patient, the reality of an "incestuous" relationship can become concrete proof that one cannot and should not ever compete with one's peers. Beyond this, the particular meanings that the incestuous relationship will have for the sibling/patients will depend, of course, on each individual's psychology and, perhaps, to a great extent on the phase of the treatment when the transgression came to light. On one extreme is the sibling/patient in a full-blown oedipal/erotic transference toward the now-transgressor; on the other end of the continuum are the sibling/patients who have already terminated and have been beyond treatment for several years.

The problem of reparation and the move to a more sanguine acceptance vis-à-vis the transgressor is much easier with greater understanding of the problem of sexual boundary transgressions in general. It cannot be said often enough that there is a universal fallibility for all practitioners toward this problem; we are all potential transgressors just as we are all potential victims. It must be wholly and truly accepted that overinvolvement of many kinds, including sexual boundary violations, are part and parcel of the dangers associated with allowing oneself to be psychologically and emotionally available. This fallibility is more acute at certain vulnerable times in one's life. Further, and the evidence amply demonstrates this, it is wholly possible for the transgressor to have conducted competent and ethically bounded treatments with his or her other patients even if or while transgressing with another (Gabbard, 1999). This is not necessarily true of all types of transgressors but is certainly true with the one-time transgressors where the transference/countertransference (mis)fit characterizes the transgression. Again, one must never blame the patient but rather understand the unconscious hook that contributes to the transgressor's egregious misconduct.

Even after one has accepted these truths and may be fully prepared to take the steps toward reparation, it is a particular kind of challenge when the transgressor was one's own caregiver. It cannot be avoided that each sibling/patient in this situation will question the adequacy of his or her treatment, even if it was previously felt to be a successful piece of work. Sibling/patients wonder to what extent a revision of judgment about the treatment is necessary, as the view of the treatment is now refracted through the lens of one's therapist being a transgressor. There are several useful ways to examine these questions that have a good likelihood to put some of these undermining and nagging questions to rest.

First, a useful question to ask is, Was your treatment wholly about you? One of the steps in the slippery slope involves the transgressor gradually revealing more and more aspects of his or her own history. Perhaps such self-disclosing was overlaid with a rationale that learning more about the therapist or analyst is a way to normalize the patient's subjective experience. Whatever the justification, the steps down this slippery slope almost always have the effect of reversing the roles of who is being treated or helped. Did you feel the talk and focus remained about you? If so, this is how it should be and there is no reason to doubt the adequacy of the treatment on these grounds.

A second question to ask may be relevant for psychodynamic and psychoanalytic therapies only. Were you able to explore your own disappointment and criticism of the treatment and the therapist or analyst himself without his becoming unduly defensive? Although fragility around negative transference is a characteristic of one-time transgressors, this is not necessarily a feature in all treatments he has conducted nor is he similarly fragile with all patients. If this is an area that was underexplored and underdeveloped in your treatment, especially if the orientation was psychodynamic or psychoanalytic, it is likely that an important phase of the treatment was not adequately experienced or worked through. Perhaps the negative transference was more pointedly avoided. Again, if the goal and purpose of the treatment is consistent with the types of issues addressed by more intensive and long-term therapies (e.g., interpersonal or relational problems, character change associated with psychological conflicts), it may be that an important area of concern was missed. If exploration of negative transference (i.e., the expression of negative feelings felt and expressed directly toward your therapist) was a prominent feature of your treatment, either concentrated in a certain phase or present throughout, it is likely that your treatment was conducted competently.

And finally, did you experience significant gains, reflected in desired changes in your outside life, as a result of the treatment? There is no reason for these to be discredited since the transgression has come to light, even if the transgression occurred in the same time frame. For some transgressors, there is a narcissistic need to have all of their patients hold them in positive regard and to be inordinately important to them all of the time. However, many transgressors' vulnerability is stirred up only within a specific treatment dyad. These are characteristics of one-time transgressors within the transgressive dyad; however, they may not be prominent features that are generalized to other sibling/patients. Because therapy is not a substitution for life, treatment gains should be observable in one's outside life and resultant from the treatment. It is, likewise, not necessary to be enjoying the treatment or feel that the therapist is the only person who can meet your needs. There is no gain in feeling that you are good at therapy but a failure at life.

If all of the above questions can be answered affirmatively—that is, in a manner that reflects positively on one's treatment—the sibling/patient can feel confident that he or she is on the road toward accepting what has transpired. If, however, these explorations, along with the integration of our knowledge about the propensity for such violations, do not seem to help, it may be that a return to therapy with a subsequent treater may be indicated. This does not have to be a long-term prospect, but the treatment should have as one of it's primary purposes to integrate the meaning of the transgression into one's view of the past treatment and one's own gains related to it.

THE CHALLENGE FOR THE PARTNER OR SPOUSE

If there ever was a tragic member of the sexual boundary violations cast, it is the part that is handed to the spouse of either the victim or the transgressor. This is a person who is (usually) caught totally unaware, is nothing short of devastated when the violation is revealed, and who is most disregarded in the aftermath. To add insult to injury, the spouse or partner is not even a major actor in this perverse drama. Although a troubled marriage is often part of the backdrop that comprises the situational stress of the transgressor, this is not always the case. Even if it is, most partners rely on their spouses to deal with marital difficulties in a direct and private way. Infidelity is probably the most challenging betrayal to any marital commitment. Adding a professional ethics violation to it complicates the matter in both gratifying and humiliating ways. (A spouse can take a perverse pleasure in the way her spouse's professional life is destroyed.) At the same time, we are all identified with our partners and share the embarrassment, humiliation, and narcissistic mortification.

Spouses are somewhat "sealed off" from the relationships their partners have with their patients. Similarly, the spouses of the victims may not be privy to the details and events of his or her partner's therapy. This varies greatly with each couple, of course. Either of these, however, become more marked partitions if and when boundaries within the treatment are violated. The transgressor may either explicitly or implicitly convey the demand "not to tell anyone" and this barrier most pointedly excludes the spouse or partner. Again, the analogy to incest and the secrecy surrounding it is apt. A kind of "hyper-confidentiality" (Celenza, 2006a) or treatment bubble is created that deprives both the transgressor and the victim of the potentially corrective influence of others or so-called thirds (see chapter 13 for a more elaborated discussion of these factors).

It is not only the transgressor who facilitates the creation of this perverse secrecy, however. The victim often is so ashamed and confused about what is occurring that she becomes fearful of exposing how the treatment has gone awry. First, she is not sure it *has* gone awry, an uncertainty that derives from her confusion about what is appropriate along with her desire and need to maintain confidence in her caregiver. One victim innocently asked her spouse, "Are therapists supposed to talk about themselves all the time?" The victim may also feel complicit and guilty since a part of her naturally wants this kind of involvement. As noted in chapter 10, most, if not all patients are vulnerable to some kind of overinvolvement and many treatments are naturally erotically tinged. Since the treatment is designed to evoke and intensify unmet and buried longings, the patient/victim is a ripe candidate for sexual involvement. Just as it is human to be a potential transgressor, it is even more human to be a victim and get caught up.

So, what about the spouse(s) and partner(s)? What are the typical sequellae and how can the partner be helped? When the spouse learns that his partner has transgressed or has been involved in a sexual boundary violation, it is usually the case that the spouse had no idea of the involvement and is totally blindsided. There may have been unaddressed difficulties in the marriage, which is not uncommon and may have served as part of the midlife stress that the transgressor was experiencing; however, the spouse, like the victim, holds no responsibility for the way in which the transgressor chose to behave, both personally and professionally. The issue for the spouse or partner, in addition to a crisis of fidelity, revolves around feeling horrified and devastated that the spouse/transgressor chose to act in this particularly humiliating way.

Obviously, the spouse of the transgressor is in a very different position from the spouse of the victim. The spouse of the transgressor is rightfully outraged and must go through enormous public humiliation because of events that he or she did not cause. One spouse worried about newspaper coverage (that did eventually surface) and the personal exposure this would incur for both herself and her children. Others may be in the mental health profession themselves, including perhaps in the same professional circles as either the spouse/transgressor and/or the victim. The profession itself, then, becomes a humiliating context and professional activities may be avoided for a period of time. This incurs more losses, in addition to the loss of the stability of the marriage, at least as it was in the past.

Even without media publicity or the loss of one's professional contacts, there is an unavoidable embarrassment that is suffered and a fear that others may view the transgression as a reflection on the marriage or even on oneself, as opposed to only the transgressor. It is a very difficult road; however, solace can be taken by remembering that it is the transgressor who committed the wrong-doing and wrought damage on his partner and family. If there were problems in the marriage (and who is without those?), there are constructive (and private) ways to address these. The transgressor chose neither to take those paths nor to dissolve an unhappy union, if that was to be the eventual outcome.

Though rare, there have been cases where marital difficulties were in the process of being actively addressed (e.g., perhaps the couple was in marital therapy, at the time of the sexual boundary violation with the patient). The more typical case involves a marriage or partnership of long-standing unhappiness that has been neglected and ignored for many years. Again, it is only the transgressor who is to be held responsible—not for the unhappiness, but for the way in which he chose to deal with it.

Some spouses of transgressors protect themselves from losing face and from losing confidence in their marriage and husband by focusing all blame on the victim. They may become rigidly fixed in the more convenient idea that the victim tricked their unsuspecting partner into a destructive (for him) relationship. These spouses become almost compulsively preoccupied with helping the transgressor get out of his predicament and may convince themselves that he is being unfairly persecuted. This, of course, is the well-worn path toward blaming the victim (see chapter 10 for a more elaborate discussion of this tendency). It may be a defensive but understandable act of desperation; however, it is seriously misguided and adds further destructiveness to the already traumatized victim. It may be necessary for the spouse to engage the help of a therapist so that she may be supported in navigating her way through her own process of recovery. Education about this problem will also be helpful and may facilitate healing as well.

The predicament for the spouse of the victim is quite different. It is normal and appropriate for the partner in this position to be outraged. It is the transgressor who committed the betrayal, not the victim who simply fell under the sway of powerful transferential desires and longings. Therapy is based on the trust the patient/client has in the therapist. To take advantage of this trust for one's own purposes is a perversion of the therapeutic process. In one case, a therapist was having sexual relations with the wife while he treated both the wife and husband in couple's therapy. Not only was the transgressor secretly betraying the husband (his client), but he also had the audacity to ask the husband for a financial loan during their therapy! Thankfully, most therapists do not exhibit or even tend toward such egregious psychopathy. It is no less outrageous, however, for a therapist to exploit the vulnerability of his patients by becoming sexually involved with them.

The most constructive use of this outrage is for the partner or spouse of the victim to support the victim in getting help, both therapeutically and through legal or professional redress. It is equally important for the spouse to educate himself about the unusual conditions of the therapeutic context so that there is no blame or responsibility placed on the victim for becoming involved with her caregiver. The same is true if the transgressor was a mentor, teacher, or supervisor. It may be important and necessary for the partner or spouse to engage a therapist for himself since he has been traumatized by the violation as well and his personal journey through the miasma should not be sidestepped or viewed solely through the lens of the victim's position. How can a spouse or partner come to terms with infidelity when it has occurred at the hands of a trusted therapist or psychoanalyst? This is a question that is unanswerable in a general or universal way but must be reckoned with by both members of the couple.

INSTITUTIONAL RECOVERY

The damage wrought on the institution (defined as any organized body in which the transgressor was a member) is difficult to measure. An institution is an abstract entity that has no existence, feelings, or even attributes outside the members that make it up. However, it does have procedures and rules, thereby making its structure a source of influence and symbols, both of which will have measurable effects on its members. Likewise, the institution can do things to facilitate, retard, or even obstruct the recovery of the members by virtue of the responses it makes to the event, the transgressor, the victim(s), and all others involved.

Again, this cannot be said forthrightly enough: The degree to which recovery is possible has everything to do with how the institution's policies, by-laws, and actual practices reflect its attitude toward rehabilitation. This attitude has some reference to the attitudes of the members of which the institution is comprised, but not fully. Often, the membership holds a diversity of opinions about rehabilitation and the procedures and rules of the institution cannot encompass them all. In addition, the procedures and rules that guide members' behavior who are charged with the responsibility of addressing ethical problems may not be up to date with the current wisdom. Many members may not know how they feel and may look to the institution for guidance. All of these attitudes, opinions, and curiosities are mutually influential: the institution will shape and influence the attitudes of the members and vice versa.

If there are no procedures that point to a route toward rehabilitation, if there has been no precedent where rehabilitation has been considered, or if transgressors are summarily expelled without an independent evaluation (including an assessment for rehabilitation potential), the institution reflects an attitude of imperiousness and disbelief in the potential for reparation. This will have a destructive effect on the outcome of any process and on the hope of recovery for anyone involved in a transgression, including analytic or therapeutic siblings, colleagues, peers, friends, and so on. In an institution of this sort, the message is, "If you commit a sexual boundary violation, you effectively walk off a cliff." No pathway toward reparation is possible to consider. This is a dangerous message to give to the membership and a difficult outcome for all to live with.

Such a denial of rehabilitation potential is an anti-therapeutic attitude and, therefore, is contradictory to what the mental health profession represents. These attitudes and procedures should not remain foregrounded in the way these problems are handled. It is the responsibility of the membership to influence the institution to reflect a more constructive and health promoting attitude. This must be reflected in its policies and procedures.

In the rest of this discussion, I will focus only on the type of sexual boundary violation that is amenable to rehabilitation and has potential for recovery and reparation. The one-time transgressor is the shorthand for this category of transgression. This type of sexual boundary transgression should be viewed in most cases as a potentially temporary and very specific impairment. Thus, the institutional procedures that I will set forth can be used as a guide in setting up structures that facilitate a healthier functioning institution. However, it should also be noted that structural change (i.e., the presence of procedures that delineate a path toward rehabilitation) are not the same thing as change itself. I have consulted to institutions where the by-laws, procedures, and appropriate committees were all in place yet the attitude of the membership was closed to such processes. The mechanisms, though present, were not utilized, and transgressors who might have been rehabilitated were not. Similarly, I have seen institutions where no such structures existed, yet the attitude of the membership reflected an openness toward rehabilitation such that transgressors who were amenable received comprehensive rehabilitation. In short, the structures are less important than the attitude of the membership and, as mentioned, these are mutually influential if attitudes of openness and curiosity are present.

The structures that need to be in place include: (1) a confidential peer review or assistance committee (with no disciplinary or rehabilitative powers), (2) access to an independent consultant/evaluator who has expertise in sexual boundary violations, (3) an ethics committee (with disciplinary and oversight powers), and (4) experts to provide treatment, supervision, and consultation to the institution. These structures should be sufficient to address and contain the various aspects of this problem. The peer review or assistance committee (PRC) should be a confidential body that may respond to credible rumors or complaints. Such rumors or complaints may be anonymous, but should have some credibility to guard against nuisance complaints. Cooperation with the PRC should be a condition of membership in the organization. This PRC is mandated to begin an investigation of the problem, with specific reference to a confidential meeting with the alleged transgressor. Though its proceedings are confidential and members are required to cooperate with the PRC, the PRC may have the power to initiate an ethics complaint if the rumors or concerns are deemed substantive.

The ethics committee and independent evaluator each plays a role only when a formal complaint has been filed. These may not be anonymous. The procedures for each of these are noted in chapters 11 and 12 of this volume; see also Celenza and Gabbard (2003), which addresses the important aspects of rehabilitation, the typical components of a rehabilitation plan, and guidelines in terms of how to go about constructing such a plan if and when it is viable. Chapter 10 addresses the important issues usually associated with helping the victims recover from a sexual boundary violation, including financial redress and subsequent therapy.

In most institutional settings, it is the PRC that is usually missing. The only way for a transgression to come to light is for the patient to file a written, formal complaint directly to the ethics committee. This may not be a problem in and of itself if the patient is strong enough to recognize the transgression early. However, this is rarely the case. In fact, most often, the transgression has been going on for some time and others in the institution are aware of the violation but do not know what to do or how to proceed. This is the need addressed by the PRC. Since it is a confidential body with no disciplinary power, it is designed to be somewhat less threatening to approach. Colleagues, peers, and supervisors alike can confidentially or even anonymously express their concern. The details of the procedures and rules may vary; however, the essential features are that the peer review committee's powers are limited, the processes are confidential, and the members are required to cooperate.

Of course, there is no avoiding the fact that the PRC can set in motion a process that may eventuate in the filing of a complaint and may have adverse effects on the alleged transgressor. This is why the healthy functioning of such a committee depends greatly on every member's attitude toward rehabilitation. Consider, for example, the committee's attitude reflected in a greeting to the alleged transgressor such as "Are you all right?" versus the attitude reflected in "We're watching you." When part of the committee's mandate is to function with the attitude of acceptance and viability for rehabilitation, the committee will more likely be viewed as a resource for help and guidance rather than a disciplinary body to be avoided. Much like the functioning of a consultative body, the PRC has the potential to be accessed more liberally by both patients and caregivers alike, ideally in the early stages of concern before it is too late.

Another mistake that institutions frequently make is in conflating the needs of the transgressor with the needs of the victim. It is important to keep these very different problems and concerns separated. There is, in effect, a boundary collapse that the institution is vulnerable to incurring. The problem to which I am referring is the institutional tendency to address the victim's concern and harm through the disciplinary actions against the transgressor. This is a category error. The two (victim and transgressor) have markedly different needs, have had qualitatively different levels of responsibility in the violation, and therefore should not be combined in the institutional response. Probably the most frequent example involves a victim who insists that she will only be healed if the transgressor is permanently expelled or is never allowed to practice again. The two concerns, her healing and his ability to practice, must be assessed separately since the issues related to the readiness of either lie in different domains. One has nothing to do with the other, though the victim may proclaim that she cannot "move on" unless she knows he is out of the profession. In fact, and this is demonstrated in case after case, the victim often cannot move on without a substantial subsequent treatment exploring the ways in which she remains psychically tied to the transgressor. Some victims will be unable to stop seeking further avenues for contact with the transgressor as long as some system allows for it (e.g., civil suits, complaints to alternative professional organizations where the transgressor is a member, etc.). The transgressor's punishment should not be viewed as an appeasement tool for the victim. It is not effective and it is not appropriate, even if it were effective. Though all victims are entitled to redress, this should not be obtained through the transgressor's punishment but rather in the form of financial support and whatever form of therapeutic healing is indicated.

Another area where institutions often go awry is instigated by the fear of lawsuits (from the transgressor and/or the victim). This often paralyzes the institution from taking effective action (see also Gabbard et al., 2001). While it is not possible to completely separate the financial solvency of the institution from these concerns, it should not be a guiding principle in how the institution responds. In general, if rules and procedures are followed, the institution will have little to no exposure to lawsuits, though these may be threatened by the transgressor and/or the victim. Sometimes, an unintended outcome is a protracted stalemate. This often occurs when an institution is threatened with a lawsuit and the various committee members are genuinely stymied about how to proceed. Further, the institution may have received legal advice to indefinitely stall the process to limit further exposure. This should be viewed as unethical in and of itself, since no prospect of recovery for anyone involved, especially the victim, will be possible. The effect on the members will be palpable as well, since the case will remain in some kind of confidential limbo and therefore will not be discussable in any useful way. The institution must find a way to move beyond the stalemate, tolerate the threat of lawsuits from either side, and continue the process of helping all parties regain their integrity.

The membership of an institution has needs for recovery. If these are not addressed in some direct manner, there will be an unhealthy level of confusion, anger, and alienation from within the institution itself. One mechanism to promote healing at the membership level is to hold small processing groups led by facilitators who are familiar with the problems associated with sexual boundary violations. The context of small groups is important since most professionals find it very difficult to reveal their private beliefs about this problem in a large group. Fear of others being judgmental is a powerful hindrance to honest disclosure of the complicated and often contradictory feelings that are likely stirred up. Idealization and loyalty (toward both the transgressor and the victim) stand in the way as well (Gabbard, 1999). It may be helpful to have a two-stage process where the first involves a consultation or large group presentation from an expert in sexual boundary transgressions with the aim of addressing general concerns. Then the membership might be invited to participate in small group discussions in order to process their thoughts and feelings on a more personal level.

IS A TIED KNOT A CLOSED LOOP?

How do we understand, think about, or possibly resolve the case of a therapist or analyst who marries a patient? There have been instances of this in contemporary times. There is no literature or any systematic study of this significant and intriguing outcome. For all intents and purposes, the members of the couple may appear to be blissfully happy. Taken at face value, it is difficult to understand this outcome if we are also devoted to the idea that transferences stimulated by virtue of the treatment structure are always potentially present. Though I hope to study this vexing problem in years to come, there are a few inescapable speculations worth considering.

As discussed at length in chapter 5, it is not the presence of transference that makes sexual involvement with a patient unethical. The modality of couple's therapy is based on the acknowledgment of transferences inevitably entangled in the relationship and the potential for couples to transcend their transference/countertransference proclivities. Rather, it is the fact that in the therapeutic setting, these transferences are *embedded in the structure of the context*, rendering them, thereby, nonnegotiable. If a therapist marries his patient, can the structure be considered dissolved and are they then facing the same challenge that all couples face?

The former therapist-patient pair will never be in the equivalent situation of a couple who did not initially meet under the auspices of a structured power imbalance. Does this power imbalance have permanence, even in the absence of the structure in which it was embedded? Does the length and intensity of the treatment matter? In the transgressor-victim couples I have seen, there is often a marked power imbalance on a personal level. As noted in chapter 2, the patient/victim is experienced (by the transgressor, at least) as the dominant member of the dyad. It is not at all unusual for the transgressor to express, "She has all the power in this relationship. I am powerless." He ignores, of course, the structured power imbalance inherent in the therapeutic matrix and is referring instead to the subjective sense of power that he (and maybe she) consciously experiences. This is the level of personal transference/

countertransference proclivities and not the professional, role-based dimension of the relationship.

However, these cannot be fully separated since the meaning the other has (to each) is imbued with the power that is experienced, no matter from where it is derived. It may be meaningful for the patient/victim to experience her therapist as "loving her so much he would give up his professional ethics and career." How to extract the meaning of this from the marital dynamics once the structure is dissolved? Was it important that Prince Edward gave up the throne to be with his lover? Are there other symbols of the therapeutic setting that shape the meaning of the romance for each member of the dyad (Celenza, 2006c)? What is left of these meanings when the structure is dissolved? These meanings cannot be erased without attempting a self-deceptive erasure of history itself.

The prospect of a relationship resulting in a long-term partnership or marriage, yet based on an unethical foundation, raises more questions than can be answered at present. There is an analogy to marriage growing out of an affair; however, this is not the whole story. It cannot be ignored that the relationship began as some form of incestuous bond. At the same time, it is not exactly analogous to a parent and a child. Assuming that the members of the couple are adults, what are the temporal limits and potential for change that might free each of them up, either alone or together? What are the conditions for change?

Another way to pose these questions is, Can the couple be rehabilitated? If the answer to this question is "yes," the statement must not be misconstrued as sanctioning or providing a loophole for sexual boundary violations. Despite my staunch belief in rehabilitation, I am certain that some couples (just as some transgressors) are not able to be rehabilitated; yet, others are. My faith in rehabilitation, for certain types of sexual boundary violations, is thoroughgoing and based on evidence, not just good wishes, confidence, or arrogance. Still, acceptance of these propositions by those individuals involved—whether it be the transgressor, the victim, or the couple—also requires the actual and genuine participation in rehabilitation efforts, not just a belief in them. These are speculations and questions I hope to consider and more fully elaborate in my future studies.

10

HELPING THE VICTIMS

[Love in the therapeutic setting] is an unavoidable consequence
. . . as inevitable as the exposure of the patient's body or the imparting of a vital secret. It is therefore plain . . . that [the therapist]
must not derive any personal advantage from it. The patient's
willingness makes no difference; it merely throws the whole responsibility on [the therapist].

—S. Freud (1915, p. 169)

Had I had any dreams? [Dr. Jordan asked]. As he was looking
forlorn, and as it were, at a loss, and as I suspected that not all
was going well with him, I did not say that I could not remember. Instead, I said that I had indeed had a dream.

—Margaret Atwood (*Alias Grace,* p. 242)

Psychoanalysis was originally founded on the principle of abstinence, the
idea that desires and needs will not be acted upon or met. The paradigm
shift associated with contemporary theorizing has transformed this basic
principle. It is now understood that therapy is comprised of a two-person,
intersubjective, and collaborative field that fosters an intense involvement in
which both therapist and patient participate. If all goes well, there will be
interpersonal gratifications, a loving attachment, and other feeling-based experiences that make up the therapeutic action. In addition, therapists and psychoanalysts have accepted that they will inevitably disclose aspects of their
own person through their presence, character traits, and style. This does not
necessarily include a therapist's disclosures about his or her personal life and
certainly does not include gratifying the therapist's needs, sexual or otherwise. The attempt is still to place all of the attention on the patient/client,
whether or not this is wholly possible, and this remains one of the defining
features of the therapeutic setting.

The attempt to direct the attention toward the patient/client has been misunderstood in the past as an attempt to reduce the analyst's presence. There is no such thing, however, as a fully sanitized (uncontaminated, as historically put), one-person relationship—the idea is an oxymoron and the pursuit of such an ideal is no longer considered viable or even advisable (Renik, 1995). The patient's awareness (made verbally explicit by the analyst or not) of the analyst's presence, routine aspects of his or her personality (Cooper, 2000a), and even on some minimal level, the therapist's or analyst's needs, is part of the negotiation between them as each adjusts to the other's presence. It is now accepted that the analyst's character, blind spots, and defensive reflexes are profound determining factors in what the patient/client will say and what he or she will allow to come to mind.

This is the unavoidable relational matrix that is unique to each dyad and is often more in the forefront of the patient's mind than the therapist's or analyst's. Can my analyst hear this now? Is he strong enough to bear my complaints and anger? Will this please him? These are typical questions that any patient will ask herself and, though these questions themselves are influenced by transference in no small measure, there is also a way in which she takes into account her experience of the analyst's character and subjectivity (see, for example, Aron, 1991; Cooper, 2000a). Patients can be astute observers of their therapist's real limitations and fluctuating need states.

It is just this capacity, based on empathy, that makes some patients or clients become victims of sexual misconduct. This capacity to sense and adjust to what the therapist wants, needs, or possibly demands is the very talent that both makes her an appealing patient and, with the wrong therapist, can lead her down a path of harm. I do not mean in any way to place responsibility on the patients or clients who have this talent; in the right hands, it is a capacity that bodes well for the efficacy of constructive and sound treatment. However, if a patient or client is engaged in a therapy with a potential transgressor (especially a psychopathic predator), this talent will be exploited for his own gain at tremendous cost to her.

One of the tragic sequellae of sexual misconduct is the way it closes the door toward help for the victim at a time when she is most in need. Because the exploitation by a therapist means being betrayed by a person imbued with trust, there is an understandable fear of trusting in this context again. The transgressor's corruption of the place of healing not only damages the victim personally, but also can bar her from being able to seek support, guidance, and reparation, at least in a therapeutic context, again. Even if able or willing to try again, many do not trust themselves to evaluate and wisely select a subsequent treater (Wohlberg, McCraith, & Thomas, 1999). Being exploited by a therapist shakes the very foundation of the victim/patient's ability to use her own judgment.

For some victims, self-help is the only avenue open, especially in the first few months of crisis. To address this problem, there are many victim-led or leaderless support groups that have arisen in response to the need for support and guidance when no professional could be trusted. The Therapist Exploitation Link Line (TELL) and Boston Association to Stop Therapist Abuse (BASTA) are two such groups in the Boston area and there are many around the country that are similarly structured. The Walk-In Counseling Center of Minneapolis, Minnesota, is a groundbreaking organization with programs designed specifically to address the consequences of therapist sexual abuse. The Walk-In Counseling Center's pioneering efforts in this area are responsible for countless victims obtaining redress and promoting the study of this problem in general.

Perhaps the biggest change in the past decade is the availability of guidance through the Internet. Victims are now able, within the privacy of their homes, to access support from other victims, gather educational materials, and find a therapist, advocate, lawyer, support group, and/or individual therapist through a variety of websites. Some of these are organized and maintained by victims themselves, in the self-help tradition, whereas others are generated and maintained by professionals or professional organizations designed to help victims. One such example includes www.advocateweb.org.

Sexual boundary transgression by mental health professionals of all sorts, including clergy, has become a less-taboo subject in the past couple of decades. Along with this, the literature in the various mental health fields has expanded, some of which has proven to be a crucial source of help for the victims. Rutter's (1989) book *Sex in the Forbidden Zone*, Gabbard and Lester's (1995a) *Boundaries and Boundary Violations in Psychoanalysis*, Gonsiorek's *A Breach of Trust* (1995), Bisbing and coauthors' (1995) *Sexual Abuse by Professionals: A Legal Guide*, and Schoener et al.'s (1989) *Psychotherapists' Sexual Involvement with Clients* have been instrumental for many victims in seeking help and reparation. For books written on the experience of female parishioners and counselees who have been victimized by clergy, see Frawley-O'Dea (2007), Frawley-O'Dea and Goldner (2007), Fairbanks (2002), and McBride (1999).

HARMFUL SEQUELLAE OF THERAPIST-PATIENT SEXUAL MISCONDUCT

Sexual involvement with one's therapist or psychoanalyst is almost always harmful. Rare cases have been reported where no harm was experienced by the patient/victim; however, it is unclear whether this is a subjective assess-ment that is sustained over time. Gutheil and Gabbard (1992) note that a little over one-third of the patients who initiated sexual contact reported that they were not adversely affected. Again, it is unclear if they would feel similarly over time. One study of former female victims found that many reported plea-surable feelings during the relationship but saw the experience as hurtful or exploitative in retrospect (Somer & Saadon, 1999; Somer & Nachmani, 2005). Little to nothing is known about the cases where a therapist has married his or her patient (see chapter 9 for a fuller discussion of this particular case). These are areas for future research.

There are several common and expectable sequellae of therapist sexual misconduct. The first is the extreme sense of shame that the victims feel in relation to having been involved in an exploitative relationship. This shame in part derives from the victim's confusion about the extent to which he or she was responsible for the abuse. In the more debilitating cases, the transgressing therapist may have malevolently told the patient that she had seduced him or somehow forced him to corrupt the therapeutic process. The one-time trans-gressor tends not to engage in such gaslighting and may confide in the victim that, though he could not stop himself, he and only he is responsible for the unethical conduct.

There is no responsibility that the patient bears for this problem. This should be stated emphatically to the patient/victim by the subsequent treater so that the burdens of guilt and shame may begin to be lessened. It is no doubt relevant that females instinctively tend to take responsibility for their relationships, whether these go well or badly.

Wohlberg et al. (1999) have written lucidly on the sequellae of sexual misconduct for the survivor/victim. They identify the following as common symptoms of therapist sexual misconduct: undermining of trust, ambivalence (about themselves, the abuser, and the abuse), isolation, guilt and shame, fear, depression, suicidality, rage, and the cluster of symptoms associated with post-traumatic stress disorder. These symptoms are reported by a number of other writers as well (Strasburger & Jorgenson, 1992; Luepker, 1989; Luepker & Schoener, 1989; Schoener et al., 1989).

Most researchers in this area have observed that the damage from sexual exploitation is not resultant solely or even primarily from the sex (Schoener et al., 1989; Strasburger & Jorgenson, 1992). The damage is largely wrought from the betrayal of trust, the demand for secrecy, the perverse reversal of roles, and the total abandonment of therapeutic aims. One transgressor was aware that he was not helping the patient with the problems for which she originally sought treatment, so he attempted (in vain) to find another therapist for *her,* but one who would not report *him.* Most transgressors do not face this dilemma, however, by virtue of the multiple rationalizations that support their belief that their love is curing the victim, despite ample evidence to the contrary.

Victims often report continuing to fear the transgressing therapist, even after the case has been adjudicated. This is especially true for those exploited by a psychopathic predator who may have threatened the patient or otherwise intimidated her during the relationship and perhaps throughout the adjudicative process as well. One patient received a bill for the last month of treatment even though the abuse had begun months before. This patient became extremely anxious about *not paying* the bill, despite knowing that the treatment was a sham. She was afraid the abuser would sue her or take her to court and ruin her credit standing. She was fearful of having any kind of contact with him, so she immediately paid the bill, feeling this was the best alternative and a way for her to obtain some peace of mind, at least in the short run.

Wohlberg et al. (1999) report victims having dreams in which they are harmed or even killed by their abusers. They also identify the single most common fear that victims universally report: that their abusers will say that the victim/survivor is "crazy" and that the victims themselves will be unable to know whether this is true or not. This fear is reflective of the enormous confusion about who is responsible for what, a confusion that can extend to the victim's ability to test reality or her entire identity and trust in herself.

When attempting to assess the harm to the patient that results from sexual misconduct, there is the complexity of differentiating between the psychological distress that was present at the beginning of treatment and presumably was the cause for seeking help in the first place, from the harm associated with the misconduct itself. In cases where the patient/victim is an incest or sexual abuse survivor, many symptoms will overlap. Finally, there is the subtle distinction between the trauma of the exploitation itself and what has been called "cessation trauma" (Gutheil & Gabbard, 1992), that is, the harm associated with the termination of the exploitative relationship. Though the latter is included as part of the harm associated with sexual misconduct, it may have qualitatively different effects that need to be recognized separately.

Luepker (1999) surveyed victim/patients of sexual misconduct through a 180-item questionnaire and attempted to differentiate preexisting problems from the sequellae of the abuse. She found posttraumatic stress disorder, major depressive disorder, suicidality, use of prescription drugs, disruptions in relationships, and disruptions in work or earning potential. All of these symptoms were exacerbated after the abuse. She also found that victims who sought subsequent treaters contacted an average of 2.4 professionals before settling in with one. Disturbingly, she also found that 18% were sexually revictimized by subsequent treaters.

Sometimes the argument is raised that social and cultural factors play a role in facilitating or sanctioning exploitative behavior by male therapists, reflecting patriarchal power structures in the society as a whole. This line of reasoning has merit, since the indisputable patriarchal elements in Western society are well-documented (see, for example, Dimen, 2003, and Harris, 2005, for outstanding reviews). These factors, however, reside on a different level of discourse than the one that encompasses the focus of this book. The problem of sexual boundary violations for any *particular* patient is only appropriately addressed on the individual level. While societal and cultural factors may play a role, even in the particular case, these do not address the difficulties of every individual, nor do they answer the vexing and lingering question of why such factors resonate with some individuals and not others.

THE PROFILE OF THE VICTIM/PATIENT: IS THERE ONE?

There has been a great furor over the diagnostic categorization or classification of the victims of sexual boundary violations. Some of my own papers on this subject have been misread as representing the idea that all victims of sexual boundary violations are difficult patients, or worse, have borderline personality organization. However, I firmly believe that just as *all* mental health professionals are potential transgressors, it is equally true that *all of us are potential victims.* Anyone who has been in an intensive psychotherapy or psychoanalysis knows the power of the transference and the way in which the therapeutic context stirs up universal and unresolved longings to be loved and to be intimate with a more powerful other. This is the design of the therapeutic context, whether the treatment makes constructive use of such intense longings or not. There is no shame in having gotten caught up in the process, either emotionally or sexually. Indeed, the fact of becoming caught up signals that the patient is or was accessible and thereby treatable! This is why it is an egregious violation for any therapist to take advantage of a victim/patient as she allows herself to be influenced and engaged in the process.

Most victims of sexual misconduct cannot be characterized. The profile of the victim/patient spans the full range of human descriptions. If any generalizations can be made, it is that most patient/victims are sensitive, empathic, and prone toward meeting the needs of others. In some and probably most cases, patient/victims are high-functioning, appealing women with a special empathic capacity that contributes to their ability to take care of the therapist.

This is consistent with Wohlberg et al.'s (1999a) statements that the only commonality found (in a casual survey of over 400 members of the TELL network) is that the victims "have been in enough pain and sufficiently vulnerable to seek therapy and risk trusting a mental health professional" (p. 185). In short, the victims are former patients and consumers of mental health treatment.

Horrifying as it is to admit, there are psychopathic predators within the mental health profession who see an attractive patient as a way to degrade the profession and have some sexual pleasure along the way (see chapter 4). This is expressly because the transgressor's primary victim (in his mind, not in reality) is the profession itself and the women are perversely exploited as a means to an end. She is usually not singled out with great specificity though she may be told that she is special and that she has been carefully selected as part of the seduction. It is here that many high-functioning and empathically attuned patients find themselves victims of such a perpetrator. It makes sense to surmise that the multiple transgressor—that is, the psychopathic predator—probably accounts for the largest number of victims. Indeed, this may be the *most common scenario for victims* since such perpetrators abuse multiple victims over a prolonged period of time. It stands to reason as well that most victims can probably be categorized as appealing, trusting, and empathic women who had the great misfortune of getting caught up with a psychopath. It is also a tribute to the courageous actions of the victims in bringing this problem forward that there may be a decline in the prevalence of psychopathically motivated transgressors.

In contrast, and as I have written elsewhere (see chapters 1–3), there is another type of transgressor where both the transgressor and the patient/victim are involved in a more specific and interlocked transference/countertransference scenario. It is this context where it is common to find a difficult patient with whom the transgressor has become overwhelmed. Though this may account for only a narrow band of victim/patients, this is the most common type of transgressor—the one-time offender who exploits only one victim/patient in a transference/countertransference destructive enactment. To put it succinctly, the psychopathic predator probably accounts for the largest number of victim/patients. The one-time transgressor, while the most prevalent type of transgressor (who thereby accounts for the largest number of transgressors), abuses only one patient/victim and probably accounts for a smaller number of victims.

It is also true, however, that transference/countertransference dynamic patterns can be identified and that certain types of women may be more vulnerable to or become involved in risky dyads. Gutheil (1989) has identified patients with borderline personality disorder as particularly likely to evoke boundary violations, including sexual acting out. Though false allegations are small in number, these patients have also been identified as the majority of patients who falsely accuse. Because there is an unconscious fit for some dyads (and this fit is the most prevalent kind of scenario *for transgressors*) does not imply that all or even the majority of victims share these characteristics.

Within the more prevalent one-time transgressor scenario, it is still difficult to discuss the characteristics of victims without appearing to be shifting responsibility to the patient/victim or, worse, blaming her. These harmful attitudes do, in fact, occur, especially in the adjudication process where the victim might be viciously cross-examined, depicted as crazy, as a shameless seductress, or outright disbelieved. Much like the cross-examination in rape trials, the victim's emotional stability and mental health history can be brought forward and used to discredit her. It is understandable that a posture of vigilance is adopted that forecloses attempts to examine the victim's dynamics.

There is also a longing for simplicity that we all share, including a resistance to a more complex understanding of this most vexing problem (Gutheil & Gabbard, 1992). This can cause a reader to jump to conclusions. Gutheil and Gabbard (1992) have helpfully clarified three axioms that should govern any attempt to understand the complex issues involved: (1) only the therapist can be culpable, blameworthy, and liable; (2) a dynamic understanding of the transference/countertransference dynamics in no way blames the patient, nor does it relieve the therapist of responsibility; and (3) careful, candid, detailed, and dynamically informed exploration of sexual misconduct will be beneficial to patients, mental health professionals, and society at large. The study of this area must be undertaken with these axioms in mind.

Many authors note that at least one group of patients is at high risk for exploitation by psychotherapists. This group is composed of patients who have a history of incest (Feldman-Summers & Jones, 1984; Gabbard, 1994a; Kluft, 1989; Pope & Bouhoutsos, 1986; Gutheil, 1989; Somer & Saadon, 1999; Margolis, 1994). Typical sequellae of an incestuous childhood history include associating caring with sexuality, fluid self-other boundaries, a tendency to experience relationships in terms of meeting the other's needs, and a conscious or unconscious need to repeat the abusive trauma. Norris, Gutheil, and Strasburger (2003) identified several factors that exacerbate patient vulnerability in this population. They reference overdependence on the therapist, seeking treatment to find an intense relationship or even "true love," and an acceptance of an abusive therapy relationship, probably due to a history of abuse in childhood. In a tragic sense, the fit of these patients with sexual exploitation makes dynamic sense.

Yet Pope and Vetter (1991) found only 32% of survivors of sexual boundary violations had a history of childhood sexual abuse. Pope (1990) stated that no systematic research has provided support for the notion that victims of

sexual misconduct have a history of incest or can be diagnosed as having borderline personality disorder. Estimates by leaders of self-help groups usually
hover around 30% (Wohlberg et al., 1999) with a few exceptions who esti-
mate higher incidences (Disch, 1989). Until systematic and controlled studies
are undertaken, however, these hypotheses (on both sides) must be treated as
speculative.

Many writers have been misinterpreted as stating that most or all victims
of sexual misconduct are either incest or sexual abuse survivors. This, however, is a misinterpretation of the clinical observation that patients with borderline personality disorder or borderline features (most of whom are thought
to have incest histories) may be particularly vulnerable to the transference/
countertransference misfit with the one-time transgressor (Gutheil, 1989;
Collins, 1989; Celenza, 1991, 1998). Again, this latter point probably refers to
a small subset of victim/patients.

BLAMING THE VICTIM

There is an unconscionable tendency to inappropriately focus or place blame
on the victims of therapist sexual misconduct. Sometimes this involves a
"shoot the messenger" kind of dynamic where the whistle-blower is targeted
for bringing the uncomfortable truth to light. Since therapist sexual misconduct is such an egregious violation, there can be a reflexive recoiling from the
awareness that a colleague or therapist/analyst might have exploited his or her
power in this way. This can result in excusing the transgressor and viewing
the victim as the responsible party. One victim reported that a friendship was
irretrievably destroyed when she reported her analyst for sexual misconduct.
Her former friend, an analytic sibling who was not sexually exploited by him,
stated directly to the victim, "You made me think badly of him and my analysis with him."

Women are often held responsible for "seducing the innocent man."
Gender stereotypes can facilitate the misguided response where the woman
is viewed as a dangerous seductress. Schoener (2005) has reviewed publicized
cases in the past couple of centuries reflective of a long history of viewing the
woman as the seductress of an innocent, blameless transgressor (see Schoener,
2005, for a thorough review). As quoted in the foreword to this volume, one
such case involved the wife of a minister who shamelessly devalued and blamed
the woman for seducing her husband (Harris, 1988, pp. 81–85).

Even Freud, in a letter to Jung (June 4, 1909) managed to focus all blame
on Sabina Spielrein, despite Freud's convictions about transference. He wrote,

"The way these women manage to charm us with every conceivable psychic perfection until they have attained their purpose is one of nature's greatest spectacles" (McGuire, 1988, p. 231).

Even more pointedly, Freud wrote to Jung (June 30, 1909) and asked Jung not to fault himself, asserting that "it was not your doing but hers" (McGuire, 1988, p. 238). Sadly, it has happened again and again that the victims of sexual misconduct are held responsible, blamed, or even vilified. (If a particular woman who has been a victim of sexual misconduct can be appropriately described as seductive, it is wise to remember that she came to treatment for help with, not to be exploited by, these very qualities.)

Gabbard (2002a) identified the typical responses to charges of abuse by colleagues in the early history of boundary violations and found many resonances in the ways in which institutions and colleagues typically respond today. First there is disbelief, soon the complainants are dismissed, then the victim is held responsible (e.g. "she was asking for it"), and then the complainants are denigrated as mentally ill. Sometimes there are rumors of a conspiracy against the transgressor that may or may not include his professional organization.

In addition, there is a gender bias in Western society, where it is easy to attack and be critical of a woman (whether she is the transgressor or the patient) as well as to excuse a man. The media is implicated in this regard as well. One case that I find illustrative of this tendency involved a female practitioner who was accused of malpractice by the family of a male former patient. This practitioner was vilified in the press and her reputation was ruined before the case was brought to a hearing or adjudicated. She left the field in shame. (Though this is an example of a transgressor being vilified in the press, I believe it was the fact that she was female that she received especially harsh treatment.)

From an opposing standpoint, there is also a politically correct notion that "men have sexual feelings and women do not" (Gutheil & Gabbard, 1992). This bias may be operative when female therapists exploit male patients and the patient is viewed as responsible by virtue of his gender. Though female transgressors represent a minority of therapists who sexually exploit patients, they are fully accountable and responsible just as the male transgressors are. Here again, the victim should never be held accountable or blamed.

SUBSEQUENT THERAPY

The most immediate problem that a subsequent treater will face revolves around the difficulty establishing trust and a workable alliance. The patient/

victim will likely be highly sensitive to any indication that the subsequent treater is judging, blaming, or disbelieving her. At the same time, it is also important that the subsequent therapist not be unduly eager to hold the transgressor accountable. The victim may not be ready to view the prior therapy in a destructive or negative light, much less go through an investigative and hearing process. It is not uncommon for victims of sexual misconduct to shop around for a subsequent therapist before they can feel comfortable. Sadly, some are never able to return to therapy.

Wohlberg et al. (1999) describe the experiences of victims, drawn from over 3,500 women and men who have contacted TELL since 1989. They report that many victims feel revictimized by potential or actual subsequent therapists who appear to discount, minimize, blame, or emotionally over- or underreact to the victim's story. Others report feeling that subsequent treaters have interrogated them about the abusive experience, demanded the name of the abuser, or imposed expectations regarding action. Subsequent treaters must be aware of and respect the victim's ambivalence toward the abuser, acknowledge and accept the victim's difficulty or inability to trust, and recognize her need for scrupulous attention to appropriate boundaries.

Because of the demands for secrecy and isolation (a common part of the exploitative relationship), the victim may now have great difficulty talking about the prior relationship at all (Luepker, 1989). It is often helpful for the therapist to verbalize some of the thoughts and feelings the victim may be struggling with, but to do so in a nonimperative, nondemanding way. For example, the ambivalence the victim is likely to be feeling toward the transgressor may cause her to be reluctant to see him as an exploiter. It is often helpful for the subsequent therapist to state simply and directly that *he or she* views the sexual relationship with the former therapist as exploitative, but that he or she has no need for the victim to see it that way. Such an intervention should be stated without a demand for acknowledgment. I usually add to this that I am aware the victim is likely to be overwhelmed with a mix of feelings, including love for the former therapist, and that it is fine for her to take her time to sort all these feelings out.

It is important to keep in mind that any statement about the destructiveness or incompetence of the transgressor will stir up doubt and uncertainty about whether the subsequent therapist holds the same judgments about the victim. One therapy patient who had been in a sexualized relationship with a former therapist began to realize that the transgressor had been very destructive in his treatment of her, as well as possibly manic at times. As we discussed these perceptions of him, she could not keep at bay enormous self-criticism about how and why she remained in treatment with him despite his obviously deteriorating mental state. Why did she not see his faults and incompetence? Where was her judgment? These questions are common in patients who have been abused by a therapist, despite our best efforts to reassure them that they are not at fault and that they were not responsible for maintaining the boundaries in the therapy.

It may be difficult to address the historical issues that brought the patient to treatment in the first place. These are usually relegated to the background for some time while the more immediate trauma of sexual exploitation is addressed. Over time, it is beneficial to recognize the relevance of the patient's early history to her current life circumstances. These links to the past may include the sexual misconduct or may not. Notman and Nadelson (1999) note that some patient/victims are never able to broaden their perspective, nor can they include the original presenting problems as areas to explore. They describe some patients who become profoundly absorbed with the posttraumatic aspects of the sexual misconduct and organize their lives around it. These patients may be very difficult to help move beyond the trauma associated with the misconduct.

If the victim has not pressed charges or filed a complaint against the former therapist, discussing the possibility of doing so should be part of the subsequent therapy *at some point*. Here, however, it is important that the subsequent therapist not have his or her own agenda but to let the victim take the lead. This does not preclude having an opinion about what would be the ethical or just way to proceed. It is possible to state in a simple and nondemanding way that the former therapist should be held accountable, but not at the expense of the victim's psychological well-being. As is well known, enduring an investigation and complaint process is grueling and risky for the complainant; the subsequent therapy can play an important role in strengthening the victim by helping her become clearer about her thoughts, feelings, and sense of integrity. The subsequent therapy will not be helpful if the victim pursues a complaint process before she is ready.

Using an "administrator" to guide the victim through a complaint process is a way to maintain the security and privacy of the therapy context. Such an administrator should be someone who is familiar with the ethical, legal, and statutory structures in the relevant locale. A referral for a consultation with a forensic expert or knowledgeable attorney will help the victim understand her legal options (Jorgenson, 1995). Awareness of the statute of limitations is important so that the patient/victim does not unwittingly lose the opportunity for legal redress. When the victim is ready to proceed with a complaint, this administrator can take more of an advocacy position and help the victim know what to expect at each step.

The spouse or partner of the victim is traumatized by the abuse as well (see chapter 9 for an elaboration of the sequellae for the spouse or partner). Various modes of help are indicated, depending on the particular circumstance and preference of the individual. It is not uncommon for the victim to elect not to inform her spouse for fear of the partner's reaction and/or to protect him from disappointment in the therapist. In one case, a victim never informed her spouse of her former therapist's sexual advances toward her because the couple had previously used him for marital counseling to beneficial effect. This choice has obvious complications in that the victim is deprived of an important source of potential support. This must be weighed against the dread of more negative retribution. If the victim decides not to inform her spouse or partner, the relationship will be constricted to some extent by the maintenance of secrecy about this profoundly traumatic event. In some ways, however, it is of even more concern when there is no secondary victim, such as a spouse or partner, because this usually means that the victim had isolated herself and was wholly absorbed in the exploitative relationship to the exclusion of other sources of support (Milgrom, 1989).

FALSE ALLEGATIONS

False allegations are rare; however, they do occur and there is some clinical lore that the frequency of false allegations may be on the rise. Sederer (1995) reported four cases in which hospitalized psychiatric patients made false allegations of sexual misconduct against therapists. Motives revolved around (a) monetary gain; (b) desire for retaliation or revenge against a clinician whom they believe has scorned, abandoned, or otherwise mistreated them; and (c) the inadvertent stimulation of psychopathology toward the enactment of childhood trauma.

Gutheil (1998) has written extensively on how to distinguish between true and false allegations. Designed for critical evaluations in the forensic context, Gutheil notes that false allegations often lack plausibility and internal consistency, and/or can be refuted by external factors or an alternative scenario. In any one case, it is helpful to have these caveats in mind. In my experience, however, it is most often the case that victims are telling the truth and their stories have all of these factors: plausibility, internal consistency, and consistency with external facts. There certainly are instances where the data cannot be proven beyond a "he said/she said" type of analysis. In these cases, the credibility of both the alleged transgressor and the alleged victim will be the decisive factor.

Part III

REHABILITATION

11

THERAPY OF THE TRANSGRESSOR

[The patient's plea for love] is a demand for love in the absence
of a capacity for loving.

—D. H. Frayn and M. Silberfeld (1986, p. 323)

The harmful effects of sexual misconduct for the patient are increasingly
well documented (see chapter 10). What is less well known is that many
transgressing therapists suffer sequellae as well, even to the point of suicide.
There is an immediate aversive reaction to therapists who have transgressed
in this way. They, like child abusers, have taken advantage of those who are
emotionally dependent on them. In addition, the iatrogenic effects of sexual
exploitation are often viewed as more reprehensible than other adverse effects
of treatment because sexual exploitation, perceived as intentional, cannot be
attributed to negligence or even ignorance. However, the assumption of in-
tentionality in these cases is overly simplistic. For many therapists, the sexual
exploitation is largely unconsciously motivated and multidetermined. Often it
involves unresolved narcissistic needs as well as conflicts with authority. Who
among us is completely without these?

This chapter discusses the long-term treatment of Dr. Burn, the transgressor introduced and described in chapter 2. As noted in that chapter, Dr.
Burn is actually a composite case of several transgressors who were selected
because their behavior and personal dynamics depict the most common findings in sexual boundary transgressions. It cannot be stated often enough that
Dr. Burn is an example of a one-time transgressor, not the psychopathic predator who lacks remorse and is not capable of rehabilitation. Dr. Burn and the
transgressors like him have all the characteristics that are good prognostic indicators for rehabilitation, including genuine remorse, introspective capacity,
and a desire to live with integrity.

Chapter 2 focused on the way in which sexual boundary transgressions happen. This chapter describes Dr. Burn's therapy, a treatment that was mandated for two years by the licensing board in his state and then voluntarily continued for another six years. What follows is a description of a long-term psychoanalytically oriented treatment aimed at the characterological factors that motivated the exploitation. While I firmly believe that such an in-depth approach is essential to any substantive rehabilitation program, other approaches may also be indicated depending on the nature of the diagnostic picture. These may be concurrent, adjunctive intervention strategies that form part of a comprehensive, multifaceted treatment program, often for more complex cases. Irons and Schneider (1994) have studied transgressors with sexual addictions and/or chemical dependency. Abel, Osborn, and Warberg (1995) provide cognitive-behavioral treatment for inappropriate sexual behavior among professionals.

CONTEXT OF THE REFERRAL

When Dr. Burn was referred to me, I received from the licensing board a copy of the written complaint against him, his response to that complaint, and a copy of the consent agreement. He had not undergone an independent comprehensive evaluation by an expert in sexual boundary violations. Though this would have been preferred, it is not an unusual omission since performing such evaluations has not become a routine procedure following an ethical complaint. The rehabilitation plan was devised by members of the licensing board based on their observations of him and the nature of the complaint. This multifaceted rehabilitation plan included restriction from independent practice, therapy for at least two years, supervision for two years, and the equivalent of 16 hours of psychoeducation on ethics.

It should be noted that the nature of this consent agreement is relatively permissive compared to how punitive and restrictive most responses are to sexual boundary violations. Even the consideration of a rehabilitation plan is unusual and I took this to be a positive reflection on the board's perception of Dr. Burn, probably revolving around his genuine remorse and willingness to take responsibility for his actions.

The rehabilitation plan stipulated that the therapy should be at least once weekly for a duration of at least two years. This mandate originally required quarterly reports from me divulging the ways in which Dr. Burn was addressing his problems, especially those that related to the transgression. Upon reading this aspect of the consent agreement, however, I notified the licensing board that such a reporting therapy was unacceptable to me since it would severely compromise the treatment. I agreed to submit quarterly reports informing the board solely that the therapy was continuing for the required period of time. I also agreed to notify the board in the event that Dr. Burn prematurely terminated the therapy. The board agreed to this modified reporting requirement. Beyond these disclosures, there were no intrusions of the confidential frame surrounding the therapy for the duration of the treatment.

After the two years of mandated therapy had elapsed and Dr. Burn had fulfilled all of the other requirements of the consent agreement, Dr. Burn was allowed to and did reapply for licensure. He was required to appear before the licensing board several times in order to assess the adequacy of his rehabilitation. This assessment included detailed written reports from his supervisor, documentation of the required psychoeducation he had obtained, and a report from me stating only that he had undergone the required two years of therapy. The members of the board also asked him to discuss the prior transgression, the gains he felt he had made in his therapy, and what he had learned from the supervision and psychoeducation. (Incidentally, all of these functions fall within the province of an independent evaluator who has expertise in sexual boundary violations, if one had been employed. The ideal situation is one where such an independent assessment is performed in the initial stages of the hearing process to determine whether the transgressor has the capacity for rehabilitation. Subsequently, a follow-up assessment, by the same examiner, assesses the adequacy of the rehabilitation and the transgressor's readiness to return to independent practice. See chapter 12 and Celenza and Gabbard [2003] for a fuller discussion of these steps.) After this series of meetings, Dr. Burn's license was reinstated.

SUMMARY OF THE TRANSGRESSION

The way in which Dr. Burn's transgression with his patient came about is fully elaborated in chapter 2. For purposes of the present chapter, a brief summary is presented here. Dr. Burn recalls feeling almost wholly isolated at the time of his involvement with his patient. His primary contact with adults, other than his girlfriend, was with the patients in his practice. Most importantly, his relationship with his girlfriend had been on a deteriorating course for several years. They were emotionally estranged and he felt little hope of regaining a more satisfying relationship.

Dr. Burn's initial understanding of his transgression revolved around a sense that he had been in love with the patient and that he had hoped to provide for her a "corrective emotional experience" (his words) in reparation for her profound history of abuse by men. They had an intensely absorbing love affair for about a year. The ending of the relationship was brought about when the patient felt certain that Dr. Burn would not leave his girlfriend, at which time the patient wrote a letter of complaint to the licensing board. This event and the disciplinary hearing that followed were highly traumatizing to both of them and it was at this point that Dr. Burn began his therapy with me.

Dr. Burn recalls that the treatment with this particular patient was difficult from the beginning. He experienced her as a hard-to-reach and withholding woman who had great difficulty trusting men. She was depressed and married to an alcoholic man who was prone to violent behavior and who had hit her on several occasions. She was quite resistant to talking about herself, and spent many sessions in silence, vigilantly watching Dr. Burn as if afraid of him.

Dr. Burn was initially respectful of her fears, but was also aware of feeling frustrated at her inability to talk to him. He offered to turn away or sit on the other side of the room, thinking this might help her feel less threatened. When this seemed only to exacerbate her anxiety, he became more overtly reassuring to her and uncharacteristically offered to hold her hand or hug her; his conscious rationale at the time had been that he was attempting to help her feel safe. At this point, Dr. Burn believed he was furthering the therapeutic process and was not responding out of his own needs. However, he also had been dimly aware of feeling increasingly helpless and had begun to view the patient as *willfully withholding*. This had echoed his experience of his mother, who had overtly resisted his attempts to engage yet had been hostile and critical if he had withdrawn. This was clearly indicative of Dr. Burn's countertransference reaction—the point at which he, in retrospect, can see that he had invested the patient with certain properties relating to his own past and having little to do with the patient, or at least with her needs. In an analogous manner, the patient's perception of Dr. Burn had paralleled her experience with her father, where she had felt intruded upon along with a continual pressure to prop up his self-esteem. At this time, however, she was greatly distressed and could not risk displeasing or losing Dr. Burn, so she responded to his advances.

Dr. Burn had become increasingly affectionate toward his patient, consciously attempting to help her feel safe and embracing the belief that she would be cured if she were loved in a constructive, caring way. The hand-holding and hugging at the end of sessions seemed to help in the sense that she began to feel better. However, Dr. Burn overlooked the appeasing effects of his efforts (Apfel & Simon, 1985) and the manner in which these served to circumvent (at least temporarily) the patient's hate and rage and prevent their emergence in her transference to Dr. Burn.

The affectionate advances began to include sitting next to the patient on the couch. She soon would lean into him and put her head on his shoulder, coinciding with a deepening of her ability to share her distress with Dr. Burn. In one particular session, she was acutely upset, saying she would kill herself if she had to bear another moment, at which point Dr. Burn kissed her and they embraced passionately. Hugging and kissing became part of each session until they were involved in a full sexual relationship. At this point, Dr. Burn terminated the therapy relationship and they continued their involvement for another year. Throughout this year, the patient had become more trusting, had exposed more of her feelings and situation to Dr. Burn, and had fallen in love with him.

Though Dr. Burn had felt conflicted about his actions due to his awareness that he was violating the ethical code, he simultaneously had felt trapped by the patient's fears, responsible for their resolution, and stimulated by the fantasy that he would be the one to save her where other therapists had failed. He rationalized his involvement through the belief that she would be cured if she were loved in a constructive and caring way. He was not aware of competitive feelings toward her husband but did consciously entertain fantasies of rescuing her from her distress and teaching her to love in nondestructive ways. He reminded himself that his training emphasized the "healing power of love," which he interpreted to mean some kind of corrective emotional experience. He told himself that she had not been helped in previous, more traditional modalities, and he thought he understood her in a special and unique way that other therapists would not understand. He knew he could not describe this therapy to anyone (a supervisor or a colleague) and he asked her to keep the treatment confidential as well. They both thereby constructed a thick insulation around their relationship from this point on.

The patient's behavior toward Dr. Burn changed to one of open affection and idealization. Dr. Burn remembers having several powerful fantasies at that time in which he felt closer to God, perhaps identified with him. He recalls a dream in which he saw himself diving from a very high place into a small bit of water, yet surviving. He recalls experiencing, in certain private moments, an oceanic feeling—a oneness fantasy in which he felt empowered by the universe and felt he could accomplish anything.

THE THERAPY

Dr. Burn and I began our meetings at a rate of once per week but it quickly became clear that he needed a more intensive treatment (for both the support and exploration). After approximately six weeks, we began meeting twice weekly. As mentioned, the therapy lasted a total of eight years, though it was mandated only for two.

Dr. Burn was middle-aged, intelligent, attractive, and carefully groomed, and had an emotionally responsive nature and quick humor. He was psychodynamically trained and primarily had conducted long-term treatments with adults. He was divorced and living with a girlfriend of several years when he became involved with his patient. At the time of his treatment with me, he was still living with his girlfriend. As part of the stipulation of the consent agreement, he was prohibited from seeing his patient in any capacity.

In addition to being mandated to treatment, Dr. Burn had his own desire for treatment at this time since he was very traumatized by the ending of the relationship with his patient and the disciplinary process itself. He feared he had "made a pathetic mess out of my life and dragged a lot of people down with me." At the time of his involvement with his patient, he was aware that his actions were unethical, but felt overcome with feelings he thought he could not control. He also harbored ill-defined notions that his involvement with his patient was therapeutic to her.

In our early meetings, Dr. Burn was extremely remorseful and self-berating. This remorse was easy to distinguish from his mortification at how he had ruined his professional career. Such narcissistic mortification was also present alongside a genuine state of regret and a conviction that he had harmed his patient rather than helped her. He was well versed in psychoanalytic jargon and often called himself "narcissistic" and "grandiose" as he recounted the story to me. He noted that he has always felt depressed and that his "self-esteem was shot." He was tearful in the early months, appeared genuinely ashamed of his actions, and feared that I would judge him harshly or be hostile toward him.

Dr. Burn depicts his childhood in stark and austere terms. He is the only son of a strictly religious couple whose beliefs about God and morality seemed to blanket the household with fear and a continual expectation of harsh judgment. He describes his mother as stern, domineering, and withholding of affection. He describes his father as well-intentioned but ineffectual, a timid man largely under his wife's thumb. According to Dr. Burn, his father was a respected professional, but had held himself back from ambitious undertakings because of a chronic illness and an accompanying fear that he might "overexert" himself. Dr. Burn's mother seemed to view the father's physical vulnerability as a weakness in his character and belittled him for it. Dr. Burn remembers his mother ridiculing his father as weak and unable to care for the family "like a real man."

The atmosphere in the house was tense and repressive. Affection was not openly expressed. Dr. Burn was discouraged from having girlfriends and recounts an incident in which his mother threatened to withhold his college tuition if he became romantically involved. Sex was taboo and he was a virgin until his 20s. At the same time, Dr. Burn remembers his mother undressing in front of him as she prepared for bed—not so much with a seductive air but as if she were asexual, denying the stimulating potential of her body.

Dr. Burn felt that his mother was depressed and chronically disappointed in her spouse. She seemed to regard her son as her savior. Yet Dr. Burn felt helpless to please her; he felt capable instead only of disappointing her or maintaining the status quo. Grandiose, compensatory rescue fantasies developed and existed alongside a view of himself as helpless and weak. He felt simultaneously cast in the role of a woman's ultimate savior and hero yet utterly helpless to have any effect.

Dr. Burn has come to recognize that part of his motivation to be a therapist derives from a wish to be everything to others—to be simultaneously a lover, therapist, teacher, parent, and even child. At the same time, he recognized a long-standing, fundamental feeling of powerlessness, especially in relation to women. It seemed the wish to be everything to others served a compensatory function, defending against deeply rooted feelings of inadequacy and powerlessness that originated in early familial patterns.

It is easy to see how Dr. Burn would be attracted to the psychotherapy profession. In the therapy hour, he is privy to the intimate details of his patients' distress, which inevitably stir his narcissistic need to rescue them, promising proof to himself and the world that he is worthwhile and capable of effecting good.

Dr. Burn is also dimly aware of an underlying fear that he is so "needy" that he could "suck the life out of a woman for his own nourishment." He fears he has a hungry, clinging child inside that must be hidden and controlled lest it emerge and engulf those around him. He refers to this part of himself at some times as shameful and childish, at other times as if he were a leper or vampire inside. He tends to become involved with women who are strongly counterdependent and who reprimand him for his neediness, providing a source of external control. Although reassuring on an unconscious level, he experiences them consciously as unresponsive and cold.

The harshness of his perceptions of himself and his family is palpable. Dr. Burn speaks of not being punished as a child, but of being "condemned." He grew up trying hard to be good and earned the reputation of a "goody-two-shoes." He had few friends and remembers a recurrent fantasy that his high school would be taken over by malicious aliens, and that he would ride in on a white horse, save everyone, and become everyone's hero.

Many therapists have difficulty tolerating rage and hate in the transference and countertransference yet do not seduce their patients. Moreover, many transgressing therapists are well aware of the unethical nature of their behavior—neither ignorance nor inadequate training explains their actions. What is it in the psychic structure of these therapists that fails to prohibit the exploitation of their patients? In order to answer this question in relation to Dr. Burn, I found it revealing to analyze his *transference to the authority of the licensing board.* Understanding this aspect of the transgressing therapist's dynamics is essential in explaining how an otherwise rather common temptation moves from the level of fantasy to action.

This question raises issues that require more history. As a child, Dr. Burn would avoid asking his mother for things he wanted, feeling sure she would not allow them. Instead, he would ask his father. Although most often sending him back to ask his mother, intermittently Dr. Burn's father would secretly give him permission, colluding with Dr. Burn against Mrs. Burn's wishes. When his mother would find out, Dr. Burn would be accused of "conning his father" and manipulating him for his own gain. Thus, the gratification of a wish because forbidden, must occur in secret; publicly he struggles with a sense of himself as manipulative, devious (a "con"), and shamefully voracious, whereas privately he feels buttressed through his identification with his father, secretly fortified and capable of pleasure.

Dr. Burn's difficulty tolerating hateful and angry feelings was conspicuous by their absence in his fantasy life as well. He consciously strove toward positive, idealized visions of himself and others, adopting a passive, if not masochistic, attitude toward conflict. For example, if someone treated him aggressively, he would admonish himself for not being able to transcend the pain and would focus on what he believed to be the other person's underlying benign intentions.

In the context of his treatment with me, the various defensive transformations discussed in relation to his patient emerged within the transference. Initially, the negative maternal transference was salient. Dr. Burn was very concerned with my judging him harshly and experienced me as withholding and silently condemning. This led to associations of experiences in childhood where "to be known was to be condemned." Strikingly, at the end of an early session, he turned to confirm our next appointment and, as he did so, he winked. I was surprised and curious at the meaning of this behavior. Was he being flirtatious? Was the wink a signal of some kind? Did he have control of himself, given that this therapy was a result of his seductive behavior or at least poor judgment?

At our next session, I brought up his wink and asked him what he had meant by it. He was unaware that he had done it and became embarrassed and self-critical at what he called his "impulsive seductive behavior." I suggested there might be other meanings and that we would try to explore them all. When we later explored this incident, Dr. Burn began to reflect on his tendency to use seduction as a way to mollify my anticipated hostility, to forestall potential retaliation, and to strengthen our connection to prevent abandonment. (Later discussions revealed additional meanings associated with the paternal transference, discussed below.)

Other aspects of his relationship to his mother were replicated in Dr. Burn's transference to me as well. Because of his grandiose, compensatory rescue fantasies of himself as a woman's ultimate savior, which existed alongside a view of himself as helpless and weak, Dr. Burns had feared exposure of this imagined incompetence; this had intensified the pressure to act in the face of perceived disappointment in the maternal figure.

This conflict emerged in the transference in the following way. On one occasion, he made a humorous remark and, in response, I laughed. After a moment, he became preoccupied with whether he had manipulated that reaction out of me and thereby caused me to lose my "analytic neutrality" or whether he had actually made up my reaction altogether. (Here, his defensive undoing momentarily caused him to question his perception of reality, that is, had I laughed or was it his fantasy?) In this way, he recapitulated the dynamic of simultaneously feeling powerful but destructive (by causing me to err) or feeling he had no effect on me at all. He was unable to enjoy giving me pleasure without attacking himself, as if the wish for me to enjoy him was bad. Instead, he rendered himself inefficacious in his mind to avoid the awareness of his forbidden and, in his mind, sadistic wish.

Despite an intense conviction that I was hostile toward him, Dr. Burn was unaware of aggressive and hostile fantasies toward me. He was exceedingly moralistic with himself and would not tolerate destructive wishes toward me or anyone else, even on a fantasy level. After several years, he reported a fantasy of revenge toward a hostile coworker. He then remarked, "I'd prefer that the image not be associated with a destructive impulse—I need something to come between . . ." as if something could prevent him from the awareness of these wishes.

Dr. Burn's conviction that I was hostile toward him also reflected facets of a paternal transference and was notable in that he was readily accepting of my perceived hostility. He frequently prompted me to agree with his poor self-image by referring to himself as narcissistic or grandiose, smiling slightly when recounting self-deprecating stories, as if attempting to induce me to agree with him that he was bad and that his masochistic attitude toward himself was good. In discussing this with him, he wondered if he were in fact seeking to be punished, feeling that he had never struggled or endured a "rite of passage" into manhood, as he imagined other boys had. He wondered if his behavior was self-castrating to compensate for the absence of the wished-for oedipal phallic father.

A recapitulation of this dynamic emerged in the transference to me, in the following way. In the first phase of treatment, Dr. Burn's transference to me and the licensing board was essentially undifferentiated and characterized by a pervasive anticipation of condemnation. In contrast, the second phase was characterized by a fantasy of my collusion with him against the licensing board. The hope for reinstatement of his license had become a wish that had taken on the quality of the forbidden. The licensing board had come to represent the withholding mother against whom he and I were in collusion.

A later development in the paternal transference occurred when he began to experience me as the more gratifying, collusive father. He remarked on my "unconventional hair," which led to a fantasy that I was conspiring with him to obtain his license back, in secret collusion with him against the licensing board. This led to memories of his father, grandfather, and uncle, who would engage in conspiratorial behaviors against his domineering mother, all carried out with the implicit demand "not to tell." This experience of me revealed another meaning of the wink, as an indirect acknowledgment of our "conspiracy." The childhood experience had apparently become internalized as a split in superego structure where gratification of wishes are prohibited in one part of consciousness yet permitted in another.

THE THERAPY BEYOND THE MANDATE

Gradually, Dr. Burn showed an increasing tolerance of his own negative transference to me. Competitive feelings, anger, and disappointment began to emerge. One recent example was triggered by my being a few minutes late for his appointment. He found himself wondering if I had forgotten him or if I was running late on purpose, perhaps in order to "frustrate the needy child in him." Momentarily, I became the sadistic mother in his eyes, whose harsh and condemning discipline was quickly rationalized as designed for his own good. At other times, feelings that referred to his relationship with his father predominated. For example, in response to perceived rejections by his current girlfriend, he often secludes himself in his office and fantasizes a closeness with Jesus or being held in a loving embrace by his father. In one session, the images of the protective and soothing arms of paternal figures stimulated associations to the movie *Ordinary People* (1980) when the father hugs his son.

He then recalled and spoke longingly of the scene in the same film in which the therapist hugged the young boy.

As Dr. Burn became more tolerant of a positive connection between us, erotic longings with underlying preoedipal wishes emerged. In one session, he expressed the wish to go to conferences together, walk along a beach, and stay in a motel. He quickly became sad and noted his avoidance of eye contact "because I want your acceptance and recognition so badly it hurts." Tearfully, he commented that the yearning would just lead to more yearning, making him feel helpless and passive. He concluded, "Therapy is a place where I can get what I want yet feel tortured at the same time."

CONCLUSION

In the case presented, the dynamic pattern (including the unconscious selection of the victim/patient) recapitulated unconscious, unresolved conflicts on the part of the therapist in relation to early paternal figures. Interestingly, the pattern emerged in his therapy with the victim when he thought that treatment was at an impasse. The seduction of the patient occurred in response to intolerable feelings in Dr. Burn's countertransference, an unconscious attempt to circumvent the negative transference and to sustain a positive, idealizing transference easier for both parties to bear. Dr. Burn's actions unconsciously served to seduce the patient away from her negative transference and to transform Dr. Burn's countertransference as well.

But this was not an awareness that Dr. Burn had when he was treating his patient. There were at least two clinical errors that played a part in Dr. Burn's perceptual process, both of which added to his defensive efforts to manage his emerging and intolerable maternal countertransference. The first involved his taking his patient's transference pleas at face value. As Freud (1915) warned, in his prescient paper on transference love,

> [The analyst] must recognize that the patient's falling in love is induced by the analytic situation and is not to be attributed to the charms of his person; so that he has no grounds whatever for being proud of such a "conquest," as it would be called outside of analysis. (pp. 160–161)

Understanding our patients' needs and desires as they are simply and directly stated sidesteps the all-important work of exploring deeper meanings, including possible defensive motives. In the case of an eroticized transference, it is tempting to feel flattered—there is always some grain of truth, some aspect of the therapist's person, that triggers the patient's reactions. Even for the seasoned therapist, the recognition of the transference dynamic as such can be fraught with ambivalence; the late Elvin Semrad is remembered to have said to an adoring female patient: "You feel this way for neurotic reasons and when you get better, I will be very sad."

The second error involved Dr. Burn's inability and perhaps unwillingness to acknowledge the patient's aggression, as it was beginning to emerge in her transference to him. This minimization of the patient's hostility is not necessarily always evident. Dr. Burn was able to accurately diagnose and treat difficult cases in the past. However, the particular transference manifestation for this patient provided an unconscious fit with Dr. Burn's unresolved countertransference tendencies, creating a blind spot in him in this case.

Nevertheless, the manifestation of an eroticized transference should be viewed as signaling a complex reaction. As noted in the epigraph, an eroticized transference is "a demand for love in the absence of a capacity for loving" (Frayn & Silberfeld, 1986, p. 323). What furthers the therapeutic process is an examination of the nature of the incapacity, not gratification of the transference demand. Often, transference love, especially eroticized transference love, represents a defense against disappointment, rage, or hate in the transference.

In Dr. Burn's treatment of his patient, it is apparent that a similar defensive process can occur in the therapist's countertransference. The therapist's countertransference love can function to circumvent or defend against disappointment, hate, or other intolerable affects in order to sustain a positive, perhaps even idealizing transference.

In addition, the analysis of the transgressing therapist's transference to the authority of the licensing board was essential in explaining his transgression of boundaries, especially given Dr. Burn's awareness that his actions were unethical. Unresolved anger toward his mother/authority supplied the motivational force and his identification with his father (who had sanctioned secret rule breaking) rendered the behavior relatively ego-syntonic, accounting for the weakness of internal prohibition against the unethical behavior.

Fantasies of sexual involvement with our patients can be exciting. As in incest, the strength of the taboo is related to the intensity of the temptation. Therapists must be able to acknowledge these feelings and must be aware of how these feelings can be unconsciously recruited in the service of other aims. In the training of psychotherapists, careful attention must be paid to the personal vulnerabilities and unresolved conflicts of the therapist. Educational efforts are clearly needed to address issues such as taking transference pleas at face value, minimizing deeper motivations on the part of both the therapist and patient, and emphasizing the care needed to ethically manage the asymmetric distribution of power and attention inherent in the therapeutic matrix.

Educational efforts are not enough, however, especially in light of the fact that many transgressing therapists admit to *knowing* their behavior was unethical. In addition, many give lip service to understanding the vicissitudes of transference and countertransference in their work. A more effective preventative measure will be obtained by examining the therapist's unresolved personal conflicts and past traumas. The case presented here especially points to the therapist's relationship to authority figures and his or her ability to tolerate the patient's transference rage and hate.

12

HELPING THE HELPERS: SUPERVISION OF THE TRANSGRESSOR

The elephant does not feel the bird under his feet.

Supervision is a major part of a comprehensive rehabilitation program if the transgressor is to be permitted to continue to practice, either independently or under the auspices of an organization or clinic. Such supervision is defined as ongoing weekly meetings, usually for at least one year's duration (most often several years) with the purpose of guiding and overseeing the transgressor/therapist's therapy practice subsequent to the transgression. The supervision may be mandated by a licensing board or overseeing professional agency, or engaged in voluntarily.

In order for the supervision to be relevant, viable, and effective for therapists who have engaged in sexual boundary violations, it is essential that the supervisor have a substantial background and orientation toward psychodynamic, if not psychoanalytic, approaches. This is not simply bias due to my own professional training but derives from a recognition that only these approaches have enough breadth and depth in examining and exploring the subtleties of interpersonal, transferential, and countertransferential aspects of the therapeutic relationship. Being the domain in which sexual boundary violations occur, it is essential that the supervisor have the requisite perspective, training, and experience to help the transgressor examine and appropriately handle the emotional challenges within this realm.

It is also important to remember that psychodynamic therapists have a lower prevalence rate of sexual boundary violations than practitioners of other orientations (Borys & Pope, 1989; Baer & Murdock, 1995; Pope et al., 1987), presumably by virtue of the fact that psychodynamic and psychoanalytic approaches prepare practitioners better in how to navigate the tumultuous interpersonal terrain. One transgressor had sought supervision *before* she

159

had engaged in a sexual relationship with her patient (a responsible move and one that I hope will become more common). She, herself, was a cognitive-behavioral therapist and chose a similarly oriented supervisor, however. In retrospect, she admits that the form of supervision was inadequate to help her manage the increasingly intense feelings she was having toward her patient. It is possible that had she sought a psychodynamic therapist, the outcome would have been the same because it is possible that she had already reached a point of no return; it is also possible that a psychodynamic supervisor would have helped her verbalize her feelings in appropriate depth and this might have prevented the catastrophe that followed.

For ease of discussion, therapist/transgressors will be referenced in this chapter simply as therapists or supervisees. Likewise, the supervisors of the therapist/transgressors will be referred to as supervisors.

ESTABLISHING THE FRAME OF THE SUPERVISION

The initial contact that the supervisor will receive is usually a call directly from the therapist. Most often, the therapist has selected the supervisor's name from a list of approved supervisors given to him or her by the licensing board or overseeing professional agency. It may also happen that the therapist has obtained the name of a supervisor from colleagues with the hope that the supervisor will be subsequently approved by the licensing board or overseeing professional agency. In either case, the frame of the supervision is dependent upon the pending overarching approval of the board or professional organization. The frame is also articulated by and embeds the specific requirements of the overseeing organization, such as frequency of meetings, periodic reporting, and the like.

When the therapist initially makes contact with the supervisor, he is usually very tentative and wary, anticipating a punitive or at least a condescending attitude from the supervisor. The hearing and processing of the complaint has at this point come to an end and the therapist most likely has been traumatized by these experiences. He does not know to what extent the prospective supervisor may be trusted and confided in; however, there is usually a certainty that the prospective supervisor is needed and must be pleased.

Right away the supervisor is faced with several dilemmas. One is that the supervisor's relationship with the therapist involves a split allegiance. The supervisor is hired by the therapist but is actually working for the licensing board or overseeing professional agency. The boundaries of confidentiality and liability are affected in complicated ways, similar to the split in the alliance for the subsequent therapist of the transgressor. To address this concern, the supervisor must appreciate that the therapist will need to feel as comfortable and safe as possible, but this safety will necessarily have limits. The goal for both supervisor and supervisee is that, within the constraints of this special context, the therapist will be able to authentically reveal aspects of his style and the details of his practice with minimal defensiveness.

During the initial call from the therapist, it is important to convey an attitude of interest in the supervisee and a receptivity to the possibility of working together, along with conveying that a final commitment to working together may take several weeks. This should be mutual, in the sense that both supervisee and supervisor have a stake in assessing the viability of the working alliance between them. This will involve much data gathering and some exposure to each other in order to assess the quality and nature of the communication and interpersonal fit. It is essential that the supervisor have a genuine interest in the supervisee as a person as well as an interest in the details of the transgression *from the supervisee's point of view*. It is not the only point of view that knowledge about the transgression will be gathered; however, it is essential to the bond between the supervisor and supervisee that the supervisor care about the supervisee's opinions, understanding, and subjective experience, especially as these relate to the transgression.

Much like therapeutic help, the path to change is from the inside out, not the other way around. It is not helpful if a supervisor has a reservoir of anger toward transgressing therapists or a political agenda against them. Supervision (and therapy) of transgressors is not the arena to express these attitudes or find an outlet for such axes. Though these may be defensible positions in other contexts, the supervisory alliance and the effectiveness of the supervision will be compromised if there is undue anger or hostility that motivates the supervisor. An unfortunate collusion may occur since many therapist/transgressors tend toward masochism, and a punitive negative feedback loop can become a destructive part of the rehabilitation. Just as in any therapeutic effort, a safe context must be established and maintained so that the therapist feels comfortable being himself.

But the supervisor's role is more complicated still; though there is much attention needed to examine the therapist's well-being and the difficulties establishing a working supervision in this context, the supervisor is actually working for the licensing board or overseeing professional agency. There is usually an expectation of periodic reports, perhaps a monitoring function, and even the expectation that the supervisor will be integral in terminating the therapist's license should misconduct reoccur. All of these constraints should be explicitly stated to the therapist and will present obstacles to the therapist's comfort and ease of disclosure to the supervisor. There is no solution to this tension. It simply must be tolerated by both supervisor and supervisee. If the supervisor's interest in the therapist's well-being is genuine, these constraints will not unduly compromise the supervision. If a safe atmosphere has been established, within these constraints, the therapist will disclose aspects of his work that he is uncertain about or uncomfortable with and preface the disclosure with something like, "I'm going to be honest with you, this is just the kind of case that got me in trouble . . ." or "I want your input—this is what I'm here for, I need your help."

Next, it is essential that the supervisor acquire *all* of the documentation involved in the transgression and review these carefully. It is important for the supervisor to be clear about what the original problems were and what the overseeing agency or licensing board expects the supervision to accomplish (Schoener, 2005). For the next several meetings, there should be a thorough and detailed discussion of the transgression. The vantage point from which this discussion emerges is primarily from the therapist's point of view, to reveal as much as possible about what the therapist was thinking, what he was trying to accomplish, and what he was aware of feeling. This is an essential part of the determination of whether the specific nature of the problem is something you, as a prospective supervisor, are comfortable with and understand.

In particular, I attempt to assess the character of the supervisee, the capacity for remorse, openness to the victim's point of view, and openness to supervisory influence. I usually offer supervisory comments and assess the therapist/transgressor's ability to take them in and be guided. All of this addresses the fundamental question of whether you think he has potential for rehabilitation, a question that should have been addressed in the evaluation, but often enough has not been evaluated comprehensively or thoroughly. Even if the therapist was evaluated in thorough detail, however, it is important to make *your own* assessment of this most basic question because, more than anything, *it is essential that you believe in your supervisee's potential.* Hopefully, the results of the evaluation will concur with your assessment.

If you do not see a capacity for remorse, empathy, honesty, or relative nondefensiveness, it is not likely that supervision will be helpful or that any component of the rehabilitation plan will be effective. *I do not take on supervisees unless these qualities are present, at least at some minimal level.* It is worth saying here that most of the therapists who present to the licensing board or overseeing professional agencies are not psychopathic predators or may have moderate to severe character disorders but are highly sympathetic, albeit narcissistically needy or neurotically distressed individuals. Sometimes a therapist will contact you for supervision without having been evaluated at all, so it is essential that these basic questions be addressed before agreeing to the supervisory contract.

Most psychopathic multiple transgressors do not agree to any aspect of a rehabilitation plan or even supervision because they continue to deny their culpability. There is a logical disconnect to such denial with any evaluative or rehabilitation effort since there is no ownership of a problem in the first place. Despite this, it is possible to receive a call from a therapist requesting supervision in order to appease a licensing board or professional agency with the idea that the supervision will be minimally intrusive and thereby tolerable. In these rare cases, it is not difficult to ascertain the superficiality of the commitment and the manipulativeness of the request for supervision on the whole. The psychopathic predator will not take responsibility for anything that may have caused the treatment to go awry, he or she will not admit to having erred, and usually abundant blame is placed on the victim. This is not a viable attitude or context in which supervision can occur and it is best to decline such a request for supervision. If the therapist cannot admit that there is any need for learning or oversight, the supervision will be a struggle and a sham. Fortunately, most requests for supervision come from therapists who have a genuine desire to get back on their professional feet, learn from their mistakes, and return to good standing within the profession.

It may be necessary for the potential supervisor to appear before the licensing board in order to be officially accepted to perform the supervisory role. The supervision is usually part of a more comprehensive rehabilitation plan and others involved in this rehabilitation may be present for the meeting before the board as well. The licensing board or overseeing professional agency should be interested to see the supervisor's thorough familiarity with the details of the transgression, a full awareness of the supervisory needs of the transgressor, as well as demonstrable expertise in the problem of boundary violations. It is important to prepare well for this meeting and be ready to demonstrate all of these factors. These issues should be explicitly stated and elaborated at the meeting.

The frame of the supervision should also be clearly spelled out at the official meeting of the oversight body. This includes the extrinsic expectations for the supervisory context, that is, the frequency of meetings, location of the supervision, type of supervision, and so forth. These should be clearly stated and agreed upon by all members of the rehabilitation plan. Since members of the rehabilitation plan should be relatively independent of the transgressor (i.e., they should not be a peer, colleague, or friend), it may be difficult to find someone with appropriate expertise within the transgressor's geographic area. It is not unusual for the supervisor or even the subsequent therapist or analyst to be at some distance from the transgressor's usual network and geographic area. There may be a long commute. It may also be necessary for the supervision to be conducted via telephone. In this latter instance, there should also be an arrangement for periodic face-to-face meetings (semiannually at professional meetings or the like).

Once I have agreed to supervise a therapist, I ask for a list of all of the patients in his practice. Though this is no guarantee that the therapist is giving you a full account, it is a helpful way to focus the sessions over time and to be sure you have heard about each case. It is true that the psychopathic predator will lie and omit problematic cases from such a list, or at least avoid discussing problematic parts of treatments when talking about troubling cases. There is no foolproof safeguard against this; however, if the prospective supervisor has followed the guidelines thus far, it is likely that such therapists would not have appeared amenable to supervision and/or would not have been recommended for rehabilitation by you or their overseeing professional organization in the first place.

The more typical scenario, with therapists who are genuinely engaged in the supervisory process, is one where they may inadvertently "forget" to discuss a case or overlook certain of their patients because they consciously believe there are no problematic issues in these cases. This is where a full list of cases can be very helpful, so that all patients are discussed at some point and the supervisor does not rely solely on the therapist's judgment of how cases are going or their need for supervisory input. Often enough, these therapists are unaware of boundary crossings since their judgment may be or has been poor in this area. Others may discuss problematic areas naively, without realizing that they are displaying the very area with which they need help. Most often, therapists have become highly self-conscious about areas of vulnerability and begin by saying, "I need to talk about this case because it feels the same way it did with Ms. X [the victim]."

It is also a good idea (and sometimes required by the licensing board) to have therapists bring in process notes to supervision. By process notes, I mean a verbatim account of what is said in the therapy hour, a word-for-word rendering of the back-and-forth exchanges between therapist and patient. *Process notes* are distinguished from *progress notes,* which are summaries and often do not reflect the therapist's unconscious assumptions about what constitutes the work of psychotherapy. Process notes, like tape recordings, give a more faithful account of how the therapist actually works, what his mode of influencing the patient is, what his beliefs of therapeutic action are, and most importantly, what he actually does, not what he says or thinks he does. (We all imperfectly approximate who we think we are, but these therapists have blind spots that must be monitored.) It is also important to know that written notes can deteriorate over time, that is, become sketchy or sparse. This is an important warning sign that the therapist may be unduly conflicted about the therapy progress or about the nature of the relationship in a particular treatment, or worse, may be hiding the process from the supervisor.

It must be acknowledged, as well, that process notes are (usually) not a simultaneous recording of the verbal exchange between therapist and client/patient. They are most often reconstructed after the hour, perhaps even several hours later. They rely on the therapist's memory and disciplined rendering of what transpired. Though all therapists probably have some experience reconstructing a therapy hour in this way, no one believes that it is an exact replica of what was said to whom at each moment. The question often comes up, Why not simply use a tape recorder so that a faithful rendering can be ensured? (The overseeing professional organization or licensing board may explicitly make this suggestion.) I do not encourage the use of a tape recorder, however, for two reasons: first, it is an intrusion in the therapy context and is usually an unfair burden to the patient/client. It is difficult enough to establish safety and a strong alliance; the presence of a mechanical device designed to replicate the process so that a third person can "listen in" works against this. Second, if the desire for a tape recording seems like the only viable method of obtaining a faithful account of the process, this may mean that the therapist is not sufficiently trusted to conduct treatment or to engage in an honest supervision at this time. If there is an overriding suspicion that the therapist's process notes will not be sufficiently faithful, it is likely that there is insufficient trust in the supervisee and the prospect of rehabilitation should be reconsidered.

As the supervisor, it is imperative to keep careful notes. There is potential liability in supervising a therapist on a form of professional probation or suspension, so detailed notes may be helpful at some future point if questions are raised about the therapist's competence. Further, the notes are helpful when it comes time to prepare reports to the licensing board or overseeing professional agency. I sometimes highlight portions of these notes as I am writing them to indicate to myself that these portions may be relevant to include in a report. I also include verbatim process in the reports that are good examples of the therapist's work.

THE SUPERVISION

If a relatively safe atmosphere is established, this paves the way for the very important work of exploring the therapist's approach, specific techniques, and most importantly, his or her countertransference or any feelings that underlie specific interventions. In this context, the term "countertransference" is used to denote all of the feelings and reactions evoked in the therapist by the patient. It is in the therapist's countertransference that the supervisor will discover the motivations for the therapist's acting out, and in this way the supervision will have some similarities to therapy. Supervisors differ in the extent to which they are comfortable exploring in depth the therapist's countertransference. This is especially true if countertransference feelings involve intense passions, either hateful or loving ones. With therapists who have engaged in sexual misconduct, the supervisor has a special responsibility to explore these feelings in depth since they are integral to the boundary violation, and in that sense, it is the heart of the work that will be done. For this reason, greater license is granted to the supervisor to gather personal information from the supervisee about his or her childhood experiences, current marital situation, and the like.

Unlike therapy, however, it is incumbent upon the supervisor to take direct and specific stances about what the therapist should and should not do or say in his practice of psychotherapy. Here is where the initial, thorough discussion of the complaint, formal charges, and any relevant lawsuit are relevant. It is very important for the supervisor to be thoroughly familiar with the problems described in the charges and complaint, as well as any other problems that the therapist may have revealed to you. The supervisor needs to know the specific vulnerabilities of the therapist, what to watch for, what the warning signs are likely to be, and what the areas of weakness are. These could be evoked by specific types of patients or certain affectively based exchanges with patients.

One therapist was charged with using unprofessional and "unempathic" language in an assessment of a patient (not the one with whom she had engaged in a sexual boundary violation). This therapist had written a report about a family and had described the father in unflattering terms. She wrote this despite the fact that she intended to give a copy of the report to the father. As her supervisor, I could see her impulsivity. However, I also saw that I needed to explore the roots of her lapse in empathy and the circumstances under which she had difficulty containing her anger. This area, the area of exploring the therapist's countertransference, is greatly enhanced if the supervisee is also in a personal therapy simultaneously. (If he or she is not—that is, if personal therapy is not part of the comprehensive rehabilitation plan—I usually suggest he or she engage in one during the supervision.)

Another aid to this aspect of the work is the comprehensive evaluation. If it is done well, there is a thorough account of the therapist's vulnerabilities. This is obtained through personal interviews with the therapist as well as interviews (perhaps by telephone) with colleagues, employers, coworkers, and family members (see Celenza & Gabbard, 2003).

Whether hired by a licensing board or overseeing professional agency or if the therapist has engaged in supervision voluntarily, the therapist may reveal boundary violations that are beyond what is already known by the oversight organization. This raises the question of whether to report the misconduct to the appropriate agency. The answer to this question is, on one level, addressed state by state. Some states have mandatory reporting, others do not, and these regulations may vary by discipline as well. Further, there are different mandates for supervision than for the therapeutic context, which also must be taken into account (see chapter 8 for a detailed discussion of these conflicting mandates). In one situation, I was the therapist for a social worker who informed me that she was involved in a sexual relationship with her former psychiatrist. I, being a psychologist, was not at all clear whose ethical guidelines applied (besides my own, of course). I called the ethics committee of my state's psychological association who attempted to provide me with guidance. I also documented all of the consultations I obtained. In the end, the question of reporting was moot because my patient was unwilling to give me the name of her psychiatrist. In any event, it is always a good idea to maintain close contact with your local ethics committees, under any auspices, as an avenue for consultation and guidance.

Beyond the question of a reporting requirement, however, is the dilemma that additional sexual boundary violations present for you as a rehabilitation supervisor. Whether there is a reporting requirement in your state for your discipline or not, you still have a responsibility to inform the overseeing professional agency that has hired you of these additional violations. But much will depend on your own assessment and perspective on these subsequently revealed boundary violations in terms of how you present them to the agency.

There are many important questions to ask and the answers will affect the continuing viability of the supervision. One is why these violations did not come to light at the time of the evaluation and hearing process. The therapist's answer may revolve around his own fear and self-protectiveness, a rational wish to minimize further discipline. In revealing these violations to you, he may be displaying a sincere attempt to get help in a more thorough and comprehensive way. This does not necessarily bode poorly for the viability of the supervision; rather, it may indicate that he trusts the process and is putting more of himself into it. Another way further violations may come to light is inadvertent, where the therapist demonstrates his areas of blind spots by revealing violations without knowing that they are just that. These too are likely to be areas of supervisory work but do not bode poorly on the continuing viability of supervision. Your report of these additional violations should include your perspective on what they mean and how they bear on the continuing viability of the supervision.

The worst case scenario, however, is when a therapist knowingly reveals violations to you that he has intentionally kept from the process thus far in the hopes that you will collude with him against further disciplinary action. This is not a way of presenting himself with integrity or an honest attitude toward the process. Whatever the case may be, the supervisor is responsible to put in perspective and convey these facts to the overseeing professional agency along with his or her understanding of the continuing viability of the supervision.

FROM THE SUPERVISOR'S POINT OF VIEW

From the supervisor's point of view, one problem to surmount is inherent in the fact that you are "overseeing a peer or colleague." In addition, the supervisee may be your senior. This presents another obstacle to establishing an alliance with the supervisee, made all the more complicated by the fact that the supervisee has probably just endured a shaming and humiliating disciplinary process. These therapists often report, understandable from their point of view, feeling abused or traumatized by the process with the licensing board or overseeing professional agency. Again, it is important to convey the attitude that you are interested in their point of view and that you care about their experience. One therapist who was initially deeply suspicious of getting any help from anyone, and became more so after his disciplinary process, was relieved to find I was genuinely interested in his well-being. After several meetings, I told him I would work with him, after which he responded, "I have been in trouble for so long and now I feel someone is finally taking notice." Many therapists have stated a similar sentiment and add, "My hope through all of this is that I will be a better therapist in the end."

Finally, it is important to realize that as a supervisor, you will be invested in the supervisee's future and success in the supervisory process. This may contribute to your own blind spots regarding his or her progress. It is important to discipline yourself to follow up on any uncertainties or vague feelings of discomfort that you may have. It is important to notice whether your recommendations are being incorporated in the supervisee's style and technique. You should see changes in the way the supervisee practices according to your influence and input. It is also important not to be naïve about the initial "gun-shyness" associated with the stunning effects of the disciplinary process. It is very likely that the supervisee will be significantly affected, even traumatized, by the disciplinary procedures, and these by themselves will have a constraining effect. However, this will be a temporary effect and will not cause deeply rooted character change. For a while, perhaps even a number of years, the therapist may carefully monitor himself while the experience of the disciplinary process is still fresh. This does not mean he has been rehabilitated. A resolution of his vulnerabilities must be observed, especially with regard to isolative tendencies, neediness, and grandiosity reflected in his routine practice and handling of difficult cases.

Regarding liability issues, according to Slovenko (1980), supervisors are responsible to provide "due care," meaning "that degree of diligence, care and skill that ordinarily prudent supervisors would exercise under like conditions." Even if this is provided, however, the supervisor should assume that anyone involved in a particular case will be liable. This is the deep pocket rule of litigation. This does not necessarily mean, however, that every participant in the rehabilitation plan will be held responsible in court. Each person's involvement and adequacy is arguable and will be determined in each particular case. For this reason, it is important that the expectations of the supervision are carefully elucidated from the beginning. This includes the timing and frequency of reports to the licensing board or overseeing professional agency as well as the specific areas to be addressed in the supervision. As discussed below, the reports to the licensing board or overseeing professional agency should be highly detailed and should demonstrate how the various issues are addressed, what the therapist currently understands about the issues, and how he or she is able to put the supervisory guidance into use at the time of each reporting period.

REPORT WRITING

A mandated supervision will usually include periodic reports to the overseeing professional organization (usually a licensing board). These may be quarterly or semiannual and should be very detailed and specific. Each report should be individualized and describe in detail the content of the supervision; I have included two sample reports at the end of this chapter to exemplify the many topics that might be covered and the way they might be described. The identity of the supervisees in these sample reports is not revealed to protect their confidentiality; however, the reports retain their coherence in the manner in which the supervision was pitched and oriented.

Regardless of the theoretical orientation of the supervisee, supervising a transgressor who has violated sexual boundaries should focus on the following themes: (1) the transgressor's overall professionalism and sensitivity to how verbal and written communications to patients or clients may be received or understood by the patients; (2) the maintenance of awareness and control over countertransference feelings, especially when treatments are challenging, eroticized, and/or aggressive; (3) the appropriate use of peers, colleagues, and other caregivers (including yourself as a current supervisor, but also as a general rule); (4) the capacity to be continually aware of the meaning of an impulse to act, especially if this arises with a feeling of urgency; (5) the integration of techniques from different theoretical perspectives (e.g., cognitive behavioral, psychopharmacologic) with a sensitivity toward how this shift in role may be experienced by the patient or client; (6) the management of boundaries, especially regarding separations, payment of fees, and termination; and (7) overall tolerance of complexity, ambiguity, and forestalling the need to come to a resolution prematurely, which may disempower the client or patient.

In addition, when the opportunity arises, it is most important that some report(s) at some point include a detailed description of an ongoing case that bears some similarity (perhaps in great measure) to the dynamics in the case in which the transgression occurred. This should take primary importance in the supervision and, as mentioned, should be described in great detail in the reports. Verbatim process should also be included, especially when similar pressures on the therapist or analyst have arisen (either from within or from the patient/client). Subtle interpersonal communications, not just frank statements, should be included as well since these often play a significant role in determining interpersonal behavior. It is also warranted to describe in detail the thoughts, ruminations, misgivings, and alternatives that may have occurred to the supervisee as interventions are considered and then finally decided upon. These have great value in demonstrating what the supervisee has learned and the extent to which he or she has taken ownership of previously problematic tendencies.

In this vein, a relevant part of any future treatment will bear on how the therapist tolerates and manages negative feelings expressed by the patient/client. These interactions should be described in detail, along with the supervisor's understanding of the supervisee's prior habits and attitudes related to negative transference. There should be a high value placed on helping the patient/client directly express disappointment, criticism, anger, or any other complaint about the therapy and/or the therapist. These aspects of the transgressor's subsequent treatments should be a major focus of the supervision.

WARNING SIGNS

Schoener (2005) has delineated a comprehensive list of potential problems in a rehabilitative supervision that can serve as grounds for additional scrutiny of the supervisee's work. Among these are:

1. The supervisee appears to be withholding key information or is unwilling to discuss a given case.
2. The supervisee is having contacts outside the professional setting with a client or spouse of a client, or otherwise socializing with clients.

3. The supervisee is being contacted frequently by a given client, with messages left, letters, postcards, unexpected visits outside of appointment times, and so forth.
4. The supervisee is continually arguing for extension of the treatment of a client well beyond normal practice limits; this can refer to length of treatment or frequency of meetings.
5. A family member of either the patient/client or therapist begins raising concerns about their relationship.
6. There is an overall breakdown of responsibilities, including an inability to keep up with record-keeping, missing supervision meetings, and so on; or unexplained absences.
7. Inappropriate gifts by the patient/client or by supervisee.
8. A relationship with the patient/client appears radically different from the supervisee's normal style, such as excessive joking, kidding, fraternizing with a patient/client in the waiting room, and so on.
9. Evidence of excessive self-disclosure by the supervisee, in terms of amount, timing, content, or frequency.
10. Claims that the supervisee and patient/client "have a lot in common" emphasized repeatedly or frequently.
11. Dressing up for the patient/client in terms of clothing or makeup.

There also may be indications of boundary crossings within the supervisory relationship itself. For some supervisees, the tendency to blur boundaries may be a more pervasive style or blind spot that may be the result of inadequate training or personality style. These may include: requesting favors of the supervisor, sliding into a therapeutic or supportive type of relationship rather than focusing on the supervisory work; and, over- or premature familiarity. However, it is difficult to draw a clear line or boundary around supervision since it is frequently reported that the most valued supervisors are those with whom the supervisee has felt a personal connection and with whom one may have socialized. However, the supervision in the context of a rehabilitation plan for sexual boundary violations should have more strongly fortified boundaries than a more casual supervision. It is important to remember that the supervisee in this context will use the supervisor's behavior and attitudes as a major source of identification and role modeling. Further, it is reasonable to assume that the supervisee who has just endured a disciplinary process is in an atypically confused and vulnerable state of mind. He will often report that he has lost his moorings and that everything about his usual way of practicing is being questioned by himself (deservedly so or not). Someone in the supervisory dyad needs to have strong reference points and stable moorings; the boundaries surrounding this relationship should be firmly in place.

SAMPLE SUPERVISORY REPORT: DR. PSYCHOANALYST

Andrea Celenza, Ph.D.
(office address)
(office telephone)

(Date)

(Name of Rehabilitation Coordinator)
(Address of Rehabilitation Coordinator)

Dear Dr. (Rehabilitation Coordinator),

This is the second report on my supervision of Dr. Psychoanalyst that, as you know, began on (date). The supervision continues on a weekly basis. We have had thirty-two supervisory sessions to date (sixteen since my last report) with one interruption in August due to my vacation.

Dr. Psychoanalyst continues to be cooperative and forthcoming in every aspect of our discussions. He continues to provide me with verbatim transcripts of his sessions with several analytic patients. We continue to focus on two female analytic patients, especially with regard to problem areas that coincide with issues that we view as potentially related to those he had encountered with the complainant. There has been no evidence of any tendency to repeat these behaviors and he continues to willingly discuss how his treatment with the complainant went awry as well as how these patients may or may not challenge him in a similar manner.

One hypothesis that we have been considering is that Dr. Psychoanalyst was having considerable difficulty with the complainant's underlying contempt for men, wherein he may have been motivated to (unconsciously) remain as a positive transference object, circumventing the emergence of the patient's hatred or hostility. This is particularly relevant for one of his current female patients as well. Dr. Psychoanalyst continues to tolerate my probing in this area and willingly addresses problems in this area, both in terms of his countertransference and in relation to questions of technique. In the past few months, the patient entered a phase of her analysis that can be described as a more intense version of transference hate that Dr. Psychoanalyst tolerated, explored deeply, and handled skillfully. This coincided with the patient's ability to make important changes in her outside life to the extent that she is considering becoming engaged to be married. (This patient entered treatment with a presenting complaint revolving around difficulties with commitment and intimacy.) We view this as a direct result of her treatment with Dr. Psychoanalyst.

Dr. Psychoanalyst continues to be introspective and revealing with me about the various factors that had caused him to inappropriately self-disclose and sexualize his relationship with the complainant. We have applied this knowledge (about his character and the vulnerable state he was in at the time) to examine potential pitfalls in his work at present. He demonstrates a keen insight into the ways in which boundaries are managed from moment to moment and to the ways in which he lost his way in the past.

I continue to believe that Dr. Psychoanalyst is genuinely and thoroughly engaged in this rehabilitative process. As I have mentioned from the beginning, there is no way I can be sure that he is revealing all of the relevant problematic cases and areas of concern to me, but in the context of what we have discussed, I believe he is handling his cases appropriately and our supervisory relationship is on the right track. In addition, I have no reason to believe that he is not being completely forthcoming in his presentation of his work; the dialogue between us feels quite open and spontaneous.

If you have any further questions or concerns, please do not hesitate to contact me.

Sincerely,

Andrea Celenza, Ph.D.

cc: Dr. Psychoanalyst

SAMPLE SUPERVISORY REPORT: DR. COGNITIVE BEHAVIORIST

Andrea Celenza, Ph.D.
(office address)
(office telephone)

(Date)

(Name of Chair of Licensing Board)
Chair
Board of Registration of Psychologists
(Address of Board)

Dear Dr. (Name of Chair) and Members of the Board,

As agreed and according to the terms of the Consent Agreement, I have been meeting with Dr. Cognitive Behaviorist weekly (50-minute sessions) for the purpose of supervising his clinical work. We began meeting on (date) and have continued weekly in a regularly scheduled manner. There was one interruption due to my vacation in

June. We met on the following dates: (list dates). To date, we have met for a total of 11 sessions.

As you know, Dr. CBT is primarily a cognitive-behavioral therapist; he defines his methods as combining respondent, operant, and social learning theories. He primarily sees clients on a short-term basis and sees clients long-term when clinically indicated. At the start of our supervision, his practice was composed of 12 psychotherapy clients, most of which were short-term cases, through the (Name of Counseling Center–NCC). He also has 3 private psychotherapy clients, all of whom are long-term cases. At this writing, 4 of his psychotherapy cases through NCC have completed their cycle of therapy and have terminated. The other 8 clients remain in treatment and he has acquired one additional case at NCC, for a total of 9 clients through NCC and the 3 continuing private clients. It is our goal to discuss one or two cases every supervisory session so that each case will be discussed at least once or twice by the end of each quarter.

Dr. CBT has been reliable and conscientious as well as open and forthcoming about his work. To his credit, he initially presented the cases he is most uncertain about in addition to those similar to the dynamics involved in the complaint. He has submitted copies of his progress notes on each case weekly, for my review. These include a summary of the presenting problem, diagnosis, a summary of current process, and the treatment plan. He has also provided process notes on cases we discuss during our supervisory hour.

In the course of his case presentations, Dr. CBT and I have had the opportunity to discuss and dissect several issues in his style of work that are relevant to the complaint. As you know, we have the added complexity that Dr. CBT's theoretical orientation is behavioral while mine is psychoanalytic; however, this has proven to be an enriching difference in our work rather than an insurmountable stumbling block. We both have had a diverse training in our histories so that we can speak each other's language to a point. (Dr. CBT has trained and worked for years in psychodynamically oriented Psychology Departments of various teaching hospitals whereas I have had years of behavioral medicine training/experience as well as work adjunctively with behaviorally oriented therapists for some of my current patients.) This melding of diverse language systems and orientations requires that we be specific about our terms with each other and also that we highlight areas of unfamiliarity that otherwise may have been overlooked. It has been my experience (with other supervisees as well) that areas of difference in background and orientation can be fruitful opportunities to examine and discuss boundaries, technical questions, and theoretical principles that serve to clarify areas of confusion or reveal hidden areas of conflict. This is proving to be a fruitful combination of differences in our case as well.

Dr. CBT has a naturally supportive style that facilitates his clients' strengths and builds confidence in a way that is continuously and helpfully in the background of his relational style with each client. He is naturally interested in the "big picture," i.e., the relational context of the therapy, and he has developed techniques described in behavioral terminology but are easily translated into psychodynamic language. For example, he describes one component of his work with each client as "expressive therapy." Upon examination, the process could equivalently be described as supportive, exploratory, and oriented around the analysis of thoughts and feelings. He is also acutely aware of nonverbal aspects of the interaction, both on his part and the client's. He attends to his own nodding, "ahems," and listening behavior, being cognizant of the ways in which these nonverbal behaviors influence or shape the interaction in behavioral terms, such as increasing the prevalence of nouns in the client's speech. In all, I have observed Dr. CBT to be a compassionate and attentive therapist who tries to promote constructive action in his clients.

Dr. CBT has a keen eye when formulating the problematic areas of his clients' presenting concerns. He tends to mix psychodynamic and behavioral formulations in ways that are reasonable and helpful. For example, with a psychotic patient who was initially paralyzed with paranoid fears, Dr. CBT understood her bizarre behavior as organized "operant compulsive behaviors based on guilt." Understood in the context of this patient's history, it became clear that Dr. CBT was honing in on the ways in which this client was overwhelmed with and guilty about her angry and hostile feelings toward her cruel and abusive father. These impulses were unacceptable to her and instead of acting on them, she developed a series of action-oriented rituals that prevented her from expressing her aggression toward her father. Dr. CBT helped her to redirect her anger in more constructive ways by providing positive reinforcement, assertiveness training, and social skills training, all in the context of a supportive relationship with Dr. CBT. Her case has been a significant success for Dr. CBT—she initially was unable to go outside and would hide under her bed. She has now received her high school diploma and has been employed outside the home.

Dr. CBT naturally takes on the role of a benevolent father figure in many of his clients' lives. When we discussed this, he said, "I try to be supportive and noncritical. I want to be a positive influence." With many of his clients, Dr. CBT becomes a person they want to please and make proud. I believe Dr. CBT's presence instinctively creates this relational mode; however, he also actively encourages it by providing supportive and reassuring "pats on the back," as well as teaching various aspects of cognitive restructuring, such as moving away from negative thoughts and changing negative attitudes to positive ones.

We have also discussed areas of concern, including the exploration of a client's sexual history and Dr. CBT's facilitative intentions and style in encouraging these types of expressions. I have stated in no uncertain terms that the sharing of sexual feelings is always inappropriate for a therapist to a client. We have discussed this at length in many ways. First, in terms of point of view, we have identified that a common pitfall for Dr. CBT was the assumption that *his intention* was the same as the client's intention. (This, by the way, is a common misconception in therapists who have boundary management problems.) In the past, Dr. CBT might have scrutinized his own intention in revealing some personal piece of history and concluded that his intent did not contain an erotic component or wish, thus justifying the disclosure. What he overlooked, however, was how the client was likely to hear his disclosure either in the moment or upon later reflection.

We have also discussed the multiple components of the therapy relationship: therapist/client, man/woman, friend/friend, teacher/student, parent/child, and person/person. We have discussed and done relevant reading on this topic as well as compared the supervisory relationship and the multiple components inherent in our own relationship. We have identified important similarities and differences. I have observed Dr. CBT become increasingly clear on the complexity of the relationships and the different ways of managing these. He has sometimes brought in reflections on his own personal therapy relationship as well as relevant readings that have sparked his interest. Finally, we have discussed in detail a prominent case of boundary mismanagement that included much inappropriate sexual disclosure by the therapist and the theoretical misunderstandings involved. Dr. CBT stated, "Behaviorism is reality-based. You would never make yourself into something you're not or never could be to a client." This is an example of Dr. CBT's increasing sensitivity to the awareness and management of the transference in relation to the client *from the client's point of view.*

Dr. CBT and I plan to continue our work in the manner described above. If you need further information from me, please do not hesitate to contact me.

Sincerely,

Andrea Celenza, Ph.D.

cc: Dr. CBT, Ph.D.

ENDNOTE

Portions of this chapter is derived from a paper presented at the annual convention of the American Psychological Association, Chicago, 1996.

Part IV

PREVENTION

13

RESPONSIBLE RESPONSIVITY

The more plainly the [therapist] lets it be seen that he is proof
against every temptation . . . the patient . . . will then feel safe
enough to allow all her preconditions for loving . . . to come to
light.

—S. Freud (1915, p. 166)

A male patient recently said, "The way you pay attention feels like love.
The attention helps, the love doesn't." This statement followed a previous
session where he had proposed that we spend an afternoon "having ecstatic
sex, fall hopelessly in love with each other, and run away together." He knows
I'm married but needed me to say no anyway. It didn't help that some therapists actually have spent such afternoons with their patients.

Today, it is a surprise to hear a patient say that the love in the therapeutic
setting is not much help. We are growing more accustomed to the corrective and healing aspects of the therapeutic situation, especially as they revolve
around loving. Love in the therapy setting is complicated, however, by the
ways in which it is entangled with power imbalances and other asymmetries.

As mentioned in chapter 4, the fundamental question a patient has of his
or her therapist is, Why can't we be lovers? In multiple ways, this is put to the
therapist with intensifying pressure as the treatment evolves. By virtue of the
structure of the therapeutic setting, this question is brought to the foreground
in an increasingly pressured way. The reader is referred to chapter 5 for a more
elaborate discussion of the two defining axes of the therapeutic setting, these
being mutuality and asymmetry (Aron, 1996). A few points discussed in that
chapter will be repeated here since it is the structure of the therapeutic setting
that defines the therapist's responsibility to the patient.

The special combination of mutual, personal engagement along with
an asymmetric distribution of attention (Aron, 1996) is highly seductive.

179

The seductiveness of the therapeutic setting inheres in multiple aspects of the structure, including (1) the offer of unconditional commitment; (2) the way in which the patient is paradoxically positioned, on the one hand as special (and thereby of elevated status) and on the other, in a desiring or needful state (thereby vulnerable and disempowered); (3) various pressures to level the hierarchy, which may arise from within the therapist as well as the patient; and (4) the evocation and persistence of transferences derived from early experience.

SEXUAL METAPHORS IN THERAPY AND PSYCHOANALYSIS

Still, it might be asked, why does the urge to level the hierarchy (prompted either by the patient or the therapist), the desire to disempower one member of the dyad, so often become played out in the sexual realm? As in sadomasochistic relations where the power play in the dyad is polarized in an equally complex way (Celenza, 2000b), this power play between therapist and patient has its own sexual tension.

The tensions between therapist and patient, revolving around power, become sexualized for several reasons. One, because power, in and of itself, is sexy. This is universal, ubiquitous, and part of what the therapist embodies in the psychotherapeutic relational matrix. It is also not gendered. By this, I refer to both the female therapist's phallic power and the seductiveness of male receptivity (Celenza, 2000a). A male patient is fond of rephrasing the Hippocratic Oath by calling it my "Hypocritical Oath." Here he refers to my ethics, my refusal to engage in a sexual relationship with him, as hypocritical, given the seductive and tempting aspects of our psychotherapeutic involvement. This is inherent in the asymmetry of the psychotherapeutic relationship, yet despite (or perhaps by virtue of) this feeling of "being done to," he feels turned on. And so he feels set up. The specific ways in which the therapist derives his or her power transcends typically Western gender stereotypes and are sexy in and of themselves.

Power is sexy because it always was, that is, because this is the way love was experienced in its first instantiation. We are born into a power relation, directing our first loving feelings toward those who have a temporal advantage, to those (parents or a parent) who have come before, so to speak. To be in a relationship with a person more powerful than oneself activates memories and expectations of love relationships structured around a power imbalance, of which the parent-child experience is the prototype. Of course, this is the transference phenomenon upon which psychoanalytic treatment is based and which this treatment aims to explore.

The seductiveness of the therapist's power is derived from multiple aspects of the treatment setting, including (1) the power inherently structured in the asymmetry of the treatment context; (2) the metaphorical nature of the power derived and constituted by the therapeutic role (to hold and penetrate the patient); and (3) the power inherently expressed in one's personality or "way of being" in relation to the patient. This last factor varies with each therapist and will be influenced by the particular match within the dyad as well.

Transference love derived from unresolved oedipal wishes or other developmental moments will be fostered by virtue of the structured asymmetry. And whenever love is in the air, sexual desire is not far behind. Love is, after all, a four-letter word.

In all, the treatment situation (perhaps any intimate relationship) lends itself to sexual metaphor. The dialectic between holding and penetration fosters a mutual deepening and this dialectic is itself a sexual metaphor. For both genders, the psychotherapeutic work on the part of the therapist is both penetrating and enveloping, incisive and holding, a firm receptivity that retains, envelops, and holds the other in one's mind.

Some time ago, a patient struggled with impotence and the internal fear that sexual feelings are dangerous. As he had been gradually allowing his sexuality to surface, he had identified a reticence to stick out, to penetrate, or to accept his desire to be inside the other. He said, "I want you, but I worry I may not be able to keep up with you. You have so many interests. And sexually too."

Hearing an allusion to his anxiety about sustaining an erection, I said, "Keep up?" He responds, "We'd have to work with me. I think I'm sexually competent. But what do women want? I think women want to be raped. A void to be filled. Women like men to be strong. An 'I'm taking you,' Tony Soprano kind of thing. But technique is a question—how long, what to touch, how. I don't know about that. My wife is depressed. She has a lot of baggage. You and I could share intellectually. You work. You're an involved woman. I do tend to feed off the other person's life. I'd get involved in what you like. I'd be interested—I'd be your surrogate."

For this man, sexual fantasies, complicated by desires to hurt and take, threaten self-annihilation in a way that is demonstrated here: he becomes his love object's surrogate. This illustrates a familiar defensive posture of submission in relation to the love object and the way in which love and power, wanting to consume and to hurt, lead to inhibition and selflessness. From my perspective, his mode of relating with me has often felt too focused on me and my thoughts, too "in me," his desire expressed as a wish to appropriate my subjectivity, to be inside me, not *to come in me*, but *to become me* (see Celenza, 2006, for a more elaborated discussion of this case).

Healthy sexuality for each individual involves a mixture of "male" and "female" modes of relating, both phallic and receptive forms of loving. Western societal convention has traditionally bifurcated these gender roles into dichotomous and polarized modes of sexual expression. In Western cultures, males tend to define their sexuality in active and phallic modalities whereas females tend to express their sexuality in passive and/or receptive modes. These stereotypes present different challenges for the therapeutic pair depending on the gender configuration (see, for example, Celenza, 2000a, 2000b; Mayer, 2001).

One way traditional gender stereotypes can be metaphorically experienced is through the expectation that the therapist will make penetrating insights while the patient will receive them or take them in. Similarly, the therapist looks, sees, and penetrates the patient with his or her gaze all the while formulating (doing it to—even sticking it to) the patient. When the therapist is female and the patient is male, the structured power imbalance in the therapeutic setting contradicts these traditional gender stereotypes, at least on an anatomical or concrete level.

For female therapists, there may be a reluctance or conflictually experienced countertransference relating to genital power in its phallic form. As I have written elsewhere (Celenza, 2006), there are culturally determined inhibitions against the full development of aggressive and erotic transferences that can play a role for the female therapist who may unconsciously and defensively foster preoedipal material. Female therapists may unconsciously foreclose awareness of the power inherent in genital sexuality, that is, the phallic nature of "doing to the other" or similar hierarchical, aggressive, and domineering aspects of lovemaking. For female patients, it is a culturally acceptable stance that women are wanting or desiring, encouraging idealization of the powerful phallic figure of the therapist who has what the (female-receptive) patient wants or needs. In contrast, male patients struggle with a powerful resistance to feeling insufficient, impotent, castrated, or as missing something that the therapist provides.

In some cases, containment and receptivity becomes eroticized while penetration is "aggressivized." This is suggested particularly in female therapist/ female patient dyads. In these cases, the therapist's "penetrating insights" can be experienced as one side of a sadomasochistic engagement while the holding/ containing transference provides safety and expresses an eroticized symbiotic longing.

One female patient longed for a previous therapist who seemed to understand her without her having to put her feelings into words. "Psychoanalysis is too intellectual, too left-brain" she complained. "I want you to know what I feel without my having to say it. The act of verbalizing puts distance between us. I want to be close, to be touched without words. She [the former therapist] knew what I was thinking, she would finish my sentences. I think you and I are too different for that to happen." When I asked in what ways she imagined we were different, she responded, "You can't understand, you can't know me, I can't trust you to see me in the way I need. I think you'll hurt me."

Here, it is possible to see the longing for merger, the wish for the therapist to be inside, that is, to know, to touch, and to be close without difference or distance. Holding and containing is conflated with similarity and knowing; difference feels jarring, exterior, and thereby threatening.

THE RESPONSIBILITY OF THERAPEUTIC LOVE AND POWER

There is a profound responsibility attached to the psychotherapist's role. This is directly related to the way in which the psychotherapeutic situation inextricably entangles (and potentially erotizes) love, attention, and power. Every gesture, sentence uttered, or glance can be imbued with sexual meaning. But as Freud so presciently stated, "The patient's falling in love is induced by the analytic situation and is not to be attributed to the charms of [the therapist's] own person" (1915, pp. 160–161). As discussed in this book, the seductiveness of the psychotherapeutic setting is derived from multiple sources and the patient's falling in love is thereby structured into the setting. This fact is definitional and must be *accepted as a given.*

What does it mean to accept the seductiveness of the psychotherapeutic situation as a given? Part of the therapist's responsibility is to keep in mind the multiple ways in which the seductive aspects of the psychotherapeutic situation are tied to the structure itself. These potentials are not caused by personal attributes of the therapist. This both frees the therapist of undue shame or guilt for the ways in which the setting is experienced as hurtful or humiliating, but it also deprives the therapist of an opportunity for narcissistic gratification associated with this power.

The therapist's responsibility begins with an *awareness of the full extent of the seductive power inherent in the psychotherapeutic role* and its multiple constituents. These especially include an appreciation of the complexities involved in the asymmetric attentiveness paid to the patient. As discussed, this asymmetry instantiates a paradox: both therapist and patient are simultaneously empowered and disempowered by it in different ways.

The therapist must continually *withstand pressures to level the asymmetric structure* of the psychotherapeutic situation, from both within himself or herself and from the patient. The decision to become a therapist is comprised of the commitment to attend to the patient unconditionally and to do so in a sustained way. This commitment will arouse in the patient universal and tenaciously held wishes to be loved totally, purely, unconditionally, and omnipotently. On the therapist's part, this commitment entails a constant frustration of the therapist's needs and wishes (see also Akhtar, 2005) that he or she is continually pushed to indulge. These are the conditions of the therapeutic setting that are accepted when a treatment is embarked upon.

The therapist's responsibility also includes helping the patient cope with the paradox of being both empowered and disempowered in relation to the therapist. It is often helpful to describe the asymmetries in the therapeutic context, elucidating what the patient is likely already feeling, in a straightforward and accepting manner. This should also convey compassion for how difficult it is to be in the patient's position. There will be pressures to disempower the therapist in relation to the patient in order to ameliorate the humiliation associated with the disempowering aspect of being in the patient's position. This can be hurtful to the patient in some ways. The therapist must accept the inherent power conferred on him or her by virtue of the asymmetry. This may include resisting gestures toward an impossible egalitarianism that essentially denies and oversimplifies the inherent asymmetry in the psychotherapeutic structure.

It is also important for therapists to recognize the ways in which power itself can become sexualized. It can be said that in psychoanalysis, an ideal is set up that both therapist and patient strive to attain: a phallic, hard receptivity (the kind that can contain any assault) along with an incisive penetration (where the therapist sees and recognizes the hard structures within). Though presented here in stark sexual terms, there is a level at which the patient may feel (consciously or unconsciously) the therapeutic process to be intimate and sexually arousing in just these ways. It is important that the therapist be attuned to these possibilities and ways of experiencing. Many an intervention has been spoken with a benign or naïve intent only to be heard by the patient in explicitly sexual terms.

This chapter has discussed the constituents of therapeutic love, especially as these dimensions relate to the power inherent in the structure of the treatment setting. In turn, erotic and aggressive feelings are often activated in relation to the desire for power, that is, the power perceived in the therapist and/or feelings of disempowerment in relation to the therapist. The constituents of therapeutic love (or any transference that develops in the patient toward the therapist) cannot be considered without reference to the unique structure of the therapeutic setting. In the treatment setting, transference develops in relation to the essential therapeutic matrix, that being the asymmetric distribution of power between therapist and patient. Both aggressive and erotic strivings in the patient will be activated in relation to this power differential, either defensively or as a direct consequence of this structure. This power, if associated with guilt and disavowed by the therapist, can cause the pair to devolve into a sadomasochistic enactment that serves to disclaim the inherent seductiveness of the psychotherapeutic situation. When this kind of dynamic emerges, it is ironic that in the therapist's desperation to restabilize the relationship, overt seduction is often used in order to establish some mode of relating that both communicates and manages the crisis (Celenza, 1991, 1998).

PREVENTING TRANSGRESSION

Many writers have emphasized multiple important preventative measures (Pope et al., 1986; APA Ethics Committee, 1988; Schoener et al., 1989; Gabbard & Lester, 1995a; Gabbard, 1996; Margolis, 1997; Strasburger & Jorgenson, 1992; Gutheil & Gabbard, 1998; Celenza, 1995; Plakun, 1999; Jackson & Nuttal, 2001; Samuel & Gorton, 1998; Gorton & Samuel, 1996). These include: (1) education about boundaries, transference, the power differential, and ethics; (2) supervision on all forms of positive and negative countertransference (the latter emphasizing aggression and hate); and (3) self-care on the part of professionals, including personal treatment for the therapist. Training recommendations suggest that these topics be incorporated into the entirety of academic and clinical education, not limited to isolated or compartmentalized courses in ethics. There should be multiple modalities in the ways in which these issues are discussed, including texts, videotapes, process group experiences, and so forth (see, for example, Gorton, Samuel, & Zebrowski, 1996). Finally, most authors encourage education for providers as well as the consumers of services.

In my experience, all of these recommendations are essential aspects of preventative measures. Sometimes the cause of sexual boundary transgressions lies primarily in the educational sphere; sometimes the lack of self-care on the transgressor's part is glaring. It is rarely solely one thing, however, and, needless to say, it is never the patient's fault.

Hamilton and Spruill (1999) believe the risk of boundary violations in training contexts is related to decline of concern over transference and countertransference, failure to educate students in client-therapist sexual attraction and consequences, and the reluctance of supervisors to deal straightforwardly with trainees' sexual feelings. Regardless of the theoretical orientation of the graduate or training program, basic training on the psychodynamic constructs of transference and countertransference is an essential preventive measure (Ehlert, 2002). Unfortunately, all researchers in this area are well aware that none of these recommendations is a panacea that will prevent sexual boundary violations. However, taken comprehensively and practiced assiduously, the rate of sexual boundary violations can be reduced significantly.

In almost all cases I have seen, however, it is fair to say that by the time the seduction is about to occur, it has already been too late for some time. The recommendations for preventative measures outlined above are endeavors that all professionals must have in place for all of their patients well before they experience trouble in any one particular case. There are two other recommendations I will outline that are also part of a comprehensive, multilayered standard about how professionals should fortify themselves in order to provide ethically based care throughout their careers.

The first involves a measure of introspection about whether and to what extent one has the risk factors that have been identified and outlined in chapter 3. These risk factors are specific enough to determine whether or not a professional falls into a category of potential vulnerability. They are not predictive; however, an empirical study has been performed validating their utility for just this purpose. Chapter 15 presents a questionnaire derived from this study to enhance the ease with which we all can self-assess. I aim to make this a part of the way we practice, and encourage us all to periodically assess ourselves, using the questionnaire attached at the end of this book, in order to help us all self-monitor and guide ourselves for further self-care if need be.

The second recommendation involves the context in which we work and the way this context is presented to ourselves, our colleagues, our patients, and the public at large. Therapy happens in real time and space. This is the concrete context of the psychodynamic process with specific reference to the limits and constraints imposed by reality, yet these reality constraints are often forgotten. Illusions are created based on unconscious wishes that can go unrecognized: the universal wish for immortality, the wish that time were endless, that the therapeutic dyad exists within some kind of ungrounded bubble—a special, safe place where time, space, and moral prohibitions do not apply. These are dangerous illusions.

As Greenberg (1999) reminds us, some analyses are too dangerous and never get started; others are too safe and never end. Similarly, Cooper (2000b) refers to the "conspiratorial timeless unconscious," the part of us that can easily engage therapy for its own sake, setting aside the important pressure and need for therapeutic gain in real time, that is, before death. These constraints are easy to resist or deny; no one wants to face mortality and limits.

Likewise, there is what I will call "the illusion of the dyad" that presents itself as a temptation to deny spatial constraints, in other words, the boundaries that exist between this relationship and all others. Boundaries demarcate one from another; essentially and primarily, boundaries mark difference. It is by virtue of a boundary that we can distinguish self from other, as well as one dyad from another and all other relationships. The boundary defines what is within and without based on similarity and difference. It is by virtue of this defining that boundaries give meaning to context. Sometimes the context is the larger set of which the dyad is a subset; sometimes what is external to the boundary is the opposite of what is internal. In this latter case, we know who we are by knowing who we are not and vice versa. An example is that the therapeutic couple is a dyad different from a marriage.

When a boundary demarcates a subset within a larger set, the boundary represents less a mark of difference than one of similarity, and in this case, can be more easily forgotten or disavowed. I refer here to the tendency to deny the context within which we all work, the context of the third, the professional community that gives our work its meaning. Just like incest is defined by the familial context, our meetings with our patients are defined by the context and structure within which they occur. The psychotherapeutic process is unusual, especially with regard to the asymmetric distribution of attention, and we can conduct this unusual way of conversing because the context is endorsed by a professional morality and way of doing things. This is a context that often remains unnamed, but is part of the background, the everyday atmosphere within which the process occurs. It gives our sessions meaning.

It is easy to deny this unnamed atmosphere and foster an illusion that the therapeutic couple exists outside of this space. In cases of sexual boundary violations, this illusion becomes its own reason for being as therapist and patient describe their experience as "special," one or the other as "exceptions," either of them as "the only persons capable of understanding the other," and finally, "a process in which the usual rules do not apply." These phrases reflect the absence of the essential grounding, contextualized meanings of the morality as defined by the therapeutic community.

Confidentiality is an essential part of the psychotherapeutic matrix that makes exploration of the unconscious possible. I am suggesting, however, that a kind of "hyper-confidentiality" occurs in cases of sexual boundary violations where either party may insist that the treatment be surrounded by an impermeable membrane. In these misalliances, such insularity is sometimes insisted upon as a condition for treatment where either the therapist or patient demands total secrecy, even excluding supervision, consultation, and the like. The patient may say, "I can't continue this treatment if you talk about me with anyone." Or the therapist may insist that the patient tell no one of what occurs between them. This has been referred to as the creation of a treatment "bubble," an insularity that is one of the last steps in the slippery slope.

However, most psychoanalyses and psychotherapies are conducted with at least a tacit understanding (on both parts) that the treatment will be periodically and anonymously reviewed in such contexts as consultation, supervision, and/or peer groups. Conducting treatment without explicit reference to these "thirds" can support the idea of the dyad as existing outside of temporal and spatial constraints, and creates the illusion of an exclusive, closed system that is at best a fantasy and at worst, a harmful reality.

Here, I do more than offer a new way of thinking about the problem of sexual boundary violations in our work. I suggest we use this understanding with specific recommendations for technique. I suggest that in all therapies and analyses we make explicit the implicit spatial context at the beginning of the treatment and throughout—not just between therapist and patient, but in real space, that is, in peer groups, consulting, and/or supervisory contexts. When we begin a treatment, I suggest that we state explicitly to the patient that the process will be periodically discussed (confidentially and anonymously) with a consultant, peer group, and/or supervisor.

What I suggest here is to make explicit that the therapeutic couple exists within a larger context and that this context will not be forgotten and that these ties and boundaries will not be severed. Mostly this occurs anyway, but it is rare, outside of control cases, that it is made known to the patient. Here it is important to note that it is one of the disturbing features in cases of sexual boundary transgressions that these ties to consultants, supervisors, or other members of the professional community are woefully and sometimes purposefully lacking, despite the fact that many writers on sexual boundary violations have emphasized the need for periodic consultations on all cases (Schoener et al., 1989; Gabbard, 1996, 2000; Gutheil & Gabbard, 1998; Plakun, 1999; Jackson & Nuttall, 2001; Davies, 2000; B. Pizer, 2000). The transgressor will often say, in retrospect, "I thought of going to a consultant, but I couldn't stop." When an analyst or therapist is sexually engaged with a patient, it is already too late. I am suggesting establishing an explicit context in real time and space from the start.

Sometimes the patient insists that the therapist must not consult with anyone about her case, ever. This may be stated by the patient at the outset. It is useful here to ask, "What is that wish about?"—the desire to create a space that is *beyond private, beyond confidential,* to create a space that is *secret,* with all its implications of a forbidden liaison, existing outside of acceptable and realistic limits. There are profound differences between privacy, confidentiality, and secrecy. Can these wishes be explored without being acted upon (that basic tenet of psychoanalysis), and can the fantasy surface for the patient even if a third is a known player in the larger context? I would say yes.

We cannot avoid participating in an enactment, but enactments differ in meaning and impact. Participating in the illusion of the dyad gratifies an omnipotent preoedipal and regressive oedipal wish: to be "the one and only" or the fantasy that there isn't competition with or envy of a third. By colluding with this omnipotent wish (either through silence or by actually avoiding consultation), we enact a childhood illusory dyadic fantasy. By acknowledging the existence of a third, we establish a triadic context and challenge the patient (and therapist) to mourn and, in this way, help the patient grow.

ENDNOTE

This chapter is derived from a forthcoming paper, A. Celenza (in press). "Analytic love and power: Responsible responsivity," *Psychoanalytic Inquiry*.

14

LOVE AND HATE IN THE COUNTERTRANSFERENCE: PREVENTING VIOLATIONS THROUGH SUPERVISION

> If all goes well, the infant can actually come to gain from the
> experience of frustration since incomplete adaptation to need
> makes objects real, that is to say, hated as well as loved. . . . Ex-
> act adaptation resembles magic and the object that behaves per-
> fectly becomes no better than an hallucination.
>
> —D. W. Winnicott (1971, p. 11)

Usually, by the time a vulnerable therapist notices he is on that dangerous slippery slope, it is already too late. This chapter aims to delineate
subtle predisposing attitudes and misunderstandings about the therapy process
that provide the feeding ground for later rationalizations. Even if a therapist
is not vulnerable to frank sexual misconduct, these concerns and misunderstandings, observable in a supervisory context, are worth taking up as points
of clarification in any case.

Not surprisingly, therapists who have engaged in sexual intimacies with
their patients present with deeper and more problematic issues than can be addressed solely in supervision or consultation. As noted in chapter 3, the motivation for the sexual transgression most often involves unconscious, split-off,
or compartmentalized conflicts (Celenza, 1998) that can only be resolved in
the context of an intensive psychotherapy or psychoanalysis. These issues are
usually related to personal vulnerabilities in the narcissistic realm and render
the therapist vulnerable to destructive enactments as intolerable helplessness,
loss of self-esteem, or even rage are evoked.

In the present chapter, common confusions of transgressing therapists (and
the unconscious function these confusions can potentially serve) are discussed

191

to assist supervisors in working with trainees of all levels, but especially those who may have difficulty with boundaries.

The most salient finding in almost all of the difficulties with which these therapists struggle involves some misunderstanding of, rationalization about, and/or unconscious defensive transformation of love and/or hate in the countertransference. On a conscious level, there are numerous rationalizations that reflect an overvaluing of countertransference love with an underlying intolerance of countertransference hate. This issue calls to mind a familiar quote (reprinted above) from Winnicott (1971) where he refers to the mother-infant dyad analogously to the therapy relationship, and the usefulness of empathic failure so that the infant learns of the mother's separateness and difference.

SUPERVISORY CONCERNS

Training for most therapists is largely inadequate in the area of tolerating and empathically responding to negative transferences. In the past ten years, there has been a decline in the concern over and training about the phenomena of transference and countertransference in general as psychology and psychiatry programs have become less psychodynamic or psychoanalytic in orientation. In addition, there is insufficient attention to intense countertransference reactions in general and much misunderstanding about countertransference love in particular. The reluctance on the part of supervisors to straightforwardly address trainees' sexual feelings has been noted for some time (Hamilton, 1999; Woolley, 1988). This is also reflected in the paucity of literature on countertransference love, which is striking when compared to the relatively more abundant literature on countertransference hate. The imbalance in the literature probably reflects a more general lack of clarity in the field. I would also suggest that because there is inherent ambiguity in and much misunderstanding about countertransference love, it can be unconsciously recruited for defensive purposes, leading the therapist to overvalue the extent to which his or her "loving feelings" for the patient can be therapeutic.

Though vulnerable therapists show an acute intolerance of the negative transference along with an intolerance of their own countertransference hate, the lack of clarity regarding countertransference love allows for certain rationalizations and defensive transformations to occur such that so-called countertransference love can mask underlying hostility or other negative feelings toward the patient. Based on countertransference or not, love is not healing in and of itself, though many offending therapists hold to that belief. As Levine (1997) has argued, it is ultimately the use to which countertransference is put that determines whether it constitutes an interference or facilitates the thera-peutic process. The idea that the love of the therapist, by itself, can cure the patient is alarmingly naïve (Twemlow & Gabbard, 1989).

It is interesting to note that Freud's papers on technique were written during a time when he was corresponding to Ernest Jones about his flagrant seductive behavior and frank sexual involvements with numerous patients (see Paskauskas, 1993; Gabbard & Lester, 1995a, for further discussion of this cor-respondence). There is an implication that Freud's development of abstinence, neutrality, and anonymity, as the hallmark components of a proper analytic stance, derived from his concern about Jones and the boundary transgressions of other analysts during this time (Gabbard & Lester, 1995a).

So why might there still be less literature on countertransference love in comparison to the literature on countertransference hate? Remarkably, the misunderstandings of each seem to coincide and I have wondered if the same issues explain both. That is, the very reasons why there *is* literature on countertransference hate may also explain the relative *absence* of literature on countertransference love. These misunderstandings occur in the same three areas, including: (1) how the alliance is conceived, (2) how therapists view themselves and their professional self-image, and (3) how the process of em-pathy is understood.

COUNTERTRANSFERENCE HATE AND THE ALLIANCE

The first point relates to the way the alliance is conceived. Therapists recognize when they feel hateful toward their patients because *hateful feelings interfere with the therapist's capacity to establish an alliance*. Countertransference hate is viewed as incompatible with the warm and positive feelings evoked in the therapist in response to the patient's wish for engagement. Countertransference hate impedes the development of the positively toned affective, relational aspect of the alliance and holding environment needed to promote an atmosphere of safety and trust.

Maltsberger and Buie (1974) have described hatred as a mixture of aver-sion and malice that is difficult to bear and may tempt the therapist to abandon the patient. This may not be a conscious impulse. For example, the therapist may question his expertise or consider transferring the patient to another col-league in pursuit of a "better match." Alternatively, countertransference hate can take the form of psychological withdrawal (feelings of boredom or fatigue during the patient's hours); the therapist might become overly anxious about the patient's safety (in reaction to his own unconscious murderous wishes), or even defensively transform his countertransference hate into its opposite and act out dramatic rescue fantasies that deprive the patient from taking appropriate responsibility for her life.

It is inevitable that countertransference feelings will be comprised of the full range of affects and the therapist's countertransference feelings must be well sorted out, conscious, and bearable for the maintenance of evenhanded and caring attention (Winnicott, 1949). Love and hate always coexist in the countertransference; tolerance of ambivalent feelings toward our patients is necessary to facilitate effective and empathic interventions. In Winnicott's important paper on hate in the countertransference (1949), he stated, "However much [the therapist] loves his patients he cannot avoid hating them, and fearing them, and the better he knows this the less will hate and fear be the motive determining what he does to his patients" (p. 69).

COUNTERTRANSFERENCE LOVE AND THE ALLIANCE

In contrast to the recognition of countertransference hate as incompatible with a positive alliance, countertransference love can be overlooked because it can be *confused with the alliance.* Therapists may view their countertransference love as an aspect of the positive and warm feelings therapists should have toward their patients in order to respond to the patient's wish for engagement.

Similarly, the patient's transference love may not be noticed or addressed because the patient's positive view of the therapist is seen as an objective appreciation of the therapeutic frame (or the therapist's person). Examples of this are the belief that a patient's positive transference helps the therapy proceed and implies that the treatment is successful. One therapist had an unusually strong reaction if a patient expressed dissatisfaction with his treatment. He typically reacted by referring the patient to another therapist or, in one case, referred the patient for psychological testing.

The therapeutic context centers on the provision of safety, warmth, care, and even love to some extent, so that the relationship is conducive to self-exploration. It can be difficult to tease apart transference manifestations from appreciation of the comforting and nurturant holding that comprise the therapeutic context. The transference and nontransference elements of such positive feelings often remain unexplored. As mentioned, they may be viewed as appropriate reactions to the therapeutic frame and are taken for granted. Such misunderstandings about the alliance and countertransference love overlook the possibility that a positive alliance can function as a resistance to probing deeper or to avoid upsetting an easy balance (Stein, 1981).

In contrast, the mark of a strong alliance is an attitude of openness toward the entire range of the patient's feelings as well as the entire range of one's own. A truly safe alliance includes permission for the patient to feel and express defiance, revenge, or devaluation of the therapist. A genuine commitment to one's patients involves an openness to all parts of them.

COUNTERTRANSFERENCE HATE AND PROFESSIONAL SELF-IMAGE

The second issue involves misunderstandings of countertransference hate and love as these feelings bear on the way therapists like to view themselves and their professional self-image. Abel, Osborn, and Warberg (1995) note cognitive distortions that serve to rationalize sexual boundary violations in order to preserve the therapist's image of himself. Along similar lines, countertransference hate is more easily recognized because it is felt to be *inconsistent with the therapist's professional self-image*. Maltsberger and Buie (1974) have discussed this aspect of countertransference hate in the following manner: "We conceive ourselves to be compassionate, caring and nonjudgemental, and often predicate our professional self-respect on not being rejecting, punitive, sadistic, murderous and disgusted with patients" (p. 628). Coupled with the extra-burdensome, often unconscious expectations held by therapists to cure all, know all, and especially, *love all*, the evocation of countertransference hate can effectively diminish our professional and personal feelings of self-worth. Further, some therapists hold themselves to the impossible standard of loving all of their patients all of the time.

Winnicott (1949) discussed countertransference hate as sometimes representing an objective and justified reaction to the patient. It is essential to establish an atmosphere in the treatment where the full complexity of the patient's experience can be explored. Hateful or angry reactions on the patient's part can be clarifying, provide a sense of purpose "vis-à-vis a world of clear-cut enemies" (Epstein, 1977, p. 451), or provide an opportunity for defensive counterattack around which a clearly defined sense of self may coalesce. In this way, the boundaries of the self are reinforced in relation to and at a safe distance from the threatening presence of the other (Epstein, 1977).

In contrast, a therapist's benevolent, loving, or benign responses to such hostility can be experienced as amorphous, seductive, or confusing for those with fragile egos and profound mistrust. Loving reactions in this context can add to an already unbearable sense of helplessness; that is, not only do these patients fail to make others love them, they also fail to make others hate them.

Hateful expressions by the patient naturally evoke hatred in the therapist in proportion to the need to be valued and liked by patients. For a therapist to feel otherwise in the face of these narcissistic injuries is inauthentic and may even appear hypocritical (Epstein, 1977).

Therapist self-disclosure is a controversial point of technique. Some analysts (see Hoffer, 1985) maintain that it is sufficient to use one's hateful reactions as a signal of a countertransference reaction. Patients cannot always take another's feelings into account, especially at times of exacerbated regression. Disclosure by the therapist can also detract from the analysis of the subjective experience of the patient. On the other hand, self-disclosure can be useful as it can diminish the authoritarian, imbalanced aspect to the relationship and acknowledges the therapist's participation in the intersubjective field. In addition, the therapist's capacity to identify his or her own aggression can be clarifying and relieving to the patient by demonstrating the therapist's tolerance of negative affective states.

Racker (1972) was concerned with the reluctance of analysts to write about countertransference in general and related it to a mythologic ideal of "objectivity" to which many analysts previously adhered. He wondered if the myth of the "analyst without anxiety or anger" might have served to diminish the analyst's fear of being overwhelmed by his own feelings, thereby losing his "objectivity." Racker described a realistic objectivity, attainable by a kind of internal division that enables the therapist to take himself as an object and observe his own countertransference reactions. Despite greater awareness of the analyst's contribution to the intersubjective field since Racker's writings, I have found that the myth of the therapist (analyst) without anger or aggression persists. For the narcissistically vulnerable therapists considered here, this myth is present as an idealized self-image and conscious value.

COUNTERTRANSFERENCE LOVE
AND PROFESSIONAL SELF-IMAGE

In contrast to the recognition of countertransference hate as incompatible with one's professional self-image, it is easy to overlook countertransference love because countertransference love is viewed as *consistent with the therapist's professional self-image*. Further, countertransference love is often felt in the context of the patient's positive transference, the so-called unobjectionable part of the transference. This aspect of the patient's feelings for the therapist can gratify the therapist's narcissistic needs and enhance his or her professional self-image, contributing to the therapist's love for the patient. Stein (1981) commented on several factors that may make the therapist unwilling to scrutinize the positive transference:

> The trusting positive attitude of the [patient] does allow the [therapy] to continue and is comfortable for both parties. . . . Second, it seems to be free of conflict. Third, it seems to make sense, to be entirely rational that one person should admire and trust another who is so worthy of it. (pp. 880–881)

Obviously, therapists feel gratified when patients view them in a positive or loving manner. Elvin Semrad is remembered as having said to an adoring patient, "You feel this way for neurotic reasons and when you get better, I will be very sad." Such positive feelings toward a therapist coincide with a wished-for self-image. A problem occurs, however, when narcissistically vulnerable therapists need their patients to sustain their self-esteem. A patient can unconsciously adapt to the needs of the therapist and can be all too willing to suppress conflict-laden, negative feelings if it is sensed that such expressions would not be tolerated. One female patient described the constraining effect of such a dynamic and reported, "I felt there was less and less I could talk about without sensing his discomfort."

COUNTERTRANSFERENCE HATE AND EMPATHY

The last issue involves how the process of empathy is understood. Countertransference hate is again more easily recognized as it is often *mistakenly viewed as unempathic*. This view derives from a misunderstanding of the process of empathy. Empathy is a skill, a neutral process—not a feeling state per se. It involves a simultaneous process of feeling resonant with the patient while remaining apart and observing one's own reactions. The capacity for empathy includes a feeling involvement—temporary and partial, but a feeling involvement all the same—that is comprised of imagining oneself in the other's experience and feeling what the other feels by finding in oneself an analogous experience.

At the same time, another part of the self observes, evaluates, analyzes, and remembers so as to make use of the experience in a comprehensive way (Schafer, 1959). There is an evaluation of the feeling state in the context of what is known about the patient, and an appreciation of the meaning the particular experience has for the patient given all else that is known about the patient, including the therapist's formulation of the patient's dynamic structure. The feeling or resonant component of empathy involves a temporary suspension of ego boundaries—a loss of self-other differentiation where there is a momentary, if not illusory (Buie, 1981), feeling of being the other—*a regression in the service of understanding* (Celenza, 1986). Empathy is a dialectical process in which the therapist constructs a unique model of the patient's experience by virtue of the therapist's use of his or her own emotional experiences. In this way, empathy is a self-mediated process which engenders a continual stream of jointly created events (Levine, 1997).

Hoffer (1985) defines empathy as the analyst's understanding of the patient's conflict in a neutral way from the patient's point of view. Failure of empathy, then, is an abandonment of this neutral position. Consistent with this is the idea that empathy itself is a *process* of understanding feelings, *not a particular feeling*. It is neutral in the sense that it has no a priori affective valence. It is a process that allows for simultaneous involvement and detachment, with concomitant subjective and objective components. It is a process that allows for an openness to whatever the patient presents. In that sense, it is essentially value-free (Basch, 1983).

COUNTERTRANSFERENCE LOVE AND EMPATHY

Countertransference hate is no more unempathic than countertransference love is empathic. Yet, countertransference love may go unrecognized because it is often *confused with empathy*. This is a misconception of the process of empathy where feeling loving toward the patient is viewed as having empathy for them. I believe this occurs as therapists feel pressured by demands within the transference to *provide* what is needed rather than *understand* what is needed. Therapeutic understanding is promoted, in part, by tolerating frustration in the face of nongratification of transference demands. Such nongratification may threaten to evoke the negative transference, signaling an opportunity for the patient to expand his or her understanding. At these moments, however, countertransference love can be unconsciously recruited to mask or circumvent countertransference hate.

CONCLUSION

Countertransference love does not always reflect a defensive process; however, when it is felt by the therapist as intensely compelling, a defensive process is likely. Ongoing consultation for all of our therapies is becoming a constant refrain, but for those patients whom we feel loving and positively toward, we may feel the need less urgently. Once the therapist's countertransference love reaches a more intense level, there can be a more overt resistance to seeking consultation. Perhaps there is a fear of exposing "inappropriate" feelings or shame at losing the capacity to maintain the boundaries of the therapeutic frame. The road to emotional stability and health, however, is not straightforward, and periodic consultation should be viewed as an expectable need. Since we know that denied or disavowed feelings are most likely to be acted out, it is incumbent upon us to provide safe contexts in which therapists can regularly process and expose their own vulnerability, especially as this involves genuine and intense engagement with their patients. It is a matter of practicing what we preach.

Supervisors notoriously have difficulty discussing a supervisee's passionate or loving feelings for their patients. When supervisees express the wish to talk about their loving or erotic feelings toward their patients, a common reaction is for supervisors to refer them to relevant literature (which is scant) or recommend they bring these issues up in their personal therapy. Gabbard's (1994c) skillful and sensitive handling of a supervisee's erotic feelings toward her patient should serve as a model for the provision of a safe context in which a supervisee may explore his or her countertransference and ultimately make use of it for the patient's benefit.

Ironically, it appears to be easier to expose one's dislike, hatred, or anger toward patients than intensely loving feelings. This may be related to the greater attention paid to countertransference hate in the literature, as if permission has been granted and there exists a language for countertransference hate that has yet to be developed for countertransference love.

I suggest as well that hatred for patients is easier to bear than love. Most people find it easier to deal with angry feelings than loving feelings because hateful and angry feelings bring with them a sense of being armed, ready for battle, and with a specific purpose (if only in fantasy). Loving feelings carry with them no such armor; rather, there is a sense of exposure, defenselessness, and vulnerability. Since all therapeutic endeavors are ultimately aimed at the enhancement of the capacity for intimacy, it is essential that therapists have the capacity to love their patients without threat, confusion, or shame. In order for this to occur, a professional atmosphere of tolerance, safety, and clarity is needed, as well as an appreciation for the complexity, ambiguity, and inherently paradoxical nature of the therapeutic dyad.

A final word needs to be said regarding a supervisor's ethical responsibility and legal liability in the context of the supervisory relationship. In these times of deep-pocket litigation, there are disturbing but necessary questions that must be addressed when efforts to prevent harm are taken up. In general, a distinction can be made between case consultation and supervision revolving largely around the extent of control over and responsibility for the treatment provided (Kaslow, 1986; Schoener et al., 1989). Case consultation is most often a time-limited, even one-time, overview of some aspect of the treatment for specific or general guidance. Case consultation does not carry with it the assumption that the consultant bears any control over or responsibility for the treatment. The supervisor, in contrast, is usually hired or assigned through an agency for a longer duration and this context does assume control over and responsibility for the treatment. Therefore, greater care must be taken to oversee the cases appropriated to the supervision.

Thus, it behooves a supervisor to take special care if he or she detects any of the warning signs discussed in this chapter. This might include a thorough discussion of the issues of concern, careful monitoring of process notes, tracking of each case for which the supervisor has oversight, requesting audiorecording of the supervisee's therapy sessions, and direct consultation with the patient either by the supervisor or a third party. For the benefit of the supervisee, it is often useful to recommend a personal psychotherapy if he or she is not already in one. Finally, the supervisor has a wider responsibility involving reporting the supervisee's vulnerabilities or areas of weaknesses to his or her training director (see chapters 12 and 14 for related discussions).

15

BOUNDARY VIOLATIONS
VULNERABILITY INDEX (BVVI)

This chapter presents the Boundary Violations Vulnerability Index (BVVI), an assessment instrument designed as a signal to practitioners of the presence or absence of several precursors of vulnerability to sexual boundary violations. The BVVI is offered as a tool for practitioners of all theoretical orientations to use either privately or with a trusted colleague or friend for self-monitoring purposes. It is hoped that this measure will aid practitioners in identifying risk factors *before* any steps on the slippery slope are taken. Ideally, this measure should be used before practitioners are licensed or ready to practice, that is, in training settings for trainees of all orientations. It is designed to self-administer and thereby identify those areas that should be a focus of attention as part of trainees' preparation to become a clinical practitioner. Many of the issues identified by this measure are grist for the therapeutic mill and thus, once identified, can be taken to one's personal therapy for further discussion, exploration, and resolution.

Equally important, this measure is offered for the seasoned clinician to periodically monitor his or her vulnerability, especially in times of stress. As has been amply demonstrated through the study of sexual boundary violations, the one-time transgressor violates boundaries when he or she has *both* long-standing vulnerabilities and acute situational stress. This measure is designed to help clinicians identify the long-standing, potential precursors. Once these have been identified, it is hoped that these issues will be brought to one's personal therapy and be effectively addressed. At the same time, it is well known that in times of stress, old patterns reemerge and there can be a reversion to familiar but less adaptive ways of coping. Therefore, if a clinician knows that he or she has the vulnerabilities that represent potential precursors of sexual boundary violations, this measure can be especially helpful in times of stress to repeatedly self-monitor one's level of risk. It is likely, for example, that scores will be higher on this measure during stressful periods since there may be a tendency to rate oneself more harshly. When old patterns are triggered, this measure can be a useful signal that a return to treatment is indicated.

The precursors that the BVVI is designed to identify are only those associated with the one-time transgressor and not the more egregious multiple offense transgressor. The vulnerabilities that underlie these precursors are presented and discussed at length in chapters 1, 2, and 3. This measure is designed to identify those factors that are associated with the narcissistically needy practitioner, the lovesick character, and/or those with a tendency toward "masochistic surrender." In addition, this measure may be helpful in identifying the precursors to sexual boundary violations in general, one that might not comprise a character type previously described, but might identify those factors that comprise a vulnerability by themselves or in another category of personality organization.

It should be noted that the BVVI does not identify psychopathic predatory character features. As noted in many instances throughout this book, psychopathic characteristics are not amenable to rehabilitation and probably do not accord with any preventative measures that the practitioner is likely to take upon noting his or her vulnerability.

The BVVI has not been empirically tested and has not been standardized, so comparison to a normative sample is not yet possible. It is also not a predictive tool since no prospective studies have been performed to date. In addition, the BVVI aims to measure those precursors that have been identified largely in male transgressors. Though female transgressors certainly do exist, they are fewer in number and preliminary studies indicate some overlap yet also some distinctive features from male transgressors. I have added items that refer to the characteristics of female transgressors; however, my sample of these is smaller and there has been no empirical study of this population. I believe, however, the BVVI will be useful for both male and female practitioners until further studies have been carried out that control for gender differences. It is hoped that all of these studies will be carried out in the future.

BVVI
Boundary Violations Vulnerability Index

This questionnaire assesses various attitudes, behaviors, and self-observations of you and/or your parents. Some refer to present-day observations; others refer to childhood experiences (before age 16). Answer each item as you know yourself *in the context of close, personal relationships* (including therapy relationships). Place a tick in the most appropriate brackets next to each question.

	Very Like	Somewhat Like	Somewhat Unlike	Very Unlike
1. My mother spoke to me with a warm and friendly voice.	( )	( )	( )	( )
2. Setting limits on others is difficult for me.	( )	( )	( )	( )
3. My mother let me do those things I liked.	( )	( )	( )	( )
4. My father was always reliable and consistent.	( )	( )	( )	( )
5. I can't say no to people.	( )	( )	( )	( )
6. If someone close to me makes me mad, I let him or her know it right away.	( )	( )	( )	( )
7. My privacy is very important to me.	( )	( )	( )	( )
8. My parents adopted a "do as I say, not as I do" kind of child-rearing.	( )	( )	( )	( )
9. My mother seemed emotionally cold to me.	( )	( )	( )	( )
10. My mother appeared to understand my problems and worries.	( )	( )	( )	( )
11. I am assertive and direct when I'm angry.	( )	( )	( )	( )
12. My mother liked me to make my own decisions.	( )	( )	( )	( )
13. My mother did not want me to grow up.	( )	( )	( )	( )
14. My father was quite variable in his responses to me; warm sometimes and cold others.	( )	( )	( )	( )
15. My mother was affectionate to me.	( )	( )	( )	( )
16. My mother did not help me as much as I needed.	( )	( )	( )	( )
17. I feel responsible for other people's problems.	( )	( )	( )	( )
18. My mother tried to control everything I did.	( )	( )	( )	( )
19. My mother invaded my privacy.	( )	( )	( )	( )
20. I am a people pleaser.	( )	( )	( )	( )
21. My parents were hypocritical in the way they lived and preached.	( )	( )	( )	( )
22. My mother appreciated ways we were different.	( )	( )	( )	( )
23. I tend to defer to what others want of me.	( )	( )	( )	( )

	Very Like	Somewhat Like	Somewhat Unlike	Very Unlike
24. My father wanted me to be the way he wanted.	( )	( )	( )	( )
25. My mother or father confided his or her problems to me.	( )	( )	( )	( )
26. My mother did not seem to understand what I needed and wanted.	( )	( )	( )	( )
27. I worry about hurting people's feelings so much that I avoid confrontation.	( )	( )	( )	( )
28. My mother let me decide things for myself.	( )	( )	( )	( )
29. I get overinvolved in other people's problems.	( )	( )	( )	( )
30. My mother made me feel I wasn't wanted.	( )	( )	( )	( )
31. I was the only one in my family who understood my mother (or father).	( )	( )	( )	( )
32. My parents were strict with me but lax with themselves.	( )	( )	( )	( )
33. My mother was attuned to my feelings.	( )	( )	( )	( )
34. My father loved me and showed it.	( )	( )	( )	( )
35. My mother tried to make me dependent on her.	( )	( )	( )	( )
36. People take advantage of me and I seem to let them.	( )	( )	( )	( )
37. My mother felt I could not look after myself unless she was around.	( )	( )	( )	( )
38. Other people's needs always come first.	( )	( )	( )	( )
39. Only I could deal with my mother's (or father's) problems.	( )	( )	( )	( )
40. At least one parent was involved in unethical or illegal behavior (e.g., infidelity, financial misdeeds, or the like).	( )	( )	( )	( )
41. My mother let me go out as often as I wanted.	( )	( )	( )	( )
42. I am too open about myself.	( )	( )	( )	( )
43. My father was unassertive.	( )	( )	( )	( )
44. My mother did not praise me.	( )	( )	( )	( )
45. I felt responsible for my mother's (or father's) well-being.	( )	( )	( )	( )

BVVI
Boundary Violations Vulnerability Index
Scoring Method

Score each item as indicated depending on the column ticked by your responses. Add up the scores for a grand total.

	Very Like	Somewhat Like	Somewhat Unlike	Very Unlike
1. My mother spoke to me with a warm and friendly voice.	(1)	(2)	(3)	(4)
2. Setting limits on others is difficult for me.	(4)	(3)	(2)	(1)
3. My mother let me do those things I liked.	(1)	(2)	(3)	(4)
4. My father was always reliable and consistent.	(1)	(2)	(3)	(4)
5. I can't say no to people.	(4)	(3)	(2)	(1)
6. If someone close to me makes me mad, I let him or her know it right away.	(1)	(2)	(3)	(4)
7. My privacy is very important to me.	(1)	(2)	(3)	(4)
8. My parents adopted a "do as I say, not as I do" kind of child-rearing.	(4)	(3)	(2)	(1)
9. My mother seemed emotionally cold to me.	(4)	(3)	(2)	(1)
10. My mother appeared to understand my problems and worries.	(1)	(2)	(3)	(4)
11. I am assertive and direct when I'm angry.	(1)	(2)	(3)	(4)
12. My mother liked me to make my own decisions.	(1)	(2)	(3)	(4)
13. My mother did not want me to grow up.	(4)	(3)	(2)	(1)
14. My father was quite variable in his responses to me; warm sometimes and cold others.	(4)	(3)	(2)	(1)
15. My mother was affectionate to me.	(1)	(2)	(3)	(4)
16. My mother did not help me as much as I needed.	(4)	(3)	(2)	(1)
17. I feel responsible for other people's problems.	(4)	(3)	(2)	(1)
18. My mother tried to control everything I did.	(4)	(3)	(2)	(1)
19. My mother invaded my privacy.	(4)	(3)	(2)	(1)
20. I am a people pleaser.	(4)	(3)	(2)	(1)
21. My parents were hypocritical in the way they lived and preached.	(4)	(3)	(2)	(1)

	Very Like	Somewhat Like	Somewhat Unlike	Very Unlike
22. My mother appreciated ways we were different.	(1)	(2)	(3)	(4)
23. I tend to defer to what others want of me.	(4)	(3)	(2)	(1)
24. My father wanted me to be the way he wanted.	(4)	(3)	(2)	(1)
25. My mother or father confided his or her problems to me.	(4)	(3)	(2)	(1)
26. My mother did not seem to understand what I needed and wanted.	(4)	(3)	(2)	(1)
27. I worry about hurting people's feelings so much that I avoid confrontation.	(4)	(3)	(2)	(1)
28. My mother let me decide things for myself.	(1)	(2)	(3)	(4)
29. I get overinvolved in other people's problems.	(4)	(3)	(2)	(1)
30. My mother made me feel I wasn't wanted.	(4)	(3)	(2)	(1)
31. I was the only one in my family who understood my mother (or father).	(4)	(3)	(2)	(1)
32. My parents were strict with me but lax with themselves.	(4)	(3)	(2)	(1)
33. My mother was attuned to my feelings.	(1)	(2)	(3)	(4)
34. My father loved me and showed it.	(1)	(2)	(3)	(4)
35. My mother tried to make me dependent on her.	(4)	(3)	(2)	(1)
36. People take advantage of me and I seem to let them.	(4)	(3)	(2)	(1)
37. My mother felt I could not look after myself unless she was around.	(4)	(3)	(2)	(1)
38. Other people's needs always come first.	(4)	(3)	(2)	(1)
39. Only I could deal with my mother's (or father's) problems.	(4)	(3)	(2)	(1)
40. At least one parent was involved in unethical or illegal behavior (e.g., infidelity, financial misdeeds, or the like).	(4)	(3)	(2)	(1)
41. My mother let me go out as often as I wanted.	(1)	(2)	(3)	(4)
42. I am too open about myself.	(4)	(3)	(2)	(1)
43. My father was unassertive.	(4)	(3)	(2)	(1)
44. My mother did not praise me.	(4)	(3)	(2)	(1)
45. I felt responsible for my mother's (or father's) well-being.	(4)	(3)	(2)	(1)

BVVI – SCORING SHEET

	Item #	Sum	Average
Overly Nurturant:	2, 6, 20, 38		
	_ _ _ _	_____ /4 =	_____
Exploitable:	5, 11, 23, 27, 36		
	_ _ _ _ _	_____ /5 =	_____
Intrusive:	7, 17, 29, 42		
	_ _ _ _	_____ /4 =	_____
Mother Cold:	1, 9, 10, 15, 16, 22, 26, 30, 33, 44		
	_ _ _ _ _ _ _ _ _ _	_____ /10 =	_____
Mother Control:	3, 12, 13, 18, 19, 28, 35, 37, 41		
	_ _ _ _ _ _ _ _ _	_____ /9 =	_____
Father Ambivalent:	4, 14, 24, 34, 43		
	_ _ _ _ _	_____ /5 =	_____
Family Hypocrisy:	8, 21, 32, 40		
	_ _ _ _	_____ /4 =	_____
Mother/Father Responsibility:	25, 31, 39, 45		
	_ _ _ _	_____ /4 =	_____

DISCUSSION

An average score of 3 or higher (4 is the maximum) for the entire test reflects the presence of the cluster of vulnerabilities found to be precursors of sexual boundary violations. While these vulnerabilities also exist in practitioners who do not eventually transgress, these are present in a large percentage of cases of sexual boundary transgressors. It should be emphasized again that these characteristics are not predictive; a causal connection has not been determined.

The average score based on the entire test, however, can be deceiving since some specific vulnerabilities may be masked by low scores on others. In addition, the average score has limited practical utility since it represents a cluster of variables that should be addressed specifically and separately. The best and most informative use of this measure is to *score each subtest separately* and in this manner, specifically identify those vulnerabilities that this measure may have identified in you. In order to do this, follow the instructions in filling out the BVVI Scoring Sheet (above). Alternatively, go back to the instrument and circle those items for which you scored 3 or 4 points. These should cluster among the following categories: Overly Nurturant, Exploitable, Intrusive, Mother Cold, Mother Overprotective, Father Ambivalent, Family

Hypocrisy, and Mother/Father Responsibility. A description of each of these clusters follows, along with the items that constitute them.

Some of the items are positively directed, where the item is phrased in such a way that a high score means the phrase is "very like you." In contrast, other items are negatively directed, where the item is phrased in such a way that a high score means it is "very unlike you." This is the reason that sometimes a high score reflects a characteristic that is very like you while for other items, a high score reflects a characteristic that is very unlike you. In either case, the scoring is directed so that a *high* score (between 3 and 4) reflects the *presence* of the characteristic described in that category.

The items for which each of these categories is comprised are listed below:

Overly Nurturant: Items # 2, 6, 20, 38
Exploitable: Items # 5, 11, 23, 27, 36
Intrusive: Items # 7, 17, 29, 42
Mother Cold: Items # 1, 9, 10, 15, 16, 22, 26, 30, 33, 44
Mother Overprotective: Items # 3, 12, 13, 18, 19, 28, 35, 37, 41,
Father Ambivalent: Items # 4, 14, 24, 34, 43
Family Hypocrisy: Items # 8, 21, 32, 40
Mother/Father Responsibility: Items # 25, 31, 39, 45

The first three categories (Overly Nurturant, Exploitable, and Intrusive) represent interpersonal styles that are currently true for you (as self-assessed). These items relate to two dimensions or axes of personality functioning: a dimension of affiliation or nurturance and a dimension of power, control, or dominance, the latter dimension ranging from submissive behavior to dominating behavior. Each subtest can be viewed as comprised of a different balance of these two dimensions (see appendix A for a more detailed description of these items and the personality traits they aim to measure).

The pole that combines these dimensions in a manner associated with therapists who have engaged in sexualized dual relationships can be described as Affiliative Submissive. If you scored 3 or 4 on most of these items in the first three categories, it is indicated that you seek psychotherapeutic help in developing a more adaptive interpersonal style. It is important to keep in mind, however, that even with therapeutic help and a substantial mastery over these characteristics, it is possible that these tendencies *will remain a regressive potential* for you under acute stress. Thus, ongoing monitoring of your own stress level is indicated, even if effective treatment has facilitated the development of a healthier interpersonal style under normal conditions. The regressive potential should be regarded as a historical fallibility in your interpersonal style. It is essential that you keep this in mind especially during times of stress when these styles may emerge or reemerge, even if you have previously had treatment and effectively dealt with these issues.

The next three categories (Mother Cold, Mother Overprotective, and Father Ambivalent) reflect ways in which you may have experienced each of your parents, especially with regard to how each parent treated you. Since these are largely matters of history and thereby are unchangeable, it is important that you have or do come to terms with the untoward consequences of these in your present character structure.

The final two categories (Family Hypocrisy and Mother/Father Responsibility) are historical experiences and memories, as subjectively experienced by you in your familial relationships. Family Hypocrisy aims to measure ways in which one or both parents violated their own stated values and expectations of themselves, despite upholding strict expectations of you. The underlying assumption is that there may be an unconscious identification where rules may be violated, despite the fact that such violations are considered forbidden. The second category, Mother/Father Responsibility, aims to measure the extent to which you may have been selected to bear the burden of responsibility for curing or rescuing a parent from his or her psychological or physical distress. The underlying assumption is that this childhood or familial experience may make you prone to inordinate rescue fantasies with certain patients in similar psychological distress.

The categories that describe family relations and experiences are likely to have been formative in your character development. As historical facts, they are not changeable with therapeutic help. You may regard them differently from a present or future vantage point; however, they are based largely on the reconstruction of your past as you view it and remember it. It is important, however, to be aware of how these historical indicators may have played a role in the formation of your character and may represent etiological determinants in the vulnerabilities associated with sexual boundary violations. Therapeutic help may be indicated in order to come to terms with how these familial experiences play a role in your current relations.

All of the characteristics measured by the BVVI represent areas of vulnerability that are amenable to therapeutic intervention. Some are interpersonal styles, and others are indicative of childhood trauma that have played a role in the formation of defensive styles, modes of relating, and overall personality functioning. Psychoanalytically oriented treatment of various kinds is designed to address these characteristics and to facilitate more adaptive modes of relating. However, it should be kept in mind that these vulnerabilities may remain as a regressive potential, especially in times of acute stress. Thus, on-going monitoring of one's level of burnout, stress, and overall well-being is essential in order to maintain the appropriate level of boundedness and ethically based professional attitudes that are conducive to performing high-quality therapeutic work.

ENDNOTE

The BVVI is a measure derived from the empirical studies discussed in the appendices. These studies comprised in-depth examinations of various subsets from a larger sample of over 100 mental health professionals. In each case, the findings were corroborated in the larger sample.

16

TEACHING BOUNDARIES, EXPERIENCING BOUNDARIES

> The voice of reason not only speaks softly . . . it whispers and
> then falls silent under the sway of desire.

In raising the question, How to teach about boundaries?, I feel a sinking in my stomach . . . a little like the prospect of hearing Sister Union, the principal of St. Robert Bellarmine Elementary School in Bayside, Queens, lecture a group of us, then eight years old, for playing hide and seek on the convent lawn. We knew the rules, yet she couldn't stop herself from going through each one, wagging her finger (I swear she did that) with a look of contempt (and did I discern slight pleasure?) on her face.

Whether or not my association is apt (interesting, by the way, that the example of hide and seek came to mind), it is hard not to notice the resistance we all have toward talking about boundaries. It's like a collective groan . . . "Oh not that again"; a kind of expectation of boredom. This is at least in part related to the anticipation that the teaching will come from a superego position: Sister Union's annoying wagging finger. Though I am reluctant to give her credit for any kind of wisdom, she did know something about human nature. *We are tempted to break the rules.*

In relation to teaching, there clearly is a reluctance to hear a lecture on boundaries, but there is also interest in this topic too. Our Task Force[1] overflowed with members. We had to close our borders after a few meetings in order to contain it. What does this tell us? *People are willing to discuss boundary issues when they are offered an experience that they themselves can shape.* I think there is a hope lurking behind this anticipation: "Maybe I'll be able to describe what happened when . . ." And also a steadying aspect; if they are allowed to place a hand on the tiller, there is a sense of some needed control.

211

I cannot stress this issue enough. When designing a course or seminar, the instructor and creator of the curriculum has a tendency to start with questions about content. What should be on the reading list? What articles, books, papers, and other related projects should be required of the students? But developing appropriate management skills with boundaries is not an intellectual or didactic achievement. There are countless cases of therapists and analysts who engaged in sexual boundary transgressions despite years and years of courses, seminars, lectures and readings on boundaries and their management. Further, as I have stressed elsewhere in this book, in almost all cases of sexual boundary transgressions, the transgressor knew very well that he or she was egregiously violating the ethical code at the time of the transgression. As the epigraph states, the voice of reason not only speaks softly . . . it whispers and then falls silent under the sway of powerful pressures and desires.

Thus, the first things to attend to, when designing a course on boundaries, are process, structure, and format. Content will come later. That said, it is wise to notice that we tend to take process for granted because a good one embodies psychoanalytic values and we think we already know these. But more pointedly, process and content are not separable and function in dialectical relation. They define each other through their mutual contrast yet imply each other and deepen as the other deepens. In the end, despite our best efforts to put the content forward, it is the process that will determine what is learned.

What do we need to think about when we teach boundaries? An atmosphere of openness where dialogue can take place to sort through complex, interweaving, and sometimes contradictory ethical obligations. Safe discussion will be key. What follows are guidelines that foster this process.

PROCESS ISSUES

1) *It takes a group* (for support) to muster the courage to speak up. We all need support to stir the hope that our questions might be heard and supported. When we teach about boundaries, we often recommend that the therapist or analyst in conflict seek private consultation, one on one, with the idea that people will feel more comfortable with only one pair of eyes looking (and judging); and, of course, we hope that they will actually get the consultation when they need it. I do not mean to discount these private consultations, but when boundary crossings are at issue, we often need to hear a range of ideas about how to respond. More importantly, we need a heft of support, thus a group can be key.

But not just any group will do. It is possible a professor or instructor may have a difficult mix of students, one that will squelch the potential for useful dialogue. Though it is usually the course or seminar leader's responsibility to monitor the level of safety in the group, there may not be a way to resolve a destructive dynamic, especially if the seminar or course is relatively brief (i.e., six or twelve weeks). The important variables to consider are the attitudes of the students and the extent to which there is openness, affirmation, and nonjudgmentalism at the forefront. *As in all teaching, it is essential that the instructor embody these attitudes.* These are essential analytic attitudes: patience for complexity, the commitment to listen, to think analytically and bring one's empathic skill to understand, no matter what the behavior was.

In this sense, attitudes are more important than structures; you can have all the mechanisms in place, including infrastructure, committees, and ombudspersons—a person in the sway of an ethical dilemma will be reluctant to use them if they are embedded in a culture that does not reward depth or complex understanding but is, on the other hand, punitive, uncompassionate, or divisive (prone to splitting or externalizing). This is true on a macro level, regarding the training institute or college as a whole, and on a micro level, in the context of your particular seminar.

2) *It takes time.* The experience in the Task Force was comprised of a group of fifteen to eighteen persons whose process evolved over one and a half years. We met, however, for a total of only ten discussion meetings. During this time, safety was cultivated; it grew and deepened. Can this happen in a six or twelve week seminar? Yes, possibly. From our experience, it seems reasonable to raise boundary issues toward the end of the seminar, when the group has developed sufficient familiarity and trust.

3) *A small, cohesive group format* fosters open dialogue more than the intimidating atmosphere of a larger group. There also needs to be a set membership with continuity of meetings over time. This is usually a given with classes that are together for multiple years such as those in clinical psychology programs, psychoanalytic institutes, and the like. Such a structure offers the opportunity to develop familiarity and safety over that time. This is an optimal condition for setting the stage.

4) *Diversity is good, actually essential.* Openness to differences in opinion is crucial to demonstrate the degree of safety in the room. Often,

there is diversity in any group of faculty where members are attached to differing theoretical traditions and students or candidates tend to be diverse as well. Seminar leaders have an opportunity to clarify where and how responses may relate to a particular school and where the boundaries are. For example, within psychoanalytic systems of thought, the interpersonal and relational schools emphasize the participatory stance of the analyst, yet these orientations do not advocate gratuitous self-disclosure. The question is more aptly stated, How and where does one draw the line? Similarly, from the vantage point of a postclassical position, it would be important to make explicit, "Within this frame, X would be considered a boundary crossing." In terms of more general boundaries, the question often comes up, Do we do things differently depending on the health or severity of disturbance of the patient? Where are the lines drawn in those situations?

The Task Force was a diverse group on both professional and personal levels. We had representatives from every level of hierarchy at our psychoanalytic institute, from Training Analysts to candidates in the most entry level program. We had members who adhere to the full range of analytic orientations. This was not made explicit, but we all knew it. We also had personal affinities and enmities. Though there was some initial anxiety about these beforehand, they did not stand in our way. Where we were homogenous was in the commitment to openness, affirmation, and analytic listening. With these commitments, diversity enriched us more than a homogenous group might have. (Similarly, professors and instructors often find that they sometimes have classes with destructive group dynamics. These are not necessarily fatal as members learn that these tensions can be tolerated, survived, and productively used.)

5) *Hierarchical issues should be differentiated and clarified.* It is important to recognize the difference between *personal* and *structural* hierarchies. Differences in power on a *personal* level exist in every relationship. These are linked to personality variables and personal values that do or do not garner respect or admiration. What one evokes will vary for each individual because people differ over styles, values and preferences. These are private negotiations and are inescapable.

In contrast, a *structured* hierarchy is one where power is assigned according to roles. These carry with them responsibilities that have institutional effects. These are not negotiable. In seminars, for example, the instructor as leader has power and the students or candidates are likely to be more aware and sensitive to that dimension than the instructor is. If the instructor is also a training analyst or chair of the program, the candidate or student may imagine the instructor has power that will have bearing on future progression within the program or institutional hierarchy. In the immediate, however, it is the instructor's responsibility to evaluate and report on the student or candidate's participation. This, by itself, will have real effects on the student's immediate progression and consequently, their level of comfort within the seminar or course. This is inescapable, but the instructor can make it more or less tolerable.

It is important to keep in mind that the professor or instructor, as faculty and evaluator, will not subjectively feel his or her power. There needs to be an agreement about how discussions for the session on boundaries will be held and/or reported upon, despite the fact that the professor or instructor may feel it is unnecessary. One avenue is to keep the discussions about boundaries confidential. If some reporting requirement is part of the instructor's role, this should be executed without attribution (i.e., who said what) and reports might be shared among members before submission. *There should be an explicit agreement that disclosures of boundary crossings will not be used in evaluating a student or candidate.* For seminar leaders who must construct an evaluation, this may be easier to do in theory because whatever happens in the seminar is going to affect how the instructor feels and thinks about a student or candidate. A distinction between judging (forming an opinion, an inescapable consequence of thinking) versus being judgmental (tending toward negative opinion) is relevant here. Leaders should make a commitment not to act on the judgments arising from the boundary discussions. Most importantly, seminar leaders should *embrace a student's willingness to reveal boundary crossings and the effort of the candidate to understand them* rather than the fact of a boundary crossing itself. Let that value remain in the forefront.

6) Finally, it is important to keep in mind that *seminars are not therapy or psychoanalysis.* We may teach analytic thinking and analytic values in seminars, but we do not *do therapy or analysis* in seminars. Analysis requires the penetration into one's character; the seminar context is not the appropriate venue for this. Analytic thinking may be employed, however it is crucial to keep in mind that a seminar is a public venue, essentially competitive and evaluative. There has not been an agreed upon contract to scrutinize one's character in this setting and the candidates have not chosen you (as seminar leader) to

be their therapist or psychoanalyst. Analyzing a candidate's character in the seminar context would be a boundary crossing itself. Further, there are no mechanisms or opportunities to work through an interpretation should one come their way. It is impossible to prevent some private reverie about a student's personality organization or quirks, however these should not be verbalized nor repeated outside the context of the seminar. So, for example, in a clinical seminar, the focus should address the trainee's or candidate's participation in an enactment. Commentary should be kept within the context of the patient/therapist dynamics and what these reveal about the patient's unconscious fantasy or object relationship that is activated.

All of the above is *a demonstration* of mindfulness about boundary issues. If these suggestions for format and process are followed, the instructor will be *demonstrating* that which he/she is teaching and concordantly, the student/candidate will *experience* sensitive boundary management.

CONTENT: THE KNOWLEDGE BASE

Once process issues are in place, content areas may be identified and discussed. First and foremost, you may want to address the fundamental question: *What is a boundary?* It is a demarcation that signals a particular mode of thinking and relating. As therapists or psychoanalysts, we are invited to share a person's inner world and to think about it (with them) analytically. Responsibilities, defined by the setting, are attendant upon this privilege. Boundaries circumscribe these responsibilities; on a content level, you could say boundaries encircle our knowledge of these inner worlds as well. This world needs to be protected. This requires psychoanalytic understanding and within that, certain ways of acting. A boundary crossing is a change in behavior that conflicts with a psychoanalytic understanding of these roles.

The expectations, obligations, and responsibilities associated with different roles or positions can be clearly delineated as well, especially those as faculty, psychoanalysts, supervisors, ombudspersons, advisors, or administrators. Particular attention should be paid to therapist/patient, supervisor/supervisee, and faculty/student relationships. For example, self-disclosure has a wider berth (indeed it can be argued that disclosure is part of how we teach) in the more educational relationships than in the therapeutic one.

A broad knowledge base should include the full range of boundary issues, including but not limited to: confidentiality, self-disclosure, gifts, negotiation of fees, extra-analytic contacts, relations to relatives and friends of either patient or therapist, and sexual boundary transgressions, to name the most common. Not all of these topics can be covered in every class but a variety should be covered by the end of seminars, especially those affiliated with clinical programs. A reading list is provided at the end of this chapter as a resource; the citations are organized by subject matter. (At the Boston Psychoanalytic Society and Institute, there are distinctions made among the different teaching tracks [i.e., theory, technique, clinical] which will define the lens through which the teaching of boundaries will be viewed. The sequence or track chairs are encouraged to organize and keep track of what topics are being covered and where, across the years.)

Discussion works best if presented around a *real but disguised vignette* that involves boundary crossings. This allows trainees and candidates to identify with the various roles and obligations, often conflicting, and to immerse themselves in the various dilemmas. It is easier to keep the complexity in mind when a vignette portrays the different dimensions. Most importantly, if you can say that the case is a real one, it is not so easily dismissed.

You might want to *use examples that were problematic for you*. One possibility is to start with one's own boundary crossing, how confusing it was, what was thought about, and who was sought out for help (or not and why not). It is often not possible to have a clean or even successful outcome—but there should be, in retrospect, clear ideas of how the dilemma should have been handled. The group or class should try to come to their own resolutions first before the teacher or instructor shares his/her retrospective vision.

Finally, as one member of our Task Force put it, you should *expect it to be messy*. When engaging in the routine denial about boundary issues, as when we think we know all we need to know, we tend to imagine discrete scenarios that imply a straightforward mandate—scenarios where a simple "no" will do. Real life dilemmas are much more complex, sometimes ethical mandates conflict with each other, and more difficult countertransference (especially erotic) comes into play. Other chapters in this book may be further help in delineating the various dimensions that have created complex, real-life dilemmas, with the attendant questions of how to handle the more subtle nuances.

READING LIST

Generic Articles and Books on Boundaries

Akhtar, S. (2005). Experiencing oneness: Pathological pursuit or normal necessity? In S. Akhtar (Ed.), *Interpersonal Boundaries: Variations and Violations* (pp. 87–97). New York: Jason Aronson.

Akhtar, S. (2006). *Interpersonal boundaries: Variations and violations*. New York: Jason Aronson.

Celenza, A. (2007). *Sexual boundary violations: Therapeutic, supervisory and academic contexts*. New York: Jason Aronson.

Gabbard, G. O., and Lester, E. (1995). *Boundaries and boundary violations in psychoanalysis*. New York: Basic Books.

Goldberg, A. (2008). Some limits of the boundary concept. *Psychoanalytic Quarterly, 77(3)*, 861–76. Commentaries by Glen Gabbard, Jay Greenberg, Warren Poland, Sharon Zalusky and Henry Friedman, 77(3), 877–919.

Green, A. (1996). Has sexuality anything to do with psychoanalysis? *International Journal of Psychoanalysis, 76*, 871–83.

Lamb, D. H., and Catanzaro, S. J. (1998). Sexual and nonsexual boundary violations involving psychologists, clients, supervisees, and students. *Professional Psychology, Research and Practice, 29(5)*, 498–503.

Lamb, D. H., Woodburn, J. R., Lewis, J. T., Strand, K. K., Buchko, K. J., and Kang, J. R. (1994). Sexual and business relationships between therapists and former clients. *Psychotherapy, 31*, 270–78.

Pope, K. S., Levenson, H., and Schover, L. R. (1979). Sexual intimacy in psychology training: Results and implications of a national survey. *American Psychologist, 34(8)*, 682–89.

Schoener, G. R., Milgrom, J. H., Gonsiorek, J. C., Luepker, E. T., Conroe, R. M., eds. (1989). *Psychotherapists' sexual involvement with clients: Intervention and prevention* (pp. 399–502). Minneapolis, MN: Walk-In Counseling Center.

Classic Papers on Transference Love

Cesio, F. (1993). The Oedipal tragedy in the psychoanalytic process: Transference love. In *On Freud's "Observations on Transference-Love": Contemporary Freud, Turning Points and Critical Issues*. New Haven, CT: Yale University Press.

Freud, S. (1915). Observation on Transference-Love. Standard Edition 12 (pp. 157–71). London: Hogarth Press.

Fees

Rothstein, A. (1986). The seduction of money: A brief note on an expression of transference love. *Psychoanalytic Quarterly, 55(2)*, 296–300.

Rothstein, A. (2004). The seduction of money: An addendum. *Psychoanalytic Quarterly, 73*, 525–27.

Sexual Boundary Transgressions

Bloom, J. D., Nadelson, C. C., and Notman, M. T., eds. (1999). *Physician Sexual Misconduct*. Washington, DC: American Psychiatric Press.

Borys, D. S., and Pope, K. S. (1989). Dual relationships between therapist and client: A national study of psychologists, psychiatrists, and social workers. *Professional Psychology: Research and Practice, 20,* 283–93.

Celenza, A. (2007). *Sexual boundary violations: Therapeutic, supervisory and academic contexts.* New York: Jason Aronson.

Garrett, T. (2002). Inappropriate therapist-patient relationships. In R. Goodwin and D. Cramer (Eds.), *Inappropriate Relationships* (pp. 147–70). Mahwah, NJ: Lawrence Erlbaum.

Gartrell, N., Herman, J., Olarte, S., Feldstein, M., and Localio, R. (1986). Psychiatrist-patient sexual contact: Results of a national survey, I: Prevalence. *American Journal of Psychiatry, 143,* 1126–131.

Jackson, H., and Nuttall, R. L. (2001). A relationship between childhood sexual abuse and professional sexual misconduct. *Professional Psychology: Research and Practice, 32(2),* 200–204.

Kroll, J. (2001). Boundary violations: A culture-bound syndrome. *Journal of the American Academy of Psychiatry and Law, 29(3),* 274–83.

Notman, M. (2007). Sexual boundary violations. Paper presented at BPSI symposium on boundary violations.

Sarkar, S. P. (2004). Boundary violation and sexual exploitation in psychiatry and psychotherapy: A review. *Advances in Psychiatric Treatment, 10,* 312–20.

Victim/Survivors

Celenza, A. (2007). Helping the victims. In *Sexual Boundary Violations: Therapeutic, Supervisory and Academic Contexts* (chapter 10). New York: Jason Aronson.

Gutheil, G. T., and Gabbard, G. O. (1992). Obstacles to the dynamics understanding of therapist-patient sexual relations. *American Journal of Psychotherapy, 46,* 515–26.

Luepker, E. T. (1999). Effects of practitioners' sexual misconduct: A follow-up study. *Journal of the American Academy of Psychiatry and Law, 27,* 51–63.

Norris, D. M., Gutheil, T. G., and Strasbourger, L. H. (2003). This couldn't happen to me: Boundary problems and sexual misconduct in the psychotherapy relationship. *Psychiatric Services, 54,* 517–22.

Wohlberg et al. (1999). Treatment subsequent to abuse by a mental health professional: The victim's perspective of what works and what doesn't. *Journal of Sex Education and Therapy, 24(4),* 252–61.

Collateral Damage

Burka, J. (2008). Psychic fallout from breach of confidentiality. *Contemporary Psychoanalysis, 44,* 177–98.

Celenza, A. (2007). Collateral damage and recovery. In *Sexual Boundary Violations: Therapeutic, Supervisory and Academic Contexts* (chapter 9). New York: Jason Aronson.

Slochower, J. (2003). The analyst's secret delinquencies. *Psychoanalytic Dialogues, 13(4),* 451–69.
Wallace, E. (2007). Losing a training analyst for ethical violations: A candidate's perspective. *International Journal of Psychoanalysis, 88,* 1275–288.

Institutional Responses

Fogel, D. (2006). The psychopathology of everyday life at psychoanalytic institutes and boundary violations. Paper presented at BPSI, December Academic Lecture.
Gabbard, G., and Peltz, M. (2001). Speaking the unspeakable: Institutional reactions to boundary violations by training analysts. *Journal of the American Psychoanalytic Association, 49(2),* 659–73.
Levine, H. and Yanof, J. (2004) Boundaries and postanalytic contacts in institutes. *Journal of the American Psychoanalytic Association, 52,* 873–901.
Reeder, J. (2004). *Hate and Love in Psychoanalytic Institutions.* New York: Other Press.
Sandler, A.-M. (2004). Institutional Responses to boundary violations: The case of Massud Khan. *International Journal of Psychoanalysis, 85,* 27–42.

Legal and Ethical Considerations

Bisbing, S. B., Jorgenson, L. M., and Sutherland, P. K. (1995). *Sexual abuse by professionals: A legal guide.* Charlottesville, VA: Michie.
Celenza, A. (2007). Reporting and other ethical responsibilities. In *Sexual Boundary Violations: Therapeutic, Supervisory and Academic Contexts* (chapter 8). New York: Jason Aronson.
Haspel, K. C., Jorgenson, L. M., Wincze, J. P., and Parsons, J. P. (1997). Legislative intervention regarding therapist sexual misconduct: An overview. *Professional Psychology, Research and Practice, 28,* 63–72.
Hedges, L. E. (2007). *Facing the challenge of liability in psychotherapy, 2nd ed.* New York: Jason Aronson.

Prevention

Celenza, A. (2007). Responsible responsivity. In *Sexual Boundary Violations: Therapeutic, Supervisory and Academic Contexts* (chapter 13). New York: Jason Aronson.
Celenza, A. (2007). Love and hate in the countertransference: Preventing violations through supervision. In *Sexual Boundary Violations: Therapeutic, Supervisory and Academic Contexts* (chapter 14). New York: Jason Aronson.
Celenza, A. (2007). Boundary violations vulnerability index (BVVI). In *Sexual Boundary Violations: Therapeutic, Supervisory and Academic Contexts* (chapter 15). New York: Jason Aronson.
Gutheil, T., and Brodsky, A. (2008). *Preventing boundary violations in clinical practice.* New York: Guilford Press.

Clergy Misconduct

Celenza, A. (2007). A 'love addiction': Psychoanalytic psychotherapy with an offending priest. In M. G. Frawley-O'Dea and V. Goldner (Eds.). *Predatory Priests, Silenced Victims: The Sexual Abuse Crisis and the Catholic Church*. Hillsdale, NJ: Analytic Press.

Celenza, A. (2007). Clergy misconduct: The search for the father. In *Sexual Boundary Violations: Therapeutic, Academic, and Supervisory Contexts*. New York: Jason Aronson.

Frawley-O'Dea, M. G., and Goldner, V., eds. (2007). *Predatory priests, silenced victims: The sexual abuse crisis and the Catholic Church*. Mahwah, NJ: Analytic Press.

Gonsiorek, J., ed. (1995). *A breach of trust: Sexual exploitation by health care professionals and clergy*. Thousand Oaks, CA: Sage.

Schoener, G. R. (2005). Clergy sexual abuse of women: Some historical perspectives. Paper presented at the Interfaith Conference on Clergy Sexual Misconduct: Helping Survivors and Communities Heal, Minneapolis, MN, January, 2005.

Rehabilitation

Celenza, A. (2007). Therapy for the transgressor. In *Sexual Boundary Violations: Therapeutic, Supervisory and Academic Contexts* (chapter 11). New York: Jason Aronson.

Celenza, A. (2007). Helping the helpers. In *Sexual Boundary Violations: Therapeutic, Supervisory and Academic Contexts* (chapter 12). New York: Jason Aronson.

Celenza, A., and Gabbard, G. O. (2003). Analysts who commit sexual boundary violations: A lost cause? *Journal of American Psychoanalytic Association, 51(2)*, 617–36.

Celenza, A. (2008). Rehabilitation of sexual boundary transgressors: A humane and knowledge-based approach. *Psychiatric Times, 25*, 36–43.

ENDNOTES

1. This chapter is an outgrowth of my experience within the Task Force on Boundaries at the Boston Psychoanalytic Society and Institute, 2008–2009, and I am indebted to the entire group for the wisdom that follows. My thanks as well to Cordelia Schmidt-Hellerau and Laura Crain for their warm cochairmanship and thoughtful suggestions on this paper.

Appendices

EMPIRICAL RESEARCH

APPENDIX A:
PERSONAL AND INTERPERSONAL
CHARACTERISTICS OF TRANSGRESSORS

Andrea Celenza, Ph.D., and Mark Hilsenroth, Ph.D.

Interest in the problem of sexualized dual relationships among mental health professionals has increased in the past decade. Interest in the transgressing professionals has resulted in several nonempirical investigations from different vantage points, including a typology of vulnerable therapists (Schoener & Gonsiorek, 1989; Levine, Risen, & Althof, 1994), common scenarios of therapist-patient sexual intimacy (Pope, 1989b), psychodynamic profiles of transgressing therapists (Strean, 1993; Gabbard, 1994a), and potential predisposing characteristics of therapist sexual misconduct (Celenza, 1998). These studies have based their observations on extensive interviews with the transgressing professional, and may also include interviews with the victim(s) and other relevant individuals and/or organizational representatives. These comprehensive evaluations most often include psychological testing, and though there have been no previous attempts to empirically derive a profile of the vulnerable therapist, most authors have, up to now, agreed that the transgressing therapist defies simple categorization based on a single diagnosis or psychodynamic profile.

Previous clinical observations have culminated in a range of profiles and diagnostic categories of the transgressing therapist. Six diagnostic categories were delineated by Schoener and Gonsiorek (1989), including: (1) uninformed/naïve, (2) healthy or mildly neurotic, (3) severely neurotic and/or socially isolated, (4) impulsive character disorders, (5) sociopathic or narcissistic character disorders, (6) psychotic or borderline personalities, and (7) bipolar disorders. Gabbard (1994a) proposed four underlying psychological profiles as an alternative classification scheme. These underlying characteristics include: (1) psychotic disorders, (2) predatory psychopathy and paraphilias, (3) lovesickness, and (4) masochistic surrender.

In addition, Celenza (1998) has described eight potential predisposing characteristics that were observed fairly consistently in each of the professionals in her sample regardless of diagnosis. These include: (1) long-standing narcissistic vulnerability, (2) grandiose (covert) rescue fantasies, (3) intolerance of negative transference, (4) childhood history of emotional deprivation and sexualized overstimulation, (5) family history of covert and sanctioned boundary transgressions, (6) unresolved anger toward authority figures, (7) restricted awareness of fantasy (especially hostile/aggressive), and (8) transformation of countertransference hate to countertransference "love." Important issues have been usefully debated, such as the predominance of sociopathy in these individuals (Pope, 1989b), the role of aggression (Celenza, 1998; Pope, 1989b), and the lack of evidence of a consistent profile (Schoener, 1995, personal communication). One study reported prospective Minnesota Multiphasic Personality Inventory (MMPI) results differentiating a large group of psychiatry residents from two psychiatrists subsequently convicted of boundary violations (Garfinkle, Bagby, Waring, & Dorian, 1997). Garfinkle et al.'s study found elevations on Hypomania, Psychopathic Deviate, and Validity subscales. To date, however, there have been only two empirical investigations that systematically measured the personality characteristics and diagnostic schemas reported in the literature on boundary transgressions (Celenza & Hilsenroth, 1997; Ehlert, 2002). The present study is an extension of Celenza and Hilsenroth's Rorschach study in an attempt to systematically measure the various clinical findings noted above.

This empirical analysis aims to (1) further delineate the personality dimensions underlying the character structure of professionals who transgress sexual boundaries; (2) identify historical factors that may predispose individuals in this group of mental health professionals (MHPs) to boundary transgressions; and (3) highlight the characteristics that might be most useful to supervisors and educators as a focus of concern in selection processes as well as in the individual's training and personal development.

METHOD

Subjects

The target sample (Sexualized Dual Relationships, SDR) is comprised of 21 mental health professionals who have engaged in one or more sexualized dual relationships. Subjects were initially referred by an overseeing professional organization or state licensing board, or by self-referral for an independent comprehensive evaluation, supervision, or consultation. The only criterion for inclusion in the study was that the professional had engaged in a sexualized dual relationship, defined as erotic contact with a patient, client, parishioner, or student. The sample includes a wide range of therapists of various disciplines, including clinical psychology, counseling psychology, pastoral counseling, and social work. All were primarily psychodynamically trained and do intensive treatment with other specialties as well. Included in the sample as well are clergy who have engaged in sexual misconduct with one or more parishioners or students. (See table A.1 for subject characteristics.)

Twenty-eight percent of the SDR subjects endorsed a psychodynamic or psychoanalytic orientation, 17% endorsed cognitive behavioral, 33% endorsed humanistic, and 22% endorsed eclectic. All see themselves as competent, experienced, and sensitive to transference/countertransference enactments.

SDR subjects' ages at the time of initial referral ranged from 44–74 with a mean age of 57 years. All SDR subjects are male. Twenty SDR subjects are Caucasian and one is Hispanic. Twenty (95%) subjects are heterosexual whose transgression(s) involved one or more heterosexual relationships. The remaining homosexual subject transgressed once during the course of his "coming out" as gay. Seventy-six percent (*n* = 16) were married at the time of the transgression(s). All subjects appeared to be highly intelligent and all were well

Table A.1. Subjects

	SDR n = 21	PC n = 24
Gender	Male	Male
Mean Age	57	47
Age Range	44–74	35–76
Education	Ph.D., M.D. DMin, MA	Ph.D., M.D. DMin, MA
Single	2 (10%)	5 (21%)
Married	16 (76%)	18 (75%)
Divorced	3 (14%)	0
Widowed	0	1 (4%)
Mean Years Prof Practice	27	18
Range Years Prof Practice	9–40	4–43
Mean Years Personal Therapy	5.8	4.8
Range Years Personal Therapy	0–13	0–20
Orientation		
Psychodynamic, Psychoanalytic	5 (28%)	17 (71%)
Cognitive Behavioral	3 (17%)	0
Humanistic	6 (33%)	3 (13%)
Eclectic	4 (22%)	4 (17%)

educated, having achieved at least one postgraduate degree (90% at the doctoral level). Years of professional experience at the time of the study ranged
from 9 years to 40 years postgraduate (mean = 27 years). Intelligence testing
has been administered. The mean IQ for this sample is in the Superior range
(Full Scale IQ, mean = 124). This mean is two standard deviations higher than
the level expected in same-age peers. This finding is consistent with previous
observations and supports the interpretation that the cause of the transgression is not simply an incapacity to comprehend the ethical code. Indeed, most
of the subjects in this sample reported being aware of committing an ethical
violation at the time of the transgression.

No subjects in the SDR sample were psychotic. None had prior psychiatric histories involving a major mental disturbance, though many had had previous psychotherapy and two had undergone lengthy psychoanalyses. Only
two reported a history of sexual trauma or incest, although all reported significant emotional abuse in their families of origin, usually involving lack of
affection or emotional deprivation. Years of personal therapy or psychoanalysis at the time of the study ranged from none to 13 years (mean = 5.8 years).

The comparison group (Professional Controls, PC) is comprised of 24
mental health professionals who had not engaged in any sexualized dual relationships. Comparison subjects were recruited from local professional institutions. Participation was entirely voluntary and anonymous with the exception
of the determination of salient demographic characteristics for matching
purposes. Similar to the SDR sample, the PC group includes a wide range of
therapists of various disciplines including clinical psychology, counseling psychology, pastoral counseling, and social work. Also similar to the SDR sample, all are psychodynamically trained and do intensive treatment. Included
in the sample as well are clergy. Seventy-one percent (*n* = 17) of the PC group
endorsed a psychodynamic or psychoanalytic orientation, 13% endorsed humanistic, and 17% endorsed eclectic.

Comparison subjects' ages at the time of initial referral ranged from
35–76; mean age was 47 years old. All comparison subjects are male. All are
Caucasian. Seventy-five percent (*n* = 18) were married at the time of participation. Most subjects are highly intelligent and all were well educated, having
achieved at least one postgraduate degree (90% at the doctoral level). Years
of professional experience at the time of the study ranged from 4 years to 43
years postgraduate (mean = 18 years). The mean IQ for this group is in the Superior range (Full Scale IQ, mean = 123). This mean is two standard deviations
higher than the level expected in same-age peers.

No subjects in the comparison sample were psychotic. None had prior
psychiatric histories involving major mental disturbance, though many had

had previous psychotherapy or had undergone lengthy psychoanalyses. The range of years in personal therapy or psychoanalysis was from none to 20; mean number of years was 4.8.

Measures

BORRTI. The Bell Object Relations and Reality Testing Inventory (Bell, Billington, & Becker, 1985) was utilized as an additional measure of internalized object relations. This scale has produced four subscales that represent underlying dimensions of object relations (Bell, Billington, & Becker, 1986). The four subscales are: (1) Alienation, (2) Insecure Attachment, (3) Egocentricity, and (4) Social Incompetence.

The Inventory of Interpersonal Problems (IIP). The Inventory of Interpersonal Problems (Horowitz, Rosenberg, Baer, Ureno, & Villasenor, 1988) is a 127-item questionnaire designed to assess interpersonal difficulties in a broad cross-section of interpersonal domains. Subjects were asked to describe the amount of distress they have experienced from a variety of interpersonal problems. Eight interpersonal problems styles are measured, including: (1) overly autocratic, (2) overly competitive, (3) overly cold, (4) overly introverted, (5) overly subassertive, (6) overly exploitable, (7) overly nurturant, and (8) overly expressive. Each scale then submitted to a circumplex analysis, based on Timothy Leary's (1957) work on personality styles, which has shown high cross-sample stability and has been cross-validated with other samples and other measures of interpersonal dispositions (e.g., Revised Interpersonal Adjective Scales; Wiggins et al., 1988).

Within the circumplex ordering underlie two basic dimensions or axes of personality functioning: a dimension of affiliation or nurturance that ranges from hostile behavior to friendly behavior, and a dimension of power, control, or dominance that ranges from submissive behavior to dominating behavior. A number of factor analytic studies have confirmed this structure by showing that these two dimensions account for a large proportion of the variance in ratings of personality traits (e.g., Becker & Krug, 1964; Conte & Plutchick, 1981; Foa, 1961; Lorr & McNair, 1963; Schaefer & Plutchick, 1966; Wiggins, 1979). Each scale of the circumplex ordering can be viewed as comprised of a different balance of these two dimensions. Thus, it is also possible to perform a quadrant analysis, combining these two dimensions at each pole: Hostile Dominant, Hostile Submissive, Affiliative Submissive, and Affiliative Dominant.

Adult Attachment Scale. This 28-item scale measures underlying adult attachment styles in accord with Hazan and Shaver's discrete categorical measure and a fourth category added by Bartholomew and Horowitz (1991). Subjects rated the extent to which each statement described their feelings on a 5-point scale (Collins & Reed, 1990). This measure classifies subjects along three dimensions of attachment, including the capacity for dependence, anxiety in relationships, comfort with closeness, and dismissive style of relating.

Family History Questionnaire. This is a semistructured questionnaire that elicits information about family history regarding salient events as well as subjective experience of childhood. Content areas include losses, separations, relationship with parents, and so forth. Responses are limited to a few sentences for each question (Bartholomew, 1990). In addition, the original questionnaire has been expanded to include items designed to probe the moral climate in the home, especially with regard to the consistency between parents' teachings and overt/covert behavior.

Parental Bonding Instrument. This is a 25-item self-report questionnaire designed to characterize relations with each parent during the first 16 years of life (Parker, Tupling, & Brown, 1979). Two dimensions are derived, including Care and Overprotection. Subjects rated on a 3-point scale the extent to which each statement described each of their parents.

Parental Care-Giving Style. This measure is comprised of three paragraphs describing the care-giving characteristics associated with a particular attachment style (Hazan & Shaver, 1986). Subjects were asked to rate on a 9-point scale the extent to which each description characterized their relationship with each parent while they were growing up.

Interpersonal Reactivity Index. This 28-item scale consists of four 7-item subscales designed to measure different dimensions of empathy (Davis, 1980). These dimensions include (1) Perspective-Taking, (2) Fantasy, (3) Empathic Concern, and (4) Personal Distress.

Self-Rated Defense Style. This is a 97-item questionnaire comprised of statements reflective of the following defense or coping mechanisms: acting out, pseudoaltruism, as-if behavior, clinging, humor, passive-aggressive behavior, regression, somatization, suppression, withdrawal, dissociation, denial, displacement, omnipotence-devaluation, inhibition, intellectualization, identification, primitive idealization, projection, reaction formation, repression, splitting, sublimation, and turning against self (Bond, Gardner, Christian, & Sigal, 1983). Subjects were asked to indicate their degree of agreement or disagreement with each statement on a 9-point scale from which four defense styles are derived, including: (1) Maladaptive Action Patterns, (2) Image-Distorting Defenses, (3) Self-Sacrificing Defenses, and (4) Adaptive Defense Style.

The Shipley Institute of Living Scale—Vocabulary and Analogies Subtests. This measure is comprised of two subtests, Vocabulary and Analytic Ability.

Procedure

All subjects were asked to fill out a demographic information form along with the packet of questionnaires. Names and other identifying data did not appear on any of the forms and subjects were randomly assigned a subject number. SDR subjects were sent the packet of materials via parcel post with return postage paid. A research assistant blind to group membership scored the questionnaires and entered the data according to subject number. T-tests were used to compare means of the two groups on each of the measures.

RESULTS

To assess the difference in object relations between the two groups, a one-way ANOVA (analyses of variance) was performed to compare means of the two groups on the BORRTI for the object relations subscales. The groups differed significantly overall (p = .001). T-tests were then performed on the four object relations subscales of the BORRTI. The subscales are Alienation, Insecure Attachment, Egocentricity, and Social Incompetence. Two of the four subscales (Insecure Attachment and Social Incompetence) yielded significant results with the SDR group scoring higher (reflecting poorer object relations) for these two subscales. Both mean differences were significant at a p value of <.05 and for the Insecure Attachment subscale, the means differed at a p value of <.001. On the Insecure Attachment subscale, SDR subjects scored higher (mean = 49.5) than comparison subjects (mean = 38.3; p = .001). On the Social Incompetence subscale, SDR subjects scored higher (mean = 47.7) than comparison subjects (mean = 40.3; p < .05). The other two subscales (Alienation and Egocentricity) yielded differences just shy of statistical significance (p = .06 for Alienation and p = .07 for Egocentricity), reflecting strong trends in an internal sense of alienation and egocentric orientation for the SDR group.

The BORRTI also assesses reality testing capacity on three subscales: Reality Distortion, Uncertainty of Perception, and Hallucinations/Delusions. One-way ANOVAs were performed to compare means of the groups on these subscales. The results of this ANOVA revealed significant differences on the Uncertainty of Perception subscale only (p < .05). The SDR group scored significantly higher (mean = 49.4) than the control subjects (mean = 41.8) on this subscale, reflecting a greater sense of uncertainty of perception for SDR subjects.

To assess differences in attachment styles between the two groups, one-way ANOVAs were performed on the three subscales of the Adult Attachment

Inventory (AAI). The four subscales are Dependency, Anxiety in Relationships, Comfort with Closeness, and Dismissive. Results reflect no significant differences between the two groups on any of the subscales of the AAI.

The Interpersonal Reactivity Index is a measure that assesses empathic capacity on four dimensions (Perspective Taking, Fantasy, Empathic Concern, and Personal Distress). One-way ANOVAs were performed to assess differences between the two groups and significant results were obtained on the Empathic Concern subscale only. SDR subjects scored lower (mean = 10.7) than comparison subjects (mean = 13.5; $p < .05$).

To assess differences in defense style, one-way ANOVAs were performed on the Self-Rated Defense Style Inventory for each of the four subscales to determine differences between the two groups. The four subscales are: Maladaptive Action Patterns, Image Distorting, Self-Sacrificing, and Adaptive Defense Style. Significant results were obtained on the Image Distortion subscale where SDR subjects scored significantly higher (mean = 43.2) than comparison subjects (mean = 31.3; $p < .01$). On the Image Distorting subscale, SDR subjects scored higher (mean = 45.4) than comparison subjects (mean = 31.4; $p < .01$).

To assess differences in parental relationships, one-way ANOVAs were performed on the two subscales of the Parental Bonding Instrument for each parent. The analyses were performed four times, one for each parent on each of the two subscales: Mother Care, Mother Overprotection, Father Care, Father Overprotection. Significant results were obtained for Mother Care and Mother Overprotection. On the Mother Care subscale, SDR subjects scored significantly lower (mean = 14.0) than comparison subjects (mean = 20.1; $p = .05$). On the Mother Overprotection subscale, SDR subjects scored significantly higher (mean = 13.2) than comparison subjects (mean = 4.6; $p < .01$).

To assess differences in parental care-giving style, one-way ANOVAs were performed on the three subscales of the Parental Care-Giving Style Instrument. The analyses were performed six times, once for each parent on each of the three subscales: Mother Warm, Mother Cold, Mother Ambivalent, Father Warm, Father Cold, and Father Ambivalent. Significant results were obtained for Father Warm (comparison subjects scoring higher) and for Father Ambivalent, Mother Cold, and Mother Ambivalent (SDR subjects scoring higher). On the Father Warm subscale, SDR subjects scored significantly lower (mean = 16.4) than comparison subjects (mean = 21.7; $p = .05$). On the Father Ambivalent subscale, SDR subjects scored significantly higher (mean = 17.2) than comparison subjects (mean = 13.1; $p = .01$). On the Mother Cold subscale, SDR subjects scored significantly higher (mean = 19.9) than comparison subjects (mean = 13.3; $p < .01$). On the Mother Ambivalent subscale, SDR subjects scored significantly higher (mean = 17.3) than comparison subjects (mean = 14.5; $p < .05$).

There were no significant differences in intellectual functioning as reflected in the nearly equal means on the two subtests of the Shipley.

One-way ANOVAs were performed to compare means of the two groups on the 12 IIP variables. The results reflect significant differences between the two groups overall (p < .05). Results confirmed significant differences on three characteristics of interpersonal problem styles. These characteristics were: Exploitable, Overly Nurturant, and Intrusive. All mean differences were significant at a p value of <.001 (see table A.2). On the Exploitable subscale, the SDR sample scored significantly higher (mean = 1.7) than comparison subjects (mean = 1.0; p < .001). On the Overly Nurturant subscale, the SDR sample scored significantly higher (mean = 1.6) than comparison subjects (mean = .8; p < .001). On the Intrusive subscale, the SDR sample scored significantly higher (mean = 1.2) than comparison subjects (mean = .5; p < .001).

In addition to proving effective in comparisons between the SDR samples at the individual variable level, the IIP also proved useful in the discrimination of the two groups utilizing the interpersonal quadrant scores. When a circumplex analysis was performed on the four interpersonal quadrants, the SDR group differed significantly from the comparison group on the Affiliative Submissive and Affiliative Dominant quadrants. Interestingly, the SDR group did not differ significantly on scales that included the hostile pole of the affiliation axis, which concurs with the clinical observation that these subjects have great difficulty seeing themselves as aggressive (see figure A.1). On the Affiliative Submissive quadrant, SDR subjects scored significantly higher (mean = 1.6) than comparison subjects (mean = .9; p < .001). On the Affiliative Dominant quadrant, SDR subjects scored significantly higher (mean = 1.0) than comparison subjects (mean = .5; p < .001; see figure A.1).

DISCUSSION

The results of this study reflect a profile comprised of several related personality characteristics and vulnerabilities that may be associated with mental health professionals who have engaged in sexualized dual relationships. Several areas of vulnerability were delineated that are related to each other and can be categorized as: (1) insecure feelings and submissive relational behavior, (2) a history of ambivalent and problematic parenting, and (3) uncertain perceptions. Robust measures from where these findings are primarily derived were the IIP, the BORRTI, Defense Style Questionnaire, Parental Care-Giving Styles, and the Parental Bonding Instrument. Many of these instruments have overlapping areas of assessment, so the consistency in the findings reflect concurrent validity as well (table A.3).

Table A.2. Group Comparisons of the IIP Circumplex Variables ($n = 60$)

IIP Variable	Means			F	p	Group Contrasts[a]
	DSR ($n = 20$)	PC ($n = 20$)	UC ($n = 20$)			
Domineering	.79	.58	.53	1.65	.20	
Vindictive	.50	.48	.57	.19	.83	
Cold	.75	.68	.67	.14	.87	
Socially avoidant	.93	.97	1.21	.95	.39	
Nonassertive	1.46	1.28	1.10	1.45	.24	
Exploitable	1.67	1.06	.96	6.13	.004	DSR > PC**, UC***
Overly nurturant	1.59	.88	.90	6.38	.003	DSR > PC***, UC***
Intrusive	1.16	.51	.63	7.28	.002	DSR > PC***, UC***
Hostile dominant	.63	.58	.62	.06	.94	
Hostile submissive	1.20	1.12	1.15	.07	.93	
Affiliative submissive	1.63	.97	.93	6.95	.002	DSR > PC***, UC***
Affiliative dominant	.98	.54	.53	5.35	.007	DSR > PC***, UC**

Note: IIP = Inventory of Interpersonal Problems.
DSR = Mental health professionals engaged in dual sexualized relationships; PC = Professional control—mental health professionals never charged with any ethical violations; UC = University control—10 advanced undergraduate psychology majors and 10 clinical psychology graduate students.
[a] Fisher's PLSD.
* $p \leq .05$. ** $p \leq .01$. *** $p \leq .005$.

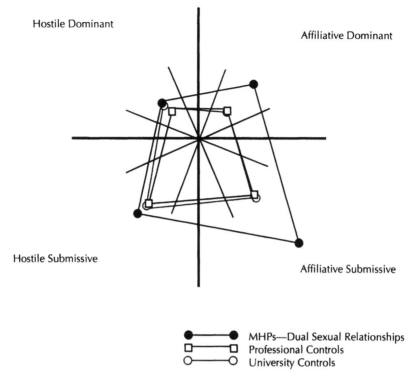

Hostile Dominant

Affiliative Dominant

Hostile Submissive

Affiliative Submissive

●————● MHPs—Dual Sexual Relationships
□————□ Professional Controls
○————○ University Controls

Figure A.1.

Relational Feelings and Behavior

Several areas of vulnerability in relational capacity (in terms of subjective feelings and behavioral tendencies) were delineated, including insecure attachment, social incompetence, exploitability, overuse of nurturance, and intrusiveness. The circumplex analysis of the IIP also revealed two prevalent interpersonal styles that capture the power dimension of relational capacity: Affiliative Submissive and Affiliative Dominant. This latter finding suggests that the SDR group may tend to exert their power in relational contexts through affiliative behaviors, a finding that is consistent with the overall understanding of the function of sexualization. It is also important to note that although the scores for the SDR group in the Affiliative Dominant quadrant varied significantly from the comparison subjects, a greater main effect was found in the Affiliative Submissive quadrant (where the mean for the SDR group was highest).

This study supports the observation that one type of therapist vulnerable to transgressing sexual boundaries may harbor a subjective sense of powerlessness that may cause him to overuse nurturance in an intrusive, exploitative

Table A.3.   SDR and PC Results

	SDR n = 21		PC n = 24		
	Mean	SD	Mean	SD	p
Relational Capacities					
Insecure Attachment (BORRTI)#	**49.5**	10.4	38.3	7.0	.0013***
Social Incompetence (BORRTI)	**47.3**	7.3	40.3	8.8	.0181*
Exploitability (IIP)#	**1.7**	.8	1.0	.5	.0009***
Overuse of Nurturance (IIP)	**1.6**	.9	.8	.5	.0012***
Intrusiveness (IIP)	**1.2**	.7	.5	.4	.0001***
Affiliative Submissive (IIP)	**1.6**	.9	.9	.5	.0007***
Affiliative Dominant (IIP)	**1.0**	.5	.5	.4	.0013***
Parenting					
Maternal Ambivalence (PCS)#	**17.3**	3.3	14.5	4.4	.0450*
Paternal Ambivalence (PCS)	**17.2**	3.8	13.1	5.1	.0123**
Mother Cold (PCS)	**19.9**	7.5	13.3	4.8	.0066**
Mother Overprotection (PBI)#	**13.2**	8.9	4.6	5.7	.0030**
Mother Care (PBI)	14.0	8.0	**20.1**	9.4	.0539*
Father Warmth (PCS)	16.4	7.1	**21.7**	7.6	.0507*
Perception					
Uncertain Perception (BORRTI)	**49.4**	9.4	41.8	7.8	.0178*
Image Distortion (DSQ)#	**43.2**	14.4	31.4	6.3	.0099**

SDR = Sexualized Dual Relationships group; PC = Professional Control group.
#BORRTI=Bell Object Relations and Reality Testing Inventory; IIP = Inventory of Interpersonal Problems; PCS = Parental Care-Giving Style; PBI = Parental Bonding Instrument; DSQ = Defense Style Questionnaire.
***$p <. 001$. **$p < .01$. *$p < .05$.

attempt to gain control of the therapy process (see chapter 2, for an in-depth case study). Though transgressing therapists are manifestly exploitative, they typically report a subjective feeling of powerlessness, an inability to tolerate negative transference, and an underlying narcissistic fragility (chapter 3). These findings suggest conflicts with aggression (manifested as passive-aggressivity, through seduction) in an indirect, inhibited manner. Further, these characteristics and vulnerabilities are consistent with previous observations emphasizing long-standing conflicts involving *interpersonal longing and deprivation,* anxiety regarding *body integrity or self-boundaries, primitive sexualization* of anxiety-provoking issues, and *depression* (Celenza, 1998; Celenza & Hilsenroth, 1997; appendix B).

Since the IIP proved a robust instrument for the variables under consideration, additional analyses were performed using the IIP with a second control group made up of 20 undergraduate students. ANOVAs were performed

Table A.4. IIP Results

Variable	SDR n = 21 Mean	PC n = 24 Mean	UC n = 20 Mean	p	Group Contrasts
Exploitability (IIP)	1.7	1.0	1.0	.0005	DSR > PC***, UC***
Overuse of Nurturance (IIP)	1.6	.8	.9	.0009	DSR > PC***, UC**
Intrusiveness (IIP)	1.2	.5	.6	.0001	DSR > PC***, UC**
Affiliative Submissive (IIP)	1.6	.9	.9	.0003	DSR > PC***, UC***
Affiliative Dominant (IIP)	1.0	.5	.5	.0016	DSR > PC***, UC**

SDR = Sexualized Dual Relationships group; PC = Professional Control group; UC = University Control group.
***p < .001. **p < .01.

to compare means of the groups on the 12 IIP variables. Table A.4 presents data concerning the ability of the IIP circumplex variables to differentiate the SDR group compared with the PC and Undergraduate Control (UC) samples. Consistent with the original findings, the results of this additional analysis confirmed significant differences on three characteristics for the SDR sample when compared to either the PC or UC groups. These characteristics were: Exploitable, Overly Nurturant, and Intrusive. All mean differences between the SDR group and the Professional Controls were significant at a p value of <.001. The mean difference between the SDR group and the Undergraduate Controls on Exploitable was significant at a p value of <.001 as well and the mean differences on Overuse of Nurturance and Intrusive were significant at a p value of <.01. Fisher Protected Least Significant Difference (PLSD) contrasts revealed higher levels on each of these mean scores for the SDR group (see figure A.2).

In addition to proving effective in comparisons between the SDR sample at the individual variable level, the IIP also proved useful in the discrimination of the three groups utilizing the interpersonal quadrant scores. When an analysis was performed on the four interpersonal quadrants, the SDR group differed significantly from the PC and UC groups on Affiliative Submissive (p < .001 for both groups) and Affiliative Dominant (p < .001 for Professional Controls and p < .01 for Undergraduate Controls). Interestingly, the SDR group did not differ significantly on scales that included the hostile pole of the affiliation axis, which concurs with the clinical observation that these subjects have great difficulty seeing themselves as aggressive (figure A.1). Finally no significant differences were found between the two control groups (PC and UC) on any of the IIP circumplex variables utilized in the study.

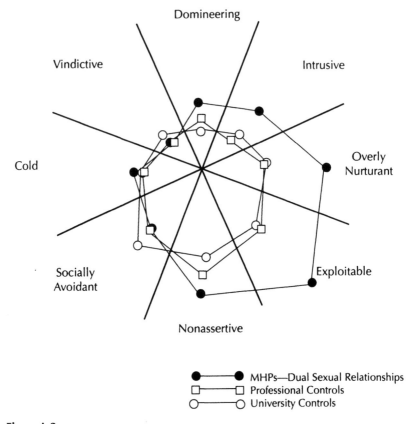

Figure A.2.

Ambivalent and Problematic Parenting

The results for this category are particularly consistent between the two measures: Parental Bonding Instrument and Parental Care-Giving Styles. The SDR group reported a higher incidence of parental ambivalence (in both maternal and paternal relationships) as well as coldness (rejection and nonresponsivity) and overprotection in maternal care-giving style. In contrast, the comparison subjects reported a higher incidence of maternal care and paternal warmth than the SDR group.

One of the most salient factors reported in the clinical literature for these individuals is the pervasive sense of unmet interpersonal longing and emotional deprivation in relational contexts. Consistent with the data from this study, these individuals appear acutely sensitive to and deprived of emotional sustenance derived from interpersonal contact, consistent with a childhood experience of emotional deprivation and lack of affection. It is reasonable to assume that this is one of the factors that contributes to a subversion of the therapeutic process such that the therapist's needs become the central focus rather than the patient's. These characteristics are consistent with Gabbard's (1994a) profile of lovesickness and may well underlie the psychodynamics of masochistic surrender as well.

The results of this study indicate that conflicts with aggression may underlie the constellation of interpersonal problems associated with sexual misconduct. This is consistent with results from Celenza and Hilsenroth's (1997) Rorschach study (see appendix B) where a low frequency of aggression was demonstrated in the protocols. The capacity to exploit another for the purpose of gratifying one's own needs is usually deemed a manifestly aggressive act and presumed to be associated with unresolved conflicts or preoccupations with aggression (Pope, 1989b). While this finding may indicate an absence of aggression in these subjects, another possible interpretation, consistent with in-depth case studies and clinical observations of this population (Celenza, 1991, 1995, 1998), postulates an unconscious defensive transformation of countertransference hate (or aggression) into countertransference love. The need for this defensive transformation has been attributed to an unconscious intolerance of countertransference hate, and the absence of aggression in these protocols might be viewed as supporting this interpretation.

Uncertainty of Perception

The data for this category are derived from the Defense Style Questionnaire and the BORRTI, both of which assess differences in the perception of reality. Scores for the two groups on the Defense Style Questionnaire revealed a significantly greater tendency to distort images by the SDR group in comparison to the control group. The image-distorting defenses include omnipotence-devaluation, primitive idealization, and splitting, all of which function to deny, manage, modulate, or otherwise transform aggression and power in relation to self and others. Consistent with this finding are the results from the BORRTI where the SDR group scored significantly higher in the subjective sense of uncertainty and doubt in the perception of self and others.

The findings also indicate that the subjects in the present study (for both groups) are not grossly impaired in most realms (a fact that may have a bearing on their appeal to patients). Cognitive functions are generally intact and they often display superior intelligence on standardized tests. Gross indications of psychopathology are absent, such as thought disorder or significant impairment in reality contact.

CONCLUSION

While generalizations from this investigation should be made cautiously, the data indicate several areas of vulnerability that require further investigation, including exploitability, intrusiveness, and submissiveness. A childhood history of emotional deprivation (maternal coldness and nonresponsivity) and parental ambivalence may also be a precursor. In addition, the results of this study do not support some clinical observations previously debated, such as the predominance of sociopathy and aggression in this population (see Pope, 1989b). Further research is needed to examine the empirical relationship between psychometric measures and clinical observation of mental health professionals who have engaged in sexualized dual relationships.

This study helps to clarify several characteristics indicating disturbance in self-development that should be a focus of concern for trainers and educators of MHPs as they progress in their training and personal development. Several areas of vulnerability may represent areas of concern, including insecure attachment, social incompetence, exploitability, overuse of nurturance, and intrusiveness. In contrast, the subjects in the present study are not grossly impaired in most realms (a fact that may have a bearing on their appeal to patients). Cognitive functions are generally intact and they often display superior intelligence on standardized tests. Gross indications of psychopathology are absent, such as thought disorder or significant impairment in reality contact.

It is tempting to view a group of individuals who have engaged in sexualized boundary transgressions as sociopathic repeat offenders who are not amenable to rehabilitation (Pope, 1989b). Though the most prevalent stereotype of offending therapists describes personality characteristics typically associated with sociopathy, repeat offenses, and calculating exploitiveness, the data from this study suggest a markedly different profile. In contrast to the individuals in the present study, sociopathic characters would be expected to score high on measures that assess personality characteristics such as domineering, vindictive, and cold. The data from the subjects in the SDR group present a contrasting constellation of interpersonal problems. This may suggest that these two groups represent contrasting, polarized, and extreme adaptations to similar conflicts in relational capacity. This study highlights the need to differentiate between these two types of offenders when performing empirical studies and when studying or proposing rehabilitation efforts.

One measure, the IIP, has been useful in delineating populations that are more or less amenable to psychotherapeutic intervention (Horowitz, 1996).

As Horowitz has described, problems of friendly submissiveness and exploitability appear to be more easily treated in brief dynamic psychotherapy than problems of hostile dominance. This implies that certain personality types of therapists who have engaged in sexual misconduct may be amenable to rehabilitation whereas others may not. In particular, the psychopathic predators who may be characterized as cold, vindictive, and dominating would not be expected to demonstrate rehabilitation effects. In contrast, the one-time offender, described variously as lovesick (Gabbard, 1994a), severely neurotic and/or socially isolated (Schoener & Gonsiorek, 1989), or narcissistically needy (Celenza, 1998) appears to be amenable to rehabilitation, and in some cases, this has been clinically demonstrated. The IIP may be useful in helping to understand these impaired professionals and may aid evaluators in the assessment of rehabilitation potential.

In addition to measures of interpersonal and attachment styles, learning tools should also include measures of behavior that may be transgressive (see, for example, Schoener, 1999). One study devised a self-assessment questionnaire designed to measure exploitive behavior by therapists (Epstein & Simon, 1990). The Exploitation Index is comprised of several subcategories of exploitive behaviors that clinicians can rate based on frequency of occurrence. To date, this scale has not been validated and though it assesses manifest behavior from slippery-slope boundary crossings to frank boundary violations, it is a useful tool for behavioral indications of boundary violations.

ENDNOTE

This study was conducted in 1999 with coinvestigator Mark J. Hilsenroth, Ph.D., and research assistants Steven Ackerman and James Rough.

APPENDIX B:
A RORSCHACH INVESTIGATION

Andrea Celenza, Ph.D., and Mark Hilsenroth, Ph.D.

Therapist sexual misconduct is now recognized as a significant problem as a result of several national studies that have reported an alarmingly high prevalence among most disciplines (see, e.g., Holroyd & Brodsky, 1977; Pope et al., 1979; Gartrell et al., 1986; Borys & Pope, 1989). Sexual misconduct is currently among the leading causes of malpractice litigation (Gabbard, 1994a). One beneficial effect of the expanded awareness of the problem is a significant rise in victims seeking help and redress.

Interest in the transgressing professionals has resulted in several investigations from different vantage points, including a typology of vulnerable therapists (Schoener & Gonsiorek, 1989; Levine et al., 1994), common scenarios of therapist-patient sexual intimacy (Pope, 1989b), psychodynamic profiles of transgressing therapists (Strean, 1993; Gabbard, 1994a), and potential predisposing characteristics of therapist sexual misconduct (Celenza, 1998). These studies have based their observations on extensive interviews with the transgressing professional, and may include interviews with the victim(s) and other relevant individuals and/or organizational representatives. These comprehensive evaluations most often also include psychological testing, and although there have been no previous attempts to empirically derive a profile of the vulnerable therapist, most authors have agreed that the transgressing therapist defies simple categorization based on a single diagnosis or psychodynamic profile.

Previous clinical observations have culminated in a range of profiles and diagnostic categories of the transgressing therapist. Six diagnostic categories were delineated by Schoener and Gonsiorek (1989), including: (1) uninformed/naïve, (2) healthy or mildly neurotic, (3) severely neurotic and/or socially isolated, (4) impulsive character disorders, (5) sociopathic or narcissistic character disorders, and (6) psychotic or borderline personalities. A seventh category, bipolar disorders, was recently added (Schoener, 1994, personal communication). Gabbard (1994a) proposed four underlying psychological profiles as an alternative classification scheme. These underlying characteristics include: (1) psychotic disorders, (2) predatory psychopathy and paraphilias, (3) lovesickness, and (4) masochistic surrender.

In addition, Celenza (1998) has described eight potential predisposing characteristics that were observed fairly consistently in each of the professionals in her sample, regardless of diagnosis. These include (1) long-standing narcissistic vulnerability, (2) grandiose (covert) rescue fantasies, (3) intolerance of negative transference, (4) childhood history of emotional deprivation and sexualized overstimulation, (5) family history of covert and sanctioned boundary transgressions, (6) unresolved anger toward authority figures, (7) restricted awareness of fantasy (especially hostile/aggressive), and (8) transformation of countertransference hate to countertransference "love." At the time of this study, there were no empirical investigations that examined the above characteristics or diagnostic schemas. Important issues have been usefully debated, such as the predominance of sociopathy in these individuals (Pope, 1989b), the role of aggression (Celenza, 1998a; Pope, 1989b), and the lack of evidence of a consistent profile (Schoener, 1995, personal communication). Up to 2001, however, there had been no systematic or controlled investigations aimed at addressing these questions, nor have studies reported the use of standardized personality assessment instruments in a systematic manner. This study is the first to do so and employed the Rorschach to systematically assess the personality characteristics noted above in evaluating such variables as emotional resources, experienced stressors, affect, interpersonal relations, ideation, mediation, cognitive processing, and self-perception.

This empirical analysis sought to (1) further delineate the personality dimensions underlying the character structure of professionals who transgress sexual boundaries; (2) identify core features, if any, of personality that may exist with this group of mental health professionals (MHPs); and (3) highlight the characteristics that might be most useful to supervisors and educators as a focus of concern in an individual's training and personal development.

METHOD

Subjects

Subjects were 20 professionals who had engaged in one or more sexualized dual relationships. Subjects were referred by an overseeing professional organization, state licensing board, or by self-referral for an independent comprehensive evaluation, supervision, or consultation. The only criterion for inclusion in the study was that the professional had engaged in a sexualized dual relationship, defined as erotic contact with a patient, client, parishioner, or student. The sample included a wide range of therapists of various disciplines, including clinical psychology, counseling psychology, pastoral counseling, and social work. Included in the sample as well were clergy who had engaged in sexual misconduct with one or more parishioners or students.

In the majority of cases (80%), testing was conducted as part of an independent comprehensive evaluation to assess rehabilitation potential within one month of a disciplinary hearing. In the remainder of cases, testing was conducted for research purposes after the subject was referred for supervision or consultation.

Subjects' ages at the time of testing ranged from 25–66. All subjects are male. Nineteen subjects are Caucasian and one is Hispanic. Ninety percent of subjects are heterosexual whose transgression(s) involved one or more heterosexual relationships, and 50% were married at the time of the transgression(s). Most subjects appeared to be highly intelligent and all were well educated, having achieved at least one postgraduate degree (90% at the doctoral level). Intelligence measures included the WAIS-R or the Shipley Institute of Living Scale–Vocabulary and Analogies subtests, the latter administered to those familiar with the WAIS-R. The mean IQ for this sample is in the Superior range (Full Scale IQ, mean = 124). This mean is two standard deviations higher than the level expected in same-age peers. This finding is consistent with previous observations and supports the interpretation that the cause of the transgression is not simply an incapacity to comprehend the ethical code. Indeed, most of the subjects in this sample reported being aware of committing an ethical violation at the time of the transgression.

Many subjects appeared to be under stress, including anxiety, depression, and, in some cases, the subjects exhibited defensiveness or oppositionality. This was understood within the context of the stressful event of the disciplinary hearing. None appeared psychotic. None had prior psychiatric histories involving a major mental disturbance, though many had had previous psychotherapy or psychoanalysis. Only two reported a history of sexual trauma or incest, although all reported significant emotional abuse in their families of origin, usually involving lack of affection or emotional deprivation.

Procedure

Each Rorschach was originally administered and scored according to the Comprehensive System (Exner, 1993) by the first author. For the purpose of interrater reliability, ten clinical protocols, also administered and scored by the first author, were interspersed in the MHP sample. Thirty protocols were subsequently scored by the second author blind to group assignment and original scoring. The two sets of scoring were then compared. Percentages of agreement were calculated for all relevant scoring categories as recommended by Exner (1991). The 80% agreement level necessary for reliability, suggested by Weiner (1991), was achieved for each scoring category, with an overall agreement level of 87%, an individual category low of 85% for Special Scores, and an individual category high of 90% for Location. The scoring by the second author was used for the tabulation of variables in the study.

Rorschach protocols were scrutinized for validity and no patients were found to have fewer than 14 responses and a Lambda above 1.0. In fact, only one protocol had 14 responses and only one other protocol had a Lambda of exactly 1.0. This indicates that this group was sufficiently engaged with the task.

RESULTS AND DISCUSSION

Tables B.1 through B.8 present descriptive statistics including mean, standard deviation, and frequency calculated for the variable clusters from the structural summary (Exner, 1993). These can be compared to the scores of 700 nonpatient adults reported by Exner (1993). These tables are organized in the format similar to Exner (1993) detailing normative and patient populations, so that direct comparisons can be made between our sample and other groups.

Four Square: Balance of Resources and Impingements

The MHP were engaged in the response process as reflected by the overall mean number of responses given (M = 28.9). This is relatively high and reflects that subjects were actively involved in producing responses for the task. Likewise, responses were often determined by more than one feature, displaying a flexible cognitive style that was complex and integrative of the stimuli. This is consistent with the levels expected from highly intelligent persons who have obtained advanced degrees. This group also displayed coping resources commensurate with normative means as reflected in the relatively high number of movement and color responses. These determinants indicate a capacity for internal reflection and affect responsiveness, respectively.

In normal protocols, however, it is typical to find a distinct coping style where an individual displays a preference for or tendency toward either reflectiveness or affective responsivity. The MHPs appeared to lack a distinct coping style, scoring equivalently for both of these characteristics, which suggests

Table B.1. Comparison of Four Square Variables of MHPs Engaged in Sexual Misconduct (n = 20) and a Normative Sample (n = 700).*

VARIABLE	Mental Health Professionals			Normative Sample		
Four Square	M	S.D.	Freq	M	S.D.	Freq
R	28.90	8.76	100%	22.67	4.23	100%
L	.36	.27	95%	.58	.26	100%
M	5.10	2.71	95%	4.30	1.92	100%
WGSum C	4.68	1.50	100%	4.52	1.79	100%
EA	9.76	3.39	100%	8.82	2.18	100%
Introversive	6		30%	251		36%
Ambitent	10		50%	143		20%
Extratensive	4		20%	306		44%
FM	4.95	2.80	100%	3.71	1.19	100%
m	2.05	1.19	95%	1.12	.85	76%
Sum C'	3.60	2.11	95%	1.53	1.25	79%
Sum T***	4.25	2.45	90%	1.03	.58	89%
Sum V	1.20	1.44	70%	.26	.58	20%
Sum Y***	4.65	4.45	90%	.57	1.00	39%
es***	20.70	7.62	100%	8.21	3.00	100%
D***	−3.35	1.66	100%	.04	1.09	100%
Adj D**	−1.75	1.29	100%	.20	.88	100%

** MHP mean > 2 S.D. from normative mean; *** MHP mean > 3 S.D. from normative mean.
# Exner, J. (1993). *The Rorschach: A comprehensive system. Vol. 1. Basic Foundations* (3rd ed.). New York: Wiley.

inefficiency in managing resources and adapting to stressors. This is particularly salient given that these individuals are experiencing extraordinary levels of distress and suggests that the stimulus demands were exceeding or threatening to exceed available emotional resources, as reflected in overall measures of current and long-standing distress. Persons with such high levels of distress scores are usually in a continuous state of stimulus overload and are vulnerable to being overwhelmed.

The high levels of distress within the protocols of this group are primarily due to an unusually high number of the four shading determinants. These include the use of the achromatic features (black, white, or gray, which are associated with depression or constrained affect); texture (tactile qualities such as fur, associated with interpersonal longing); vista (a shading response that incorporates perspective, distance, or dimensionality, associated with painful introspection); and darkness or lightness (associated with diffuse or ill-defined dysphoria). All of these shading determinants indicate intense dysphoria and affective constraint in general. However, because a great extent of the impinging dysphoria is due to a very large number of light/dark and texture determinants, these shading determinants lend a particular cast to the depression revolving

Table B.2.   Comparison of Affective Variables between MHPs Engaged in Sexual Misconduct (*n* = 20) and a Normative Sample (*n* = 700).[#]

VARIABLE	Mental Health Professionals			Normative Sample		
Affect	M	S.D.	Freq	M	S.D.	Freq
FC	5.30	2.72	100%	4.09	1.88	99%
CF	2.00	1.11	90%	2.36	1.27	96%
C	.05	.22	5%	.08	.28	7%
Afr	.50	.12	100%	.69	.16	100%
S	2.40	1.47	95%	1.47	1.21	86%
Blends	9.10	3.84	100%	5.16	1.93	100%
CP	0.00	0.00	0%	.02	.14	2%

[#] Exner, J. (1993). *The Rorschach: A comprehensive system. Vol. 1. Basic Foundations* (3rd ed.). New York: Wiley.

around feelings of helplessness, lack of clarity, and interpersonal longing. Given the current situational stressors these professionals were experiencing during their evaluations, it is not surprising that feelings of insecurity, loss of control, and in particular helplessness and withdrawal were reflected in their protocols. Though texture responses, like the more diffuse light/dark, are affected by situational stressors, especially interpersonal loss, these responses may also be indicative of character-based emotional neediness. In this regard, it is interesting to note that while approximately 50% reported undergoing the loss of a significant other or relational distress *at the time of the transgression,* only 20% reported undergoing interpersonal loss *at the time of testing.* Thus, the findings support the hypothesis that the high texture scores may in part reflect chronic or long-standing distress associated with affective/object hunger and neediness.

This hypothesis is further supported when the overall measure of distress is adjusted for situational factors by subtracting the scores associated with acute distress. The Adjusted Distress score is still significantly beyond the level expected and reflects a highly vulnerable, although improved capacity to access internal resources when situational factors are held constant. Thus, the adjusted score of distress may indicate premorbid vulnerability and long-term adjustment problems. Further, since much of the dysphoria is accounted for by excessively frequent texture responses, it can be concluded that the premorbid vulnerability resides primarily in the interpersonal sphere and is comprised of emotional neediness and object-hunger.

Affect

Overall measures of affect responsivity fall within the normative range, reflecting affective stability and a capacity for impulse control. The data do

Table B.3.   Comparison of Interpersonal Variables between MHPs Engaged in Sexual Misconduct (*n* = 20) and a Normative Sample (*n* = 700).#

VARIABLE	Mental Health Professionals			Normative Sample		
Interpersonal	M	S.D.	Freq	M	S.D.	Freq
COP	.75	.97	45%	2.07	1.52	79%
AG	1.15	1.35	60%	1.18	1.18	67%
Food	.70	1.08	35%	.23	.50	19%
Isolate	.15	.10	100%	.20	.09	100%
H	3.50	2.40	90%	3.39	1.80	99%
CG**	3.45	2.50	90%	1.29	.93	82%
Sx***	1.75	1.94	65%	.07	.39	4%

** MHP mean > 2 S.D. from normative mean; *** MHP mean > 3 S.D. from normative mean.
# Exner, J. (1993). *The Rorschach: A comprehensive system. Vol. 1. Basic Foundations* (3rd ed.). New York: Wiley.

reflect slight constriction in these individuals, who may exercise more effort at affect modulation than is typical. This may suggest a tendency to withdraw from situations that could be potentially stimulating, as reflected in the relatively low number of affect responsivity scores on cards that contain this stimulus potential. Conversely, an avoidance of affective stimuli may be the result of concerns about control, and this is often seen in individuals who are detached and/or isolated from others. This orientation may not be pathological given that there is not an excessive disproportion between scores reflecting adequate and inadequate affect modulation, but more likely is representative of a slightly obsessive character style. In addition, the affective constriction observed in this group may reflect an attempt to contain acute emotional distress.

Interpersonal

Measures of cooperation in interpersonal contexts as well as measures of aggression toward others differ little from the normative mean. Nonetheless, the measure of cooperation is slightly lower than expected and occurred in only 45% of the sample. This may belie a discomfort in or distance from interpersonal situations and may indicate a pessimism concerning having their needs met by others. However, the aggression score for this group is almost identical to the normative sample and indicates that while these individuals do not have a great deal of positive interactions with others, they also do not indicate an increased likelihood for aggressive behaviors and hostile or negative attitudes toward others. Given the sexual boundary transgressions with their patients, it is of diagnostic interest to note that these actions, while severe, are not based simply on poorly controlled aggressive impulses or an internal

Table B.4. Comparison of Ideational Variables between MHPs Engaged in Sexual Misconduct (*n* = 20) and a Normative Sample (*n* = 700).[#]

VARIABLE	Mental Health Professionals			Normative Sample		
Ideation	M	S.D.	Freq	M	S.D.	Freq
a (active)	10.95	5.07	100%	6.48	2.14	100%
p (passive)	1.25	.91	80%	2.69	1.52	94%
Ma	4.40	2.30	95%	3.03	1.59	97%
Mp	.50	.76	35%	1.31	.94	81%
Intellect	1.05	1.76	100%	1.56	1.29	100%
M***	.70	.98	40%	.03	.18	3%
Sum6	1.95	2.72	65%	1.59	1.25	80%
Lvi-2	.20	.41	20%	.03	.18	3%
WSum6	5.45	7.54	65%	3.28	2.89	100%
M none	0.00	0.00	0%	.01	.11	1%

** MHP mean > 2 S.D. from normative mean; *** MHP mean > 3 S.D. from normative mean.
[#] Exner, J. (1993). *The Rorschach: A comprehensive system. Vol. 1. Basic Foundations* (3rd ed.). New York: Wiley.

world besieged by hostile or malevolent objects. As noted by Celenza (1991, 1995, 1998), the role of aggression in these individuals is complex and may involve a subtle defensive transformation. This is further discussed below.

The number of humans perceived by this group is almost identical to the normative sample. This implies an interest in and sensitivity to others. With regard to several other scores pronounced in the Interpersonal constellation, it is important to note that the ability to perceive humans does not necessarily imply involvement with others. Some subjects who perceive humans may simply be sensitive to or perceptive of others. This finding is not surprising given that this sample is comprised of mental health professionals.

The number of clothing and sexual content scores are particularly salient for this group. The MHP group developed a significantly high number

Table B.5. Comparison of Meditational Variables between MHPs Engaged in Sexual Misconduct (*n* = 20) and a Normative Sample (*n* = 700).[#]

VARIABLE	Mental Health Professionals			Normative Sample		
Mediation	M	S.D.	Freq	M	S.D.	Freq
P	6.95	1.67	100%	6.89	1.38	100%
X+%	.61	.11	100%	.79	.08	100%
F+%	.56	.29	90%	.71	.17	100%
X–%	.14	.07	100%	.07	.05	86%
S–%	.18	.31	45%	.08	.23	15%
Xu%	.25	.11	100%	.14	.07	95%

[#] Exner, J. (1993). *The Rorschach: A comprehensive system. Vol. 1. Basic Foundations* (3rd ed.). New York: Wiley.

of clothing responses and this score occurred at least once in almost all of the protocols. This may suggest a sensitivity to external appearance and social convention as well as fears of exposure, attempts to shore up self-boundaries, or concerns about sexual issues. This latter interpretation is accentuated when examining the prominent amount of sex content in the sample as compared to the normative sample. Increased sexual ideation might be expected from MHPs who have engaged in sexualized dual relationships, indicating sexualization of anxiety-related issues. Furthermore, a large number (77%) of the sexual content responses were not perceived as integrated aspects of whole human responses. Rather, these responses took the form of body parts in isolation and were often associated with primitive, morbid, or aggressive content (i.e., "a bleeding vagina, it looks like it's splashing, ejecting with some force," "an erect penis that's not quite right, it feels explosive," "a penis that's not fully developed," "a scrotum with just testicles, no sack"). These data suggest a primitive stance toward sexuality that is relatively unmodulated and resistant to delaying intense or blatant wishes for gratification (Holt, 1977). This data is also consistent with clinical observations that these individuals exhibit a developmentally regressed part-object level of relatedness (Gabbard, 1994a).

Ideation/Mediation

Idiosyncratic, but not gross reality distortion is observed in the MHP group, particularly within the interpersonal sphere, suggesting that these individuals have odd interpretations of human interactions. These subjects produced slightly more unconventional thoughts as indicated by the elevated measure of unusual percepts in contrast to frank reality distortions. Furthermore, this group's

Table B.6.　Comparison of Processing Variables between MHPs Engaged in Sexual Misconduct (*n* = 20) and a Normative Sample (*n* = 700).[#]

VARIABLE	Mental Health Professionals			Normative Sample		
Processing	M	S.D.	Freq	M	S.D.	Freq
Zf	11.4	4.48	100%	11.81	2.59	100%
Zd	−.98	5.27	100%	.72	3.06	100%
W	9.50	3.71	100%	8.55	1.94	100%
D	17.10	7.77	100%	12.89	3.54	99%
Dd	2.40	2.52	65%	1.23	1.70	65%
DQ+	4.95	3.72	95%	7.31	2.16	100%
DQv***	5.50	2.82	95%	1.30	1.26	68%

** MHP mean > 2 S.D. from normative mean; *** MHP mean > 3 S.D. from normative mean.
[#] Exner, J. (1993). *The Rorschach: A comprehensive system. Vol. 1. Basic Foundations* (3rd ed.). New York: Wiley.

idiosyncratic perception of human interactions does not impact on otherwise intact capacities to perceive reality in conventional ways when stimuli are not overly stimulating or complex. Consistent with recent observations (Celenza, 1998), the data also indicate a tendency toward activity rather than fantasy use as reflected in the relatively high number of active movement compared to passive movement responses. This action-proneness appears rigid and inflexible with little ability to examine ideas and events from different perspectives.

Processing

The scores representative of cognitive style for this group were unremarkable and the various location features approximated the distribution of the normative sample. However, the sample did exhibit a decreased capacity to organize the stimulus field in meaningful ways.

Self-Perception

Content scores reflected a preoccupation with body integrity, feelings of damage, and vulnerability as displayed in the preponderance of percepts involving anatomy, x-ray, and morbid content. The high number of morbid responses may also be an additional indication of the pervasive dysphoria these MHPs were experiencing at the time of testing. Surprisingly, however, these individuals did not display an unusually high degree of self-focus, nor was there evidence of deficiency in self-regard as suggested by the relatively low number of reflection and pair responses, which was almost identical to the normative sample. Also interesting to note is the relatively low number of scores representative of depth, distance, or dimension that are not based on shading (i.e., dysphoria), possibly indicative of the inability to introspect

Table B.7. Comparison of Self Perception Variables between MHPs Engaged in Sexual Misconduct (*n* = 20) and a Normative Sample (*n* = 700).[a]

VARIABLE Self-Perception	Mental Health Professionals			Normative Sample		
	M	*S.D.*	*Freq*	*M*	*S.D.*	*Freq*
3r + (2)/R	.38	.12	100%	.39	.07	100%
Fr + rF	.15	.49	10%	.08	.35	7%
FD	.35	.67	25%	1.16	.87	79%
An + Xy	1.70	1.72	65%	.45	.65	35%
MOR	1.50	1.43	60%	.70	.82	51%

[a] Exner, J. (1993). *The Rorschach: A comprehensive system. Vol. 1. Basic Foundations* (3rd ed.). New York: Wiley.

Table B.8. Comparison of Constellation Indicies between MHPs Engaged in Sexual Misconduct (*n* = 20) and a Normative Sample (*n* = 700).[#]

Constellations	Mental Health Professionals		Normative Sample	
SCZI = 6	0	0%	0	0%
SCZI = 5	0	0%	0	0%
SCZI = 4	0	0%	2	0%
DEPI = 7	0	0%	1	0%
DEPI = 6	3	15%	3	0%
DEPI = 5	8	40%	21	3%
CDI = 5	1	5%	3	0%
CDI = 4	3	15%	18	3%
S-Con Positive	0	0%	0	0%
HVI Positive	1	5%	13	2%
OBS Positive	0	0%	14	2%

[#] Exner, J. (1993). *The Rorschach: A comprehensive system. Vol. 1. Basic Foundations* (3rd ed.). New York: Wiley.

without concomitant feelings of worthlessness and negative self-appraisal (in contrast to the more frequent vista response, as noted earlier).

Constellations

Not surprisingly, no indication of formal thought disorder was found among the MHP sample. Scores associated with schizophrenia or other measures of psychotic states reflected no flagrant or gross distortions of reality testing. As mentioned, the quality of the distortion that did occur was idiosyncratic and unconventional.

More than half of the sample met criteria for depression on the Depression Index, a compilation of scores associated with major depressive disorders. A review of the variables associated with this index suggests that both acute and long-standing factors account for this elevation.

Only 20% of the sample appeared to be experiencing a destabilization in coping resources as assessed by the Coping Index. This finding argues against the interpretation that the depressive affect is due to current stressors alone, given that acute crises are usually associated with measures of destabilization. In addition, the mean score on the suicide constellation was moderate, yet none of the MHPs was positive on this index, nor had any attempted suicide since the evaluation process. This again supports the contention that this group does have resources available to them and that the data is indicative of a long-standing adjustment to a moderate level of dysphoria.

CONCLUSION

The data from this study reflect a profile comprised of several related personality characteristics and vulnerabilities that appear to be associated with MHPs who have engaged in sexualized dual relationships. Seven Rorschach variables were greater than three standard deviations from the normative mean. These included measures of distress (especially texture, diffuse shading such as light/dark, and generalized measures of dysphoria), primitive sexualization, and idiosyncratic reality contact. Other indicators differing by two standard deviations from the normative mean included measures of vulnerable self-boundaries and long-standing, characterologic dysphoria.

The subjects in the present study are not grossly impaired in most realms (a fact that may have a bearing on their appeal to patients). Cognitive functions are generally intact and they often display superior intelligence on standardized tests. Gross indications of psychopathology are absent, such as thought disorder or significant impairment in reality contact. As reflected in the high score of generalized dysphoria, the data indicate that these individuals were undergoing acute distress at the time of testing such that the stimulus demands were threatening to exceed their coping capacities. This is not surprising given that most were in the midst of facing professional disciplinary actions at the time of testing, and is consistent with data from other studies examining Rorschach indicators of acute distress (Sloan, Arsenault, Hilsenroth, Harvill, & Handler, 1995). Much, but not all, of this disturbance, however, is attributable to situational stress given the significant diminution of this score when adjusted for situational factors. For the most part, these individuals appear to have adequate coping resources, though they may cope at times in idiosyncratic ways that may become more unconventional under stress.

Despite otherwise intact functioning, however, there are multiple indications of disturbance. In addition, an overall measure of distress can be adjusted for situational exacerbation by subtracting out the pressures associated with acute factors. The resultant adjusted score is still highly negative, indicating long-standing adjustment problems even in the absence of situational exacerbation. Several additional indices provide a profile of vulnerability comprised of a cluster of scores reflecting impairment primarily in self-development. These include long-standing conflicts involving *interpersonal longing and deprivation*, anxiety regarding *body integrity or self-boundaries, primitive sexualization* of anxiety-provoking issues, and *depression*. While it can be argued that some of these issues are expected given the acute situational stress these subjects were undergoing at the time of the study, the data reflect long-standing unresolved issues in these realms. In addition, many of these factors are not typically associated with acute distress (e.g., primitive sexualization, interpersonal longing, trait indicators of depression).

One of the most salient factors observed in these individuals is the pervasive sense of unmet interpersonal longing and emotional deprivation in relational contexts. Consistent with the data from this study, these individuals appear acutely sensitive to and deprived of emotional sustenance derived from interpersonal contact. It is reasonable to assume that this is one of the factors that contribute to a subversion of the therapeutic process such that the therapist's needs become the central focus rather than the patient's. This may be exacerbated by idiosyncratic, unconventional, or odd interpretations of interpersonal interactions. These characteristics are consistent with Gabbard's (1994a) profile of lovesickness and may well underlie the psychodynamics of masochistic surrender as well.

Interestingly, there was not a concomitant compromise in self-focus (either above or below the normal range). In this regard, there was not a high occurrence of reflection, pair or personalized responses, suggesting a capacity to perceive external stimuli as separate and distinct from the self. One hypothesis for this interesting juxtaposition of factors is that these individuals are sufficiently empathically attuned such that they are capable of recognizing aspects of the other and may identify with the other when similar needs to their own are presented. A loss of boundaries manifested by overinvolvement or overidentification could presumably occur, however, with the recognition of self-related needs in the other, even when this perception is to some extent rooted in reality. Though aspects of the dyad that may have stimulated transference/countertransference enactments were not an area of focus in the present study, these will be a focus of investigation in the future.

It is tempting to view a group of individuals who have engaged in sexualized boundary transgressions as sociopathic repeat offenders who are not amenable to rehabilitation (Pope, 1989b). However, recent Rorschach investigations on pathological narcissism (Hilsenroth, Hibbard, Nash, & Handler, 1993; Hilsenroth, Fowler, Padawer, & Handler, 1995) and sociopathic disorders (Gacono & Meloy, 1994) suggests a markedly different profile for the sociopathic character than is derived from the present group of subjects. In contrast to the individuals in the present study, sociopathic characters display little or no acceptance of interpersonal need, low levels of anxiety and depression, and little tolerance for ambiguity related to internal dysphoria. Further, like narcissistic disorders, sociopathic characters are markedly self-focused. The data from the present group of subjects indicate significantly high interpersonal longing, high levels of depression and anxiety, and a lack of self-focus, all of which might be characterized as a "narcissistically needy" constellation of vulnerabilities. Though the profile of this group does not conform to DSM-IV criteria for Narcissistic Personality Disorder on a descriptive level, the extent of narcissistic vulnerability in these subjects might be regarded as representative of narcissistic issues or disturbances in self-development from a psychoanalytic viewpoint. It is also generally acknowledged that some sociopathic treaters do exist, yet none of the MHPs in our sample displayed this Rorschach profile. It is possible that the apparent preponderance of predatory repeat offenders may be overstated in the extant literature due to the widespread perceptions furthered by a few, well-publicized cases.

One unexpected finding was the relatively low frequency of aggression perceived in the protocols. The capacity to exploit another for the purpose of gratifying one's own needs is usually deemed a manifestly aggressive act and presumed to be associated with unresolved conflicts or preoccupations with aggression (Pope, 1989b). While this finding may indicate an absence of aggression in these subjects, another possible interpretation, consistent with in-depth case studies and clinical observations of this population (Celenza, 1991, 1995, 1998), postulates an unconscious defensive transformation of counter-transference hate (or aggression) into countertransference love. The need for this defensive transformation has been attributed to an unconscious intolerance of countertransference hate and the absence of aggression in these protocols might be viewed as supporting this interpretation.

Though introspection is thought to be the hallmark of psychological mindedness and presumably is one of the most important personality characteristics of therapists, this group appears capable only of painful introspection. For these subjects, the capacity to reflect upon themselves occurs only in association with internal dysphoria. Despite the fact that perspective-taking is an essential skill in psychotherapy, these therapists appear incapable of introspection without experiencing negative affect. In the context of interpersonal relations, introspection often leads to idiosyncratic reality contact as well.

It is not surprising that there were multiple indications of self-boundary disturbance, primitive sexualization, and a preference for action over fantasy use. Anxiety concerning body integrity, fantasies of damage, and attempts to shore up the self were common. Gender confusion was also evident in some protocols. Since sexualized boundary transgressions occur in a context where the MHP has inherent power, these contexts can become a tempting arena for acting out these conflicts. It is also a reasonable conjecture that sexualization may occur for some of these individuals as an attempt to reestablish self-cohesion, interpersonal connection, or to reassure the individual of gender-related concerns.

Some limitations in this study should be noted. The use of 700 nonpatient adults as a comparison group may limit the generalizability of this study. Future research might compare MHPs who cross sexual boundaries with samples of nonoffending MHPs and another group of MHPs who have been charged with an ethical violation of a nonsexual nature. This study is also limited by the size of the sample and consists of only male transgressors. However, when addressing issues within special populations, it is not always possible to obtain as large a sample as one might wish to collect. Our sample is comparable in size to recent investigations utilizing the Rorschach (Ganellen, 1994; Kaser-Boyd, 1993; Sloan et al., 1995) that make contributions to the understanding of various special populations. In addition, this is the first empirical investigation that examines this population and utilizes standardized personality assessment instruments.

Despite these limitations, we feel the findings of this study support the use of the Rorschach as a valuable instrument in detecting some of the personality characteristics of mental health professionals who have engaged in sexualized dual relationships. While generalizations from this investigation should be made cautiously, the data indicate several areas of vulnerability that require further investigation, including long-standing conflicts of interpersonal longing and deprivation, anxiety concerning body integrity and self-boundaries, primitive sexualization, and depression. While these vulnerabilities reflect impairment in the narcissistic realm, the data from the present study do not support the view that MHPs who transgress sexual boundaries are Narcissistic or Antisocial Personality Disorders compared with past Rorschach investigations of these two disorders. Nonetheless, this study clarifies several characteristics indicating disturbance in self-development that should be a focus of concern for trainers and educators of MHPs as they progress in their training and personal development. Finally, this study highlights the need for further research to examine the empirical relationship between psychometric measures and clinical observation of MHPs who have engaged in sexualized dual relationships.

ENDNOTE

This paper was previously published as A. Celenza and M. Hilsenroth, "Personality Characteristics of Mental Health Professionals Who Have Engaged in Sexualized Dual Relationships: A Rorschach Investigation," *Bulletin of the Menninger Clinic, 61*(1) (1997), 1–20.

REFERENCES

Abel, G. G., Osborn, C. A., & Warberg, B. (1995). Cognitive-behavioral treatment for professional sexual misconduct. *Psychiatric Annals, 25*(2), 106–112.

Adler, G. (1989). Transitional phenomena, projective identification, and the essential ambiguity of the psychoanalytic situation. *Psychoanalytic Quarterly, 58,* 81–104.

Akamatsu, T. J. (1988). Intimate relationships with former clients: National survey of attitudes and behavior among practitioners. *Professional Psychology: Research and Practice, 19,* 454–458.

Akhtar, S. (2005). Experiencing oneness: Pathological pursuit or normal necessity? In S. Akhtar (Ed.), *Interpersonal boundaries: Variations and violations* (pp. 87–97). New York: Jason Aronson.

Albrecht, J. M. (2003). Eros defiled: Sexual exploitation of female clients by their female therapists. (Doctoral dissertation, Pacifica Graduate Institute, CA.) *Dissertation Abstracts International: Section B: Sciences and Engineering, 63*(7-B), 3462.

Allen, C. (1991). *Women and men who sexually abuse children: A comparative analysis.* Orwell, VT: Safer Society Press.

American Psychiatric Association. (2006). Principles of medical ethics with annotations applicable to psychiatry. Arlington, VA.

APA Ethical Principles of Psychologists and Code of Conduct. (2002). Washington, DC: American Psychological Association.

APA Ethics Committee. (1988). Trends in ethics cases, common pitfalls and published resources. *American Psychologist, 43,* 564–572.

Apfel, R. J., & Simon, B. (1985). Patient-therapist sexual contact: I. Psychodynamic perspectives on the causes and results. *Psychotherapy and Psychosomatics, 43,* 57–62.

Aron, L. (1991). The patient's experience of the analyst's subjectivity. *Psychoanalytic Dialogues, 1,* 29–51.

Aron, L. (1996). *A meeting of minds: Mutuality in psychoanalysis.* Hillsdale, NJ: Therapeutic Press.

Aron, L. (1999). Clinical choices and the relational matrix. *Psychoanalytic Dialogues, 9,* 1–30.

Atwood, M. (1996). *Alias Grace.* New York: Doubleday.

259

Bach, S. (1994). *The language of perversion and the language of love.* Northvale, NJ: Jason Aronson.

Baer, B. E., & Murdock, N. L. (1995). Nonerotic dual relationships between therapists and clients: The effects of sex, theoretical orientation, and interpersonal boundaries. *Ethics and Behavior, 5*(2), 131–145.

Bartholomew, K. (1990). Family history questionnaire. Unpublished doctoral dissertation, Davis: University of California.

Bartholomew, K., & Horowitz, L. M. (1991). Attachment styles among young adults: A test of a four category model. *Journal of Personality and Social Psychology, 61,* 226–243.

Basch, M. (1983). Empathic understanding: A review of the concept and some theoretical considerations. *Journal of the American Psychoanalytic Association, 31,* 101–126.

Bataille, G. (1986). *Erotism: Death and sensuality.* San Francisco: City Lights.

Becker, W. C., & Krug, R. S. (1964). A circumplex model for social behavior in children. *Child Development, 35,* 371–396.

Bell, M., Billington, R., & Becker, B. (1985). A scale for the assessment of reality testing: Reliability, validity, and factorial invariance. *Journal of Consulting and Clinical Psychology, 53,* 506–511.

Bell, M., Billington, R., & Becker, B. (1986). A scale for the assessment of object relations: Reliability, validity, and factorial invariance. *Journal of Clinical Psychology, 42,* 733–741.

Benjamin, J. (1988). *The bonds of love.* New York: Pantheon Books.

Benjamin, J. (2002). Sameness and difference: An "overinclusive" view of gender constitution. In M. Dimen & V. Goldner (Eds.), *Gender in psychoanalytic space* (pp. 181–206). New York: Other Press.

Benjamin, J. (2004). Beyond doer and done to: An intersubjective view of thirdness. *Psychoanalytic Quarterly, 73,* 5–46.

Benowitz, M. (1995). Comparing the experiences of women clients sexually exploited by female versus male psychotherapists. In J. Gonsiorek (Ed.), *A breach of trust: Sexual exploitation by health care professionals and clergy* (pp. 213–224). London: Sage.

Bera, W. H. (1995). Betrayal: Clergy sexual abuse and male survivors. In J. C. Gonsiorek (Ed.), *A breach of trust: Sexual exploitation by health care professionals and clergy* (pp. 91–111). London: Sage.

Bisbing, S. B., Jorgenson, L. M., & Sutherland, P. K. (1995). *Sexual abuse by professionals: A legal guide.* Charlottesville, VA: Michie Co.

Blackmon, R. (1984). The Hazards of Ministry. Unpublished doctoral dissertation, Fuller Theological Seminary.

Blatt, S. (2001). The therapeutic process and professional boundary guidelines: Commentary. *Journal of the American Academy of Psychiatry and Law, 29*(3), 290–293.

Blatt, S. J., Wein, S. J., Chevron, E., & Quinlan, D. (1979). Parental representations and depression in normal young adults. *Journal of Abnormal Psychology, 78,* 388–397.

Bloom, J. D., Nadelson, C. C., & Notman, M. T. (1999). *Physician sexual misconduct.* Washington, DC: American Psychiatric Press.

Bollas, C. (1987). *The shadow of the object.* New York: Columbia University Press.

Bond, M., Gardner, S. T., Christian, J., & Sigal, J. J. (1983). Empirical study of self-rated defense styles. *Archives of General Psychiatry, 40*, 333–338.

Borys, D. S., & Pope, K. S. (1989). Dual relationships between therapist and client: A national study of psychologists, psychiatrists, and social workers. *Professional Psychology: Research and Practice, 20*, 283–293.

Bouhoutsos, J., Holroyd, J., Lerman, H., Forer, B., & Greenberg, M. (1983). Sexual intimacy between psychotherapists and patients. *Professional Psychology, 14*, 185–196.

Brabant, E., Falzeder, E., & Giampieri-Deutsch, P. (Eds.). *The Correspondence of Sigmund Freud and Sándor Terenczi* (Vol. 1, 1908–1914, P. I. Hoffer, Trans.). Cambridge, MA: Harvard University Press.

Bradley, Rev. P. J. (1953). *The Holy Bible: Catholic Action edition.* Gastonia, NC: Good Will Publishers.

Bradshaw, S. L. (1977). Ministers in trouble: A study of 140 cases evaluated at the Menninger Foundation. *Journal of Pastoral Care, 31*(4), 230–241.

Britton, R. (2004). Subjectivity, objectivity, and triangular space. *Psychoanalytic Quarterly, 73*, 47–61.

Brodsky, A. M. (1986). The distressed psychologist: Sexual intimacies and exploitation. In R. R. Kilburg, P. E. Nathan, & R. W. Thoreson (Eds.), *Professionals in distress: Issues, syndromes, and solutions in psychology* (pp. 153–171). Washington, DC: American Psychological Association.

Bryant, C. (2002). Psychological treatment of priest sex offenders. *America* (April 1), 14–17.

Buie, D. (1981). Empathy: Its nature and limitations. *Journal of the American Psychoanalytic Association, 29*, 281–307.

Burka, J. (2008). Psychic fallout from breach of confidentiality. *Contemporary Psychoanalysis, 44*, 177–198.

Butler, S., & Zelen, S. L. (1977). Sexual intimacies between therapists and clients. *Psychotherapy: Theory, Research and Practice, 14*(2), 139–145.

Celenza, A. (1986). *Empathy: Ego boundaries and deficits in the sense of self.* (Unpublished doctoral dissertation, Boston University.)

Celenza, A. (1991). The misuse of countertransference love in cases of sexual intimacies between therapists and patients. *Psychoanalytic Psychology, 8*(4), 501–509.

Celenza, A. (1995). Love and hate in the countertransference: Supervisory concerns. *Psychotherapy: Theory, Research and Practice, 32*(2), 301–307.

Celenza, A. (1998). Precursors to therapist sexual misconduct: Preliminary findings. *Psychoanalytic Psychology, 15*, 378–395.

Celenza, A. (1999). *Personality characteristics of therapists who have engaged in sexual boundary violations: An empirical study.* Unpublished manuscript.

Celenza, A. (2000a). Postmodern solutions and the limit-opportunity dialectic: The challenge of female penetration and male receptivity. *Gender and Psychoanalysis, 5*(4), 347–359.

Celenza, A. (2000b). Sadomasochistic relating: What's sex got to do with it? *Psychoanalytic Quarterly, 69*(3), 527–543.

Celenza, A. (2004). Sexual boundary violations in the clergy: The search for the father. *Studies in Gender and Sexuality, 5*(2), 213–232.

Celenza, A. (2005). Vis-à-vis the couch: Where is psychoanalysis? *International Journal of Psycho-Analysis, 86*(6), 1645–1659.

Celenza, A. (2006a). *Hyper-confidentiality and the illusion of the dyad.* Paper presented at the Philadelphia Center for Psychoanalysis, January.

Celenza, A. (2006b). The threat of male to female erotic transference. *Journal of the American Psychoanalytic Association, 54*(4), 1207–1231.

Celenza, A. (2006c). Sexual boundary violations in the office: When is a couch just a couch? *Psychoanalytic Dialogues, 16*(1), 113–128.

Celenza, A. (2007). A love addiction: Psychoanalytic psychotherapy with an offending priest. In M. G. Frawley-O'Dea & V. Goldner (Eds.), *Predatory priests, silenced victims: The sexual-abuse crisis and the Catholic Church.* Mahwah, NJ: Analytic Press.

Celenza, A. (in press). Analytic love and power: Responsible responsivity. *Psychoanalytic Inquiry.*

Celenza, A., & Gabbard, G. O. (2003). Analysts who commit sexual boundary violations: A lost cause? *Journal of the American Psychoanalytic Association, 51*(2), 617–636.

Celenza, A., & Hilsenroth, M. (1997). Personality characteristics of mental health professionals who have engaged in sexualized dual relationships: A Rorschach investigation. *Bulletin of the Menninger Clinic, 61*(1), 1–20.

Celenza, A., & Hilsenroth, M. (1999). Personal and interpersonal characteristics of transgressors: An Empirical investigation. Unpublished manuscript.

Chassaguet-Smirgel, J. (1983). Perversion and the universal law. *International Review of Psycho-Analysis, 10*, 293–301.

Code of Ethics of the National Association of Social Workers. (1999). Washington, DC: National Association of Social Workers.

Coen, S. J. (1992). *The misuse of persons: Analyzing pathological dependency.* Hillsdale, NJ: Analytic Press.

Collins, D. T. (1989). Sexual involvement between psychiatric hospital staff and their patients. In G. O. Gabbard (Ed.), *Sexual exploitation in professional relationships* (p. 156). Washington, DC: American Psychiatric Press.

Collins, N. L., & Reed, S. J. (1990). Adult attachment, working models, and relationship quality in dating couples. *Journal of Personality and Social Psychology, 58*, 644–663.

Conroe, R., Schank, J., Brown, M., DeMarinis, V., Loeffler, D., & Sanderson, B. (1989). Prohibition of sexual contact between clinical supervisors and psychotherapy students: An overview and suggested guidelines. In B. Sanderson (Ed.), *It's never O.K.: A handbook for professionals on sexual exploitation by counselors and therapists* (pp. 125–131). St. Paul: Minnesota Department of Corrections.

Conte, H. R., & Plutchick, R. (1981). A circumplex model for interpersonal personal traits. *Journal of Personality and Social Psychology, 40*, 701–711.

Cooper, S. H. (2000a). Mutual containment in the analytic situation. *Psychoanalytic Dialogues, 10*, 169–194.

Cooper, S. H. (2000b). *Objects of hope: Exploring possibility and limit in psychoanalysis.* Hillsdale, NJ: Analytic Press.

Cozzens, D. B. (2000). *The changing face of the priesthood: A reflection on the priest's crisis of soul.* Collegeville, MN: Liturgical Press.

Davidson, V. (1977). Psychiatry's problem with no name: Therapist-patient sex. *American Journal of Psychoanalysis, 37,* 43–50.

Davies, J. M. (1994). Love in the afternoon: A relational reconsideration of desire and dread in the countertransference. *Psychoanalytic Dialogues, 4*(2), 153–170.

Davies, J. M. (2000). Descending the therapeutic slopes—Slippery, slipperier, slipperiest: Commentaries on papers by B. Pizer and G. O. Gabbard. *Psychoanalytic Dialogues, 10,* 219–229.

Davies, J. M. (2004). Whose bad objects are we anyway? Repetition and our elusive love affair with evil. *Psychoanalytic Dialogues, 14,* 711–732.

Davis, M. (1980). A multidimensional approach to individual differences in empathy. *JSAS Catalogue of Selected Instruments in Psychology, 10,* 85.

Dehlendorf, C. E., & Wolfe, S. M. (1998). Physicians disciplined for sex-related offenses. *Journal of the American Medical Association, 279,* 1883–1888.

Diamond, D., Kaslow, N., Coonerty, S., & Blatt, S. J. (1990). Changes in separation-individuation and intersubjectivity in long-term treatment. *Psychoanalytic Psychology, 7,* 363–397.

Dimen, M. (2003). *Sexuality, intimacy, power.* Hillsdale, NJ: Analytic Press.

Disch, E. (1989). One day workshops for female survivors of sexual abuse by psychotherapists. In G. R. Schoener, J. H. Milgrom, J. C. Gonsiorek, E. T. Luepker, & R. M. Conroe (Eds.), *Psychotherapists' sexual involvement with clients: Intervention and prevention* (pp. 209–213). Minneapolis, MN: Walk-In Counseling Center.

Ehlert, D. (2002). *A comparison of psychologists who engage in nonsexual and sexual dual relationships with psychologists who do not.* (Unpublished doctoral dissertation, West Virginia University.)

Epstein, L. (1977). The therapeutic function of hate in the countertransference. *Contemporary Psychoanalysis, 13,* 442–461.

Epstein, R. S. (2002). Posttermination boundary issues. *American Journal of Psychiatry, 159*(5), 877–878.

Epstein, R. S., & Simon, R. L. (1990). The Exploitation Index: An early warning indicator of boundary violations in psychotherapy. *Bulletin of the Menninger Clinic, 54,* 450–465.

Epstein, R. S., Simon, R. L., & Kay, G. G. (1992). Assessing boundary violations in psychotherapy: Survey results with the Exploitation Index. *Bulletin of the Menninger Clinic, 56,* 150–166.

Exner, J. (1991). *The Rorschach: A comprehensive system. Vol. 2. Current research and advanced interpretation* (2nd ed.). New York: Wiley.

Exner, J. (1993). *The Rorschach: A comprehensive system. Vol. 1. Basic foundations* (3rd ed.). New York: Wiley.

Eyman, J. R., & Gabbard, G. O. (1991). Will therapist-patient sex prevent suicide? *Psychiatric Annals, 21,* 669–674.

Fairbanks, C. (2002). *Hiding behind the collar.* Baltimore, MD: America House.

Feldman-Summers, S., & Jones, G. (1984). Psychological impacts of sexual contact between therapists or other health care professionals and their clients. *Journal of Consulting and Clinical Psychology, 52,* 1054–1061.

Foa, U. G. (1961). Convergences in the analysis of the structure of interpersonal behavior. *Psychological Review, 68,* 341–353.

Fogel, D. (2006). *The psychopathology of everyday life at psychoanalytic institutions and boundary violations.* Paper presented at the Boston Psychoanalytic Society and Institute, December.

Fortune, M. (1989). *Is nothing sacred?* New York: Harper & Row.

Frawley-O'Dea, M. G. (2005). The role of suffering and sadomasochism in the Catholic sexual abuse scandal. In M. G. Frawley-O'Dea & V. Goldner (Eds.), *Predatory priests, silenced victims: The sexual-abuse crisis and the Catholic Church.* Mahwah, NJ: Analytic Press.

Frawley-O'Dea, M. G. (2007). *Perversion of power: Sexual abuse in the Catholic Church.* Nashville, TN: Vanderbilt Universities Press.

Frawley-O'Dea, M. G., & Goldner, V. (Eds.). (2007). *Predatory priests: The sexual-abuse crisis and the Catholic Church.* Mahwah, NJ: Analytic Press.

Frayn, D. H., & Silberfeld, M. (1986). Erotic transferences. *Canadian Journal of Psychiatry, 31,* 323–327.

Freud, S. (1911). *Formulations on the two principles of mental functioning.* Standard Edition, Vol. 12, 218–22. London: Hogarth Press.

Freud, S. (1927). *The future of an illusion.* Standard Edition, Vol. 21 (p. 53). London: Hogarth Press.

Freud, S. (1915). *Observations on transference-love. (Further recommendations on the technique of Psycho-Analysis, III),* Standard Edition, Vol. 12 (pp. 157–171). London: Hogarth Press.

Gabbard, G. O. (1994a). Psychotherapists who transgress sexual boundaries with patients. *Bulletin of Menninger Clinic, 58*(1), 124–135.

Gabbard, G. O. (1994b). Sexual misconduct. In J. M. Oldham & M. Riba (Eds.), *Annual review of psychiatry* (pp. 433–456). Washington, DC: American Psychiatric Press.

Gabbard, G. O. (1994c). Sexual excitement in the analyst. *Journal of the American Psychoanalytic Association, 42*(4), 1083–1106.

Gabbard, G. O. (1995a). *Love and hate in the analytic relationship.* Northvale, NJ: Jason Aronson.

Gabbard, G. O. (1995b). The early history of boundary violations. *Journal of the American Psychoanalytic Association, 43,* 1115–1136.

Gabbard, G. O. (1996). Lessons to be learned from the study of sexual boundary violations. *American Journal of Psychotherapy, 50,* 311–323.

Gabbard, G. O. (1997). Challenges in the analysis of adults who were sexually abused as children. *Canadian Journal of Psychoanalysis, 5,* 1–25.

Gabbard, G. O. (1999). Boundary violations and the psychoanalytic training system. *Journal of Applied Psychoanalytic Studies, 1*(3), 207–221.

Gabbard, G. O. (2000). Consultation from the consultant's perspective. *Psychoanalytic Dialogues, 10,* 209–218.

Gabbard, G. O. (2001). Boundaries, culture and psychotherapy: Commentary. *Journal of the American Academy of Psychiatry and Law, 29*(3), 284–286.

Gabbard, G. O. (2002a). Boundary violations and the abuse of power: Commentary on paper by Philip Kuhn. *Studies in Gender and Sexuality, 3,* 379–388.

Gabbard, G. O. (2002b). Post-termination sexual boundary violations. *Psychiatric Clinics of North America, 25*(3), 593–603.

Gabbard, G. O. (2003). Miscarriages of psychoanalytic treatment with suicidal patients. *International Journal of Psychoanalysis, 84,* 249–261.

Gabbard, G. O., & Lester, E. (1995a). *Boundaries and boundary violations in psychoanalysis.* New York: Basic Books.

Gabbard, G. O., & Lester, E. (1995b). Institutional responses. In G. O. Gabbard & E. Lester (Eds.), *Boundaries and boundary violations in psychoanalysis* (pp. 175–195). New York: Basic Books.

Gabbard, G. O., Peltz, M., & COPE Study Group on Boundary Violations. (2001). Speaking the unspeakable: Institutional reactions to boundary violations by training analysts. *Journal of the American Psychoanalytic Association, 49*(2), 659–673.

Gacono, C., & Meloy, J. (1994). *The Rorschach assessment of aggressive and psychopathic personalities.* Mahwah, NJ: Lawrence Erlbaum.

Ganellen, R. J. (1994). Attempting to conceal psychological disturbance: MMPI defensive response sets and the Rorschach. *Journal of Personality Assessment, 63,* 423–437.

Garfinkle, P. E., Bagby, R. M., Waring, E. M., & Dorian, B. (1997). Boundary violations and personality traits among psychiatrists. *Canadian Journal of Psychiatry, 42,* 758–763.

Garrett, T. (2002). Inappropriate therapist-patient relationships. In R. Goodwin & D. Cramer (Eds.), *Inappropriate relationships* (pp. 147–170). Mahwah, NJ: Lawrence Erlbaum.

Garrett, T., & Davis, J. (1998). The prevalence of sexual contact between British clinical psychologists and their patients. *Clinical Psychology and Psychotherapy, 5,* 253–256.

Gartrell, N., Herman, J., Olarte, S., Feldstein, M., & Localio, R. (1986). Psychiatrist-patient sexual contact: Results of a national survey, I: Prevalence. *American Journal of Psychiatry, 143*(9), 1126–1131.

Gartrell, N., Herman, J., Olarte, S., Feldstein, M., & Localio, R. (1987). Reporting practices of psychiatrists who knew of sexual misconduct by colleagues. *American Orthopsychiatric Association, 57*(2), 287–295.

Gechtman, L. (Ed). (1989). *Sexual contact between social workers and their clients.* Washington, DC: American Psychiatric Press.

Gechtman, L., & Bouhoutsos, J. (1985). *Sexual intimacy between social workers and clients.* Paper presented at the annual meeting of the Society for Clinical Social Workers, Universal City, California.

266   *References*

Ghent, E. (1990). Masochism, submission, surrender. *Contemporary Psychoanalysis, 26,* 108–136.

Gill, M. (1984). Psychoanalysis and psychotherapy: A revision. *International Review of Psychoanalysis, 11,* 161–179.

Glaser, R. D., & Thorpe, J. S. (1986). Unethical intimacy: A survey of sexual contact and advances between psychology educators and female graduate students. *American Psychology, 41,* 43–51.

Goldner, V. (2002). Toward a critical relational theory of gender. In M. Dimen & V. Goldner (Eds.), *Gender in psychoanalytic space* (pp. 63–90). New York: Other Press.

Gonsiorek, J. (1989). Sexual exploitation by psychotherapists: Some observations on male victims and sexual orientation issues. In G. Schoener, J. H. Milgrom, J. C. Gonsiorek, E. T. Luepker, & R. M. Conroe (Eds.), *Psychotherapists' sexual involvement with clients: Intervention and prevention* (pp. 113–119). Minneapolis, MN: Walk-In Counseling Center.

Gonsiorek, J. (Ed.). (1995). *A breach of trust: Sexual exploitation by health care professionals and clergy.* Thousand Oaks, CA: Sage.

Gonsiorek, J., & Schoener, G. R. (1987). Assessment and evaluation of therapists who sexually exploit clients. *Professional Practice of Psychology, 8*(2), 79–93.

Gorton, G. E., & Samuel, S. E. (1996). A national survey of training directors about education for prevention of psychiatrist-patient sexual exploitation. *Academy of Psychiatry, 20,* 92–98.

Gorton, G. E., Samuel, S. E., & Zebrowski, S. M. (1996). A pilot course for residents on sexual feelings and boundary maintenance in treatment. *Academy of Psychiatry, 20,* 43–55.

Gottlieb, M. C., Sell, J. M., & Schoenfeld, L. S. (1988). Social/romantic relationships with present and former clients: State licensing board actions. *Professional Psychology: Research and Practice, 19,* 459–462.

Greenberg, J. (1999). Analytic authority and analytic restraint. *Contemporary Psychoanalysis, 35,* 25–41.

Greenson, R. R. (1967). *The technique and practice of psychoanalysis.* New York: International Universities Press.

Groth, A. N., & Birnbaum, H. J. (1979). *Men who rape: The psychology of the offender.* New York: Plenum Press.

Gutheil, T. G. (1989). Borderline personality disorder, boundary violations and patient-therapist sex: Medico-legal pitfalls. *American Journal of Psychiatry, 146,* 597–602.

Gutheil, T. G. (1998). *The psychiatrist as expert witness.* Washington, DC: American Psychiatric Press.

Gutheil, T. G., & Gabbard, G. O. (1992). Obstacles to the dynamic understanding of therapist-patient sexual relations. *American Journal of Psychotherapy, 46,* 515–526.

Gutheil, T. G., & Gabbard, G. O. (1993). The concept of boundaries in clinical practice: Theoretical and risk management dimensions. *American Journal of Psychiatry, 150,* 188–196.

Gutheil, T. G., & Gabbard, G. O. (1998). Misuses and misunderstandings of boundary theory in clinical and regulatory settings. *American Journal of Psychiatry, 155,* 409–414.

Gutheil, T. G., & Simon, R. I. (1995). Between the chair and the door: Boundary issues in the therapeutic "transition zone." *Harvard Review of Psychiatry, 2,* 336–340.

Hamilton, J. (1999). Identifying and reducing risk factors related to trainee-client sexual misconduct. *Professional Psychology: Research and Practice, 30*(3), 318–327.

Hamilton, J. C., & Spruill, J. (1999). Identifying and reducing risk factors related to trainee-client sexual misconduct. *Professional Psychology: Research and Practice, 30*(3), 318–327.

Hanly, C. M. T. (2004). The third: A brief historical analysis of an idea. *Psychoanalytic Quarterly, 73,* 267–290.

Harris, A. (2005). *Gender as soft assembly.* Hillsdale, NJ: Analytic Press.

Harris, C. (1988). *The circuit rider's wife.* Wilmore, KY: Bristol Books. (Originally published as *A Circuit Rider's Wife,* 1910.)

Haspel, K. C., Jorgenson, L. M., Wincze, J. P., & Parsons, J. P. (1997). Legislative intervention regarding therapist sexual misconduct: An overview. *Professional Psychology: Research and Practice, 28,* 63–72.

Havens, L. (1997). A linguistic contribution to psychoanalysis: The concept of performative contradictions. *Psychoanalytic Dialogues, 7,* 523–534.

Hazan, C., & Shaver, P. (1986). *Parental care-giving style questionnaire.* Unpublished questionnaire.

Herzog, J. (2001). *Father hunger.* Hillsdale, NJ: Analytic Press.

Hilsenroth, M., Fowler, C., Padawer, J. R., & Handler, L. (1995). Narcissism in the Rorschach revisited: Some reflections upon empirical data. *Psychological Assessment, 9,* 113–121.

Hilsenroth, M., Hibbard, S., Nash, M., & Handler, L. (1993). A Rorschach study of narcissism, defense, and aggression in borderline, narcissistic and cluster c personality disorders. *Journal of Personality Assessment, 60,* 346–361.

Hoffer, A. (1985). Toward a definition of psychoanalytic neutrality. *Journal of the American Psychoanalytic Association, 33*(4), 771–795.

Hoffman, I. (1994). Dialectical thinking and therapeutic action in the psychoanalytic process. *Psychoanalytic Quarterly, 63,* 187–218.

Hoffman, I. Z. (1998). *Ritual and spontaneity in the psychotherapeutic process.* Hillsdale, NJ: Therapeutic Press.

Holroyd, J. C., & Brodsky, A. M. (1977). Psychologists' attitudes and practices regarding erotic and nonerotic physical contact with patients. *American Psychology, 32,* 843–849.

Holt, R. (1977). A method for assessing primary process manifestations and their control in Rorschach responses. In M. A. Rickers-Ovsiankina (Ed.), *Rorschach psychology* (pp. 375–420). New York: Krieger.

Horowitz, L. M. (1996). The Study of Interpersonal Problems. A LEARY legacy. *Journal of Personality Assessment, 66*(2), 283–300.

Horowitz, L. M., Rosenberg, S. E., Baer, B. A., Ureno, G., & Villasenor, V. (1988). Inventory of Interpersonal Problems: Psychometric properties and clinical applications. *Journal of Consulting and Clinical Psychology, 36,* 885–892.

Hulme, W. E. (1989). Sexual boundary violations of clergy. In G. O. Gabbard (Ed.), *Sexual exploitation in professional relationships* (pp. 177–191). Washington, DC: American Psychiatric Press.

Irons, R. R., & Schneider, J. P. (1994). Sexual addiction: Significant factor in sexual exploitation by health care professionals. *Sexual Addiction and Compulsivity, 1,* 4–21.

Jackson, H., & Nuttall, R. L. (2001). A relationship between childhood sexual abuse and professional sexual misconduct. *Professional Psychology: Research and Practice, 32* (2), 200–204.

Jorgenson, L. M. (1995). Countertransference and special concerns of subsequent treating therapists of patients sexually exploited by a previous therapist. *Psychiatric Annals, 25,* 525–563.

Kardener, S. H., Fuller, M., & Mensh, I. (1973). A survey of physicians' attitudes and practices regarding erotic and non-erotic contact with clients. *American Journal of Psychiatry, 130,* 1077–1081.

Kaser-Boyd, N. (1993). Rorschachs of women who commit homicide. *Journal of Personality Assessment, 60,* 458–470.

Kaslow, F. (1986). Seeking and providing consultation in private practice. In F. Kaslow (Ed.), *Supervision and training: Models, dilemmas and challenges.* New York: Haworth Press.

Kerr, (1993). *A most dangerous method: The story of Jung, Freud and Sabina Spielrein.* NY: Knopf.

Kluft, R. P. (1989). Treating the patient who has been sexually exploited by a previous therapist. *Psychiatric Clinics of North America, 12,* 483–500.

Kochansky, G. E. (2005). *Narcissistic character pathology and criminal and civil law.* Paper presented at the 29th International Congress on Law and Mental Health, Paris, France.

Kochansky, G. E., & Cohen, M. (2005). Priests who sexualize male minors: Psychodynamic, characterological, and clerical cultural considerations. In M. G. Frawley-O'Dea & V. Goldner (Eds.), *Predatory priests, silenced victims: The sexual-abuse crisis and the Catholic Church* (p. xx). Mahwah, NJ: Analytic Press.

Kochansky, G. E., & Herrmann, F. (2004). Shame and scandal: Clinical and canon law perspectives on the crisis in the priesthood. *International Journal of Law and Psychiatry, 27,* 299–319.

Kris, A. O. (2005). The lure of hypocrisy. *Journal of the American Psychoanalytic Association, 53,* 7–22.

Kroll, J. (2001). Boundary violations: A culture-bound syndrome. *Journal of the American Academy of Psychiatry and Law, 29*(3), 274–283.

Lamb, D. H., & Catanzaro, S. J. (1998). Sexual and nonsexual boundary violations involving psychologists, clients, supervisees, and students. *Professional Psychology, Research and Practice, 29*(5), 498–503.

Lamb, D. H., Woodburn, J. R., Lewis, J. T., Strand, K. K., Buchko, K. J., & Kang, J. R. (1994). Sexual and business relationships between therapists and former clients. *Psychotherapy, 31*(2), 270–278.

Leary, T. F. (1957). *Interpersonal diagnosis of personality.* New York: Ronald Press.

Levine, H. (1997). The capacity for countertransference. *Psychoanalytic Inquiry, 17,* 44–68.

Levine, H. B., & Yanof, J. A. (2004). Boundaries and postanalytic contacts in institutes. *Journal of American Psychoanalytic Association, 52*(3), 873–901.

Levine, S. B., Risen, C. B., & Althof, S. E. (1994). Professionals who sexually offend: Evaluation procedures and preliminary findings. *Journal of Sexual Marital Therapy, 20,* 288–302.

Lon, M. & McNair, D. M. (1963). An interpersonal behavior circle. *Journal of Abnormal and Social Psychology, 67,* 68–75.

Lothstein, L. M. (2004). Men of the flesh: The evaluation and treatment of sexually abusing priests. *Studies in Gender and Sexuality, 5,* 167–195.

Lothstein, L. M., & Rosetti, S. (1990). Myths of the child molester. In S. Rosetti (Ed.), *Slayer of the soul: Child sexual abuse and the Catholic Church* (pp. 9–18). Mystic, CT: Twenty-third Publications.

Luepker, E. T. (1989). Sexual exploitation of clients by therapists: Parallels with parent/child incest. In B. Sanderson (Ed.), *It's never O.K.: A handbook for professionals on sexual exploitation by counselors and therapists* (pp. 15–17). St. Paul: Minnesota Department of Corrections.

Luepker, E. T. (1999). Effects of practitioners' sexual misconduct: A follow-up study. *Journal of the American Academy of Psychiatry and the Law, 27*(1), 51–63.

Luepker, E. T., & Schoener, G. R. (1989). Sexual involvement and the abuse of power in psychotherapeutic relationships. In G. Schoener, J. H. Milgrom, J. C. Gonsiorek, E. T. Luepker, & R. M. Conroe (Eds.), *Psychotherapists' sexual involvement with clients: Intervention and prevention* (pp. 65–72). Minneapolis, MN: Walk-In Counseling Center.

Malcolm, J. (1981). *Psychoanalysis: The impossible profession.* New York: A. A. Knopf.

Maltsberger, J. T., & Buie, D. (1974). Countertransference hate in the treatment of suicidal patients. *Archives of General Psychiatry, 30,* 625–633.

Margolis, M. (1994). Incest, erotic countertransference, and analyst-analysand boundary violations. *Journal of the American Psychoanalytic Association, 42*(4), 985–989.

Margolis, M. (1997). Therapist-patient sexual involvement: Clinical experiences and institutional responses. *Psychoanalytic Inquiry, 17*(3), 349–370.

Maroda, K. J. (1998). *Seduction, surrender, and transformation: Emotional engagement in the analytic process.* Hillsdale, NJ: Analytic Press.

Mayer, E. M. (2001, Spring). *Sexual abuse of patients and problems in our psychotherapeutic theory of technique.* Presented at a scientific meeting, Boston Psychotherapeutic Society and Institute, Boston, Massachusetts.

McBride, T. (1999). *From the shepherd's mouth: A study of sexual abuse in the church.* Wellington, New Zealand: Trish McBride.

McGuire, W. (Ed.). (1988). *The Freud/Jung letters: The correspondence between Sigmund Freud and C. G. Jung.* Cambridge, MA: Harvard University Press.

McQuiston, J., II (1996). *Always we begin again: The Benedictine way of living.* Ridgefield, CT: Morehouse.

Milgrom, J. H. (1989). Advocacy: Assisting the sexually exploited client through the process. In B. Sanderson (Ed.), *It's never O.K.: A handbook for professionals on sexual exploitation by counselors and therapists* (pp. 29–34). St. Paul: Minnesota Department of Corrections.

Mitchell, S. (1993). *Hope and dread in psychoanalysis.* New York: Basic Books.

Modell, A. (1990). *Transference and levels of reality: Other times, other realities* (pp. 44–59). Cambridge, MA: Harvard University. Press.

Modell, A. (1991). The therapeutic relationship as a paradoxical experience. *Psychoanalytic Dialogues, 1,* 13–28.

Noel, M. M. (1986). *Sexual misconduct by psychologists: Who reports it?* (Unpublished doctoral dissertation, Antioch-New England Graduate School, Keene, NH.)

Norris, D. M., Gutheil, T. G., & Strasburger, L. H. (2003). This couldn't happen to me: Boundary problems and sexual misconduct in the psychotherapy relationship. *Psychiatric Services, 54*(4), 517–522.

Notman, M. T., & Nadelson, C. C. (1999). Psychotherapy with patients who have had sexual relations with a previous therapist. In J. D. Bloom, C. C. Nadelson, & M. T. Notman (Eds.), *Physician sexual misconduct* (pp. 247–262). Washington, DC: American Psychiatric Press.

Ogden, T. (1994). *Subjects of analysis.* Northvale, NJ: Jason Aronson.

Parker, G., Tupling, H., & Brown, L. B. (1979). A parental bonding instrument. *British Journal of Medical Psychology, 52,* 1–10.

Parsons, J. P., & Wincze, J. P. (1995). A survey of client-therapist sexual involvement in Rhode Island as reported by subsequent treating therapists. *Professional Psychology: Research and Practice, 26,* 171–175.

Parsons, M. (2000). *The dove that returns, the dove that vanishes.* Philadelphia, PA: Routledge.

Paskauskas, R. A. (Ed.). (1993). *The complete correspondence of Sigmund Freud and Ernest Jones, 1908–1939.* Cambridge, MA: Belknap Press of Harvard Universities Press.

Perr, I. N. (1975). Legal aspects of sexual therapies. *Journal of Legal Medicine, 3,* 33–38.

Perry, J. A. (1976). Physicians' erotic and non-erotic physical involvement with patients. *American Journal of Psychiatry, 133,* 838–840.

Pizer, B. (2000). The therapist's routine consultations: A necessary window in the treatment frame. *Psychoanalytic Dialogues, 10,* 197–207.

Pizer, S. (2000). The role of consultations in the prevention of boundary violations: Introduction to panel. *Psychoanalytic Dialogues, 10,* 195–196.

Plakun, E. (1999). Sexual misconduct and enactment. *Journal of Psychotherapy, Practice and Research, 8*(4), 284–291.

Pope, K. S. (1989a). Teacher-student sexual intimacy. In G. O. Gabbard (Ed.), *Sexual exploitation in professional relationships* (pp. 163–176). Washington, DC: American Psychiatric Press.

Pope, K. S. (1989b). Therapists who become sexually intimate with a patient: Classifications, dynamics, recidivism and rehabilitation. *Independent Practitioner, 9,* 28–34.

Pope, K. S. (1989c). Sexual intimacies between psychologists and their students and supervisees: Research, standards, and professional liability. *Independent Practitioner, 9,* 33–41.

Pope, K. S. (1990). Therapist-client sexual involvement: A review of the research. *Clinical Psychology Review, 10,* 477–490.

Pope, K. S. (1993). Licensing disciplinary actions for psychologists who have been sexually involved with a client: Some information about offenders. *Professional Psychology: Research and Practice, 24*(3), 374–377.

Pope, K. S., & Bouhoutsos, J. C. (1986). *Sexual intimacy between therapists and patients.* New York: Praeger.

Pope, K. S., Keith-Spiegel, P., & Tabachnick, B. G. (1986). Sexual attraction to clients: The human therapist and the (sometimes) inhuman training system. *American Psychologist, 41,* 147–158.

Pope, K. S., Levenson, H., & Schover, L. R. (1979). Sexual intimacy in psychology training: Results and implications of a national survey. *American Psychologist, 34,* 682–689.

Pope, K. S., Tabachnick, B. G., & Keith-Spiegel, P. (1987). Ethics of practice: The beliefs and behaviors of psychologists as therapists. *American Psychologist, 42,* 993–1006.

Pope, K. S., & Vetter, V. A. (1991). Prior therapist-client sexual involvement among clients seen by psychologists. *Psychotherapy, 28,* 429–438.

Racker, H. (1972). The meanings and uses of countertransference. *Psychoanalytic Quarterly, 41,* 487–506.

Renik, O. (1995). The ideal of the anonymous analyst and the problem of self-disclosure. *Psychoanalytic Quarterly, 64,* 466–495.

Renik, O. (1999). Playing one's cards face up in analysis: An approach to the problem of self-disclosure. *Psychoanalytic Quarterly, 68,* 521–540.

Richards, A. F. C. (2004). Sexual boundary violations by clergy in the Episcopal Church. *Studies in Gender and Sexuality, 5,* 139–166.

Robinson, W. L., & Reid, P. T. (1985). Sexual intimacies in psychology revisited. *Professional Psychology, 16,* 512–520.

Robison, L. H. (2004). The abuse of power: A view for sexual misconduct in a systemic approach to pastoral care. *Pastoral Psychology, 52*(5), 395–404.

Rodolfa, E., Hall, T., Holms, V., Davena, A., Komatz, D., Antunez, M., & Hall, A. (1994). The management of sexual feelings in therapy. *Professional Psychology: Research and Practice, 25*(2), 168–172.

Rosetti, S. (Ed.). (1990). *Slayer of the soul: Child sexual abuse and the Catholic Church.* Mystic, CT: Twenty-third Publications.

Ross, J. M. (1995). The fate of relatives and colleagues in the aftermath of sexual boundary violations. *Journal of the American Psychoanalytic Association, 43,* 959–961.

Russell, R. (1984). *Social worker's awareness of and response to the problem of sexual contact between client and helping professional.* (Unpublished master's thesis, University of Washington.)

Rutter, P. (1989). *Sex in the forbidden zone: When therapists, doctors, clergy, teachers and other men in power betray women's trust.* Los Angeles: Jeremy P. Tarcher.

Samuel, S. E., & Gorton, G. E. (1998). National survey of psychology internship directors regarding education for prevention of psychologist-patient sexual exploitation. *Professional Psychology: Research and Practice, 29,* 86–90.

Sandler, A.-M. (2004). Institutional responses to boundary violations: The case of Masud Khan. *International Journal of Psychoanalytic, 85,* 27–42.

Sandler, J. (1960). The background of safety. *International Journal of Psychoanalysis, 41,* 352–356.

Sandler, J. (1976). Countertransference and role-responsiveness. *International Review of Psychoanalysis, 3,* 43–47.

Sarkar, S. P. (2004). Boundary violation and sexual exploitation in psychiatry and psychotherapy: A review. *Advances in Psychiatric Treatment, 10,* 312–320.

Schaefer, E. S. & Plutchik, R. (1966). Interrelationships of emotions, traits, and diagnostic constructs. *Psychological Reports, 18,* 399–410.

Schafer, R. (1959). Generative empathy in the treatment situation. *Psychoanalytic Quarterly, 28,* 342–373.

Schoener, G. R. (1995). Assessment of professionals who have engaged in boundary violations. *Psychiatric Annals, 25,* 95–99.

Schoener, G. R. (1999). Preventive and remedial boundaries training for helping professionals and clergy: Successful approaches and useful tools. *Journal of Sex Education and Therapy, 24,* 209–217.

Schoener, G. R. (2005). *Clergy sexual abuse of women: Some historical perspectives.* Paper presented at the Interfaith Conference on Clergy Sexual Misconduct: Helping Survivors and Communities Heal, Minneapolis, MN, January, 2005.

Schoener, G. R., & Gonsiorek, J. (1989). Assessment and development of rehabilitation plans for the therapist. In G. R. Schoener, J. H. Milgrom, J. C. Gonsiorek, E. T. Luepker, & R. M. Conroe (Eds.), *Psychotherapists' sexual involvement with clients: Intervention and prevention* (pp. 401–420). Minneapolis, MN: Walk-In Counseling Center.

Schoener, G. R., Milgrom, J. H., Gonsiorek, J. C., Luepker, E. T., & Conroe, R. M. (Eds.). (1989). *Psychotherapists' sexual involvement with clients: Intervention and prevention* (pp. 399–502). Minneapolis, MN: Walk-In Counseling Center.

Schwartz, R. S., & Olds, J. (2002). A phenomenology of closeness and its application to sexual boundary violations: A framework for therapists in training. *American Journal of Psychotherapy, 36*(4), 480–493.

Searles, H. F. (1979). *Countertransference and related subjects.* Madison, CT: International Universities Press.

Sederer, L. (1995). False allegations of sexual misconduct: Clinical and institutional considerations. *Psychiatric Services, 46*(2), 160–163.

Shipley, B. (1967). *The Shipley Institute of Living Scale.* Los Angeles: Western Psychological Services.

Simon, R. I. (1995). The natural history of therapist sexual misconduct: Identification and prevention. *Psychiatric Annals, 25*, 90–94.

Simon, R. I. (1999). Therapist-patient sex: From boundary violations to sexual misconduct. *Psychiatric Clinics of North America, 22*(1), 31–47.

Slavin, J., Oxenhandler, N., Seligman, S., Stein, R., & Davies, J. M. (2004). Dialogues on sexuality in development and treatment. *Studies in Gender and Sexuality, 5*(4), 371–418.

Sloan, P., Arsenault, L., Hilsenroth, M., Harvill, L., & Handler, L. (1995). Rorschach measures of posttraumatic stress in Persian Gulf war veterans. *Journal of Personality Assessment, 64*, 397–414.

Slovenko, R. (1980). Legal issues in psychotherapy supervision. In K. Hess (Ed.), *Psychotherapy supervision: Theory, research and practice* (pp. 453–473). New York: John Wiley.

Smith, S. (1977). The golden fantasy: A regressive reaction to separation anxiety. *International Journal of Psychoanalysis, 58*, 311–324.

Smith, S. (1984). The sexually abused patient and the abusing therapist: A study in sadomasochistic relationships. *Psychoanalytic Psychology, 1*(2), 89–98.

Somer, E., & Nachmani, I. (2005). Constructions of therapist-client sex: A comparative analysis of retrospective victim reports. *Sexual Abuse: A Journal of Research and Treatment, 17*(1), 47–62.

Somer, E., & Saadon, M. (1999). Therapist-client sex: Clients' retrospective reports. *Professional Psychology: Research and Practice, 30*(5), 504–509.

Spezzano, C. (1998). The triangle of clinical judgment. *Journal of American Psychoanalysts Association, 46*, 365–388.

Stake, J. E., & Oliver, J. (1991). Sexual contact and touching between therapist and client: A survey of psychologists' attitudes and behavior. *Professional Psychology: Research and Practice, 22*(4), 297–307.

Stechler, G. (2003). Affect: The heart of the matter. *Psychoanalytic Dialogues, 13*(5), 711–726.

Stein, M. (1981). The unobjectionable part of the transference. *Journal of the American Psychoanalytic Association, 29*, 869–892.

Stein, R. (2004). The poignant, the excessive and the enigmatic in sexuality. *International Journal of Psychoanalysis, 79*, 253–268.

Stepansky, P. E. (Ed.). (1988). *The memoirs of Margaret S. Mahler.* New York: Free Press.

Stern, D. B. (1997). *Unformulated experience: From dissociation to imagination in psychoanalysis.* Hillsdale, NJ: Analytic Press.

Stoller, R. J. (1979). *Sexual excitement.* New York: Pantheon.

Stoller, R. J. (1985). *Observing the erotic imagination*. New Haven, CT: Yale University Press.

Stone, A. A. (1983). Sexual misconduct by psychiatrists: The ethical and clinical dilemma of confidentiality. *American Journal of Psychiatry, 140,* 195–197.

Strasburger, L. H. (1999). "There oughta be a law": Criminalization of psychotherapist-patient sex as a social policy dilemma. In J. D. Bloom, C. C. Nadelson, & M. T. Notman (Eds.), *Physician sexual misconduct* (pp. 19–36). Washington, DC: American Psychiatric Press.

Strasburger, L. H., & Jorgenson, L. (1992). The prevention of psychotherapist sexual misconduct: Avoiding the slippery slope. *American Journal of Psychotherapy, 46,* 544–556.

Strean, H. S. (1993). *Therapists who have sex with their patients: Treatment and recovery.* New York: Brunner/Mazel.

Sullivan, H. S. (1953). *The interpersonal theory of psychiatry*. New York: W. W. Norton.

Tillinghast, E., & Cournos, F. (2000). Assessing the risk of recidivism in physicians with histories of sexual misconduct. *Journal of Forensic Sciences, 45*(6), 1184–1189.

Tschan, W. (2005). *Missbrauchtes Vertrauen*. Basel: Karger.

Twemlow, S. W., & Gabbard, G. O. (1989). The lovesick therapist. In G. O. Gabbard (Ed.), *Sexual exploitation in professional relationships*. Washington, DC: American Psychiatric Press.

Vinson, J. S. (1984). *Sexual contact with psychotherapists: A study of client reactions and complaint procedures*. (Unpublished doctoral dissertation, California School of Professional Psychology.)

Vitz, P. C., & Gartner, J. G. (1984). Christianity and psychoanalysis, Part I: Jesus as the anti-oedipus. *Journal of Psychological Theology, 12*(1), 4–14.

Wallace, E. (2007). Losing a training analyst for ethical violations: A candidate's perspective. *International Journal of Psychoanalysis, 88,* 1275–1288.

Weiner, I. B. (1991). Editor's note: Interscorer agreement in Rorschach research. *Journal of Personality Assessment, 56,* 1.

Westen, D. (1995). *Social Cognition and Object Relations Scale: Q-sort for projective stories (SCORS-Q)*. Unpublished scale. Cambridge, MA: Cambridge Hospital, Harvard Medical School.

Wheelis, J., Michels, R., Celenza, A., & Gabbard, G. O. (2003). *How could this happen to me? Panel on sexual boundary violations among psychoanalysts*. New York: American Psychoanalytic Association.

Wiggins, J. S. (1979). A psychological taxonomy of trait-descriptive terms: The interpersonal domain. *Journal of Personality and Social Psychology, 37,* 395–342.

Wiggins, J. S., Trapnell, P., & Phillips, N. (1988). Psychometric and geometric characteristics of the revised interpersonal adjective scales (IAS-R). *Multivariate Behavioral Research, 23,* 517–530.

Williams, M. H. (1997). Boundary violations: Do some contended standards of care fail to encompass commonplace procedures of humanistic, behavioral and eclectic psychotherapies? *Psychotherapy, 34*(3), 238–249.

Winnicott, D. W. (1949). Hate in the countertransference. *International Journal of Psychoanalysis, 30,* 69–74.

Winnicott, D. W. (1971). *Playing and reality.* New York: Basic Books.

Wohlberg, J. W., et al. (1999b). Treatment subsequent to abuse by a mental health professional: The victim's perspective of what works and what doesn't. *Journal of Sex Education and Therapy, 24*(4), 252–261.

Wohlberg, J. W., McCraith, D. B., & Thomas, D. R. (1999a). Sexual misconduct and the victim/survivor: A look from the inside out. In J. D. Bloom, C. C. Nadelson, & M. T. Notman (Eds.), *Physician sexual misconduct* (pp. 181–204). Washington, DC: American Psychiatric Press.

Woolley, S. T. (1988). *Transference, countertransference, erotic issues and the female therapist.* (Unpublished doctoral dissertation, Harvard Graduate School of Education.)

INDEX

ABOUT THE AUTHOR

Andrea Celenza, Ph.D., is an assistant clinical professor at Harvard Medical School, and on the faculty of Boston Psychoanalytic Society and Institute and the Massachusetts Institute for Psychoanalysis. Dr. Celenza has authored and presented numerous papers on the evaluation and treatment of therapists who have engaged in sexual boundary violations, with a focus on training, supervisory, and rehabilitation issues. She has treated, evaluated, supervised, and/or consulted on over 100 cases of sexual boundary violations. She is the primary consultant to the Northeast Episcopal Diocese and several other clergy organizations as well as licensing boards on issues of sexual misconduct in the clergy and to licensing boards of professionals in the northeast.

Dr. Celenza is a member of the Committee on Psychoanalytic Education of the American Psychoanalytic Association, currently focusing on the establishment of training criteria on boundary issues to be adopted by psychoanalytic institutes nationwide. She is the recipient of The Felix & Helene Deutsh Prize (2006), The Karl A. Menninger Memorial Award (2006), and the Symonds Prize. She is in private practice in Lexington, Massachusetts.

Made in the USA
Middletown, DE
26 February 2018